D1641062

Space(s) of the Fantastic

This book provides a series of new addresses to the enduring problem of how to categorize the Fantastic. The approach taken is through the lens of spatiality; the Fantastic gives us new worlds, although of course these are refractions of worlds already in being. In place of 'real' spaces (whatever they might be), the Fantastic gives us imaginary spaces, although within those spaces historical and cultural conflicts are played out, albeit in forms that stretch our understanding of everyday location, and our usual interpretations of cause and effect. Many authors are addressed here, from a variety of different geographical and national traditions, thus demonstrating how the Fantastic – as a mode, a genre, a way of thinking, imagining and writing – continually traverses borders and boundaries. We hope to move the ongoing debate about the Fantastic forward in a scholarly as well as an engaging way.

David Punter is Professor of Poetry Emeritus and Senior Research Fellow in the Institute of Advanced Studies at the University of Bristol, UK.

C. Bruna Mancini is Associate Professor of English Literature at the University of Calabria.

Space(s) of the Fantastic
A 21st Century Manifesto

Edited by David Punter and
C. Bruna Mancini

Routledge
Taylor & Francis Group

NEW YORK AND LONDON

First published 2021
by Routledge
52 Vanderbilt Avenue, New York, NY 10017

and by Routledge
2 Park Square, Milton Park, Abingdon, Oxon, OX14 4RN

Routledge is an imprint of the Taylor & Francis Group, an informa business

© 2021 Taylor & Francis

Library of Congress Cataloging-in-Publication Data
Names: Mancini, C. Bruna, editor. | Punter, David, editor.
Title: Space(s) of the fantastic : a 21st century manifesto / edited
    by Bruna Mancini & David Punter.
Description: New York, NY : Routledge, 2021. | Includes
    bibliographical references and index. | Summary: "In this
    book, we provide a number of accounts, with examples, of
    how we might consider the Fantastic as a mode of writing
    with both historical depth and immediate contemporary
    relevance"—Provided by publisher.
Identifiers: LCCN 2020042720 | ISBN 9780367680282
    (hardback) | ISBN 9780367680305 (ebook)
Subjects: LCSH: Fantastic, The, in literature. | Fantastic, The.
Classification: LCC PN56.F34 S64 2021 |
    DDC 809.3/8766—dc23
LC record available at https://lccn.loc.gov/2020042720

ISBN: 978-0-367-68028-2 (hbk)
ISBN: 978-0-367-68030-5 (ebk)

Typeset in Sabon
by Apex CoVantage, LLC

Contents

Introduction
Space and Fantastic

David Punter and C. Bruna Mancini

Of Margins, Transgressions, Abnormalities

What is the Fantastic? This is the main question this book tries to answer. Specifically, is it possible to define it using contemporary Literary Geography Studies? Is it conceivable to circumscribe such a magmatic, fluid, fleeing argument once and for all? As the Fantastic is what transgresses the normality of the so-called real, and goes beyond the known and everyday events of our lives, can it really be a norm, bounded, and defined? And, in particular, can the real itself be a site of the Fantastic, if we take into account uncanny and eccentric perspectives/narrations centred on the darker, more frightful and shifty spaces and places of our everyday existences? In fact, crossing the borders between the real and the unreal is in some ways easier than we expect. It outlines an uncertain, dangerous path from our living world to an occult, an unknown universe. Such a liminal and fleeing movement from our reassuring places to the spaces of the unusual and the unfamiliar/*das Unheimlich*, with the subjects almost unaware of having passed the threshold between the two, produces a limit-situation that can transform itself into a hallucinating phantasmagoria, similar to the visions of an outsider. That unsure path, full of forks, drops, and coves, is where the Fantastic most haunts and attracts us.

The language of the Fantastic can evoke, exorcise, seize the fears, the uncertainties, the contradictions that usually appear in moments of crisis. In fact, the Fantastic offsets the linear or jagged chronotope of everyday life thus leading towards what is uncertain and undetermined. The Fantastic uses a language impregnated with snares, *trompe l'oeil*, ambiguities, allusions, abnormal comparisons, sudden mutations, and overturnings. It is the very language that focuses on the evocative power of the words and on the strength of the imagination both of authors and readers. In "*La paura, atto e spazio dell'interdetto. Il fantastico tra sacro e profano*"/"Fear, deed and space of the forbidden. The fantastic between sacred and profane", Romolo Runcini writes that:

> [T]he fantastic plays with the fear for the different, the other from oneself, and, even if it ambiguously alludes to the supernatural

plane (the unreal), it keeps its fabling discourse to the terrestrial setting (the real), insinuating a descent to the underworld or a fall into the abysses of the language that suspends any judgment about the described event in order to charm the reader into a labyrinth of infinite choices without any safety route.

(p. 107, my translation)

The pleasure of the text permits the pleasure of fear, of transgression, of the uncanny to go ahead. The subversion of the ordinary world order pushes the reader of the Fantastic towards a difficult, ambivalent, dangerous itinerary that emphasizes the ambiguities of the real and makes us prey to our own imagination by breaking through the horizon towards which we are all plunging.

Following in Hegel's footsteps, Runcini identifies a fluid, hidden, elusive zone of human consciousness in which the subject is no more the master of her/himself, and yet preserves a shadow of the Ego, the Ego's double. Hegel's viewpoint is that horror comes from the most paradoxical and illogical part of the human soul (the one that a century later would be called the unconscious) unable to control the real. Fear – which is the instinctive and emotional reaction to the impact of alterity, of the unknown, of a dominating phenomenon we cannot decode – can destabilize the subjective and collective identity that is strictly linked to everyday reality. Fantastic is the writing of inner reality, rich in impulses and chaos. It is the language of freedom and transgression, ambiguity and charm, under the spell of a fear aroused by any existential and/or collective crisis. Fantastic writing insinuates itself into the magmatic fault between body and soul, conscious and unconscious, real and unreal, and acquires a dynamism that moves away from the so-called real. As a matter of fact, in these marginal and extreme regions some extraordinary, uncanny, and monstrous characters appear as figures of freedom: the witch, the ghost, the (un)dead, the lunatic, the hybrid, the mad scientist, demons and doubles, and so on and so forth. In the essay "*La linea del mostro*"/"The Line of the Monster", Toni Negri writes that every time power declares that history has ended and nature experiences an ultimate order, so that only those who adapt to measure, who obey and believe, can truly be happy, monsters necessarily appear in order to disavow any normality, obedience, and belief. The monster is an adventuring knight that beckons us towards the most dangerous places, frees us from dogmatism, and incites us to create new worlds. Monsters are philosophical heroes, powers of creativity/creation; they represent the return of the repressed, the threshold of metamorphosis, the ultimate testimony of our capability to transform the world. The angel who could save us from the inadequacies of our everyday life has to be monstrous in order to be recognized. In his monstrous body all our fears and anxieties unite, even those desires and ambitions that our societies have repressed from our lives. He represents the scarring of all the wounds that the 'dark side' inflicts on the order of reality.

1 Magissatopia
The Place of the Witch

David Punter

It is tempting to begin this chapter with a history of the witch; or of the witches, because plurality is often of the essence of the witch; or of witchcraft. But it also impossible, because there is, in a sense, no such history. What there is instead is a narrative compounded of patriarchal accusation; female abjection; the stifling of attempts at rebellious power; returns and recrudescences of 'natural magic'; lives lived and lost in Gothic shadows – and other matters, many of which can be defined as tests of the limits of justice and power and intrinsically linked to place, as typically in the Salem witch trials of 1692–3 (see Macfarlane 1970; Hutton 1999).

There is no escaping the length of the shadow which these trials – although they were typical of many – have cast over history. It is not only that, as far as can be told, a large number of women – and a few men – were put to death on flimsy evidence, or rather no evidence at all; the trials underscore the unreliability of the whole nature of 'evidence' as conceived in Western jurisprudence. That the trials stand as a prime, and haunting, example of communal injustice has only been underlined and magnified by the enduring fame of Arthur Miller's 1953 play *The Crucible*, which demonstrates how society's dealings with supposed witches can be taken as an emblem of that same society's dealings with any outlawed group – so that the witch comes to be a figure for the abused, the relegated, the physically marginal.

This then is both the strength and the weakness of the witch: strength in that the haunting voice which comes back from the margins, from the shadows, appears to hold an ancient wisdom which we ignore at our peril; weakness in that the weapons by means of which witchcraft may appear to wish to preserve its power, its sources of knowledge, are continually demonstrated to be ineffectual, incapable of resisting authority, an authority vested in the State from at least the seventeenth century onwards but also vested in our reading selves as we transmute ourselves into the witchfinder-general, that savage and weak-kneed parody of a military man whose only success consists of further abjecting those already, by virtue of poverty, gender, and age, excluded from social space.

So: there are no witches, the space of the witch is empty; they are the creation of an over-burdened, frightened patriarchal imagination. Is this so? It might alternatively be that the witch comes to remind us of much of what post-structuralism claims, that we are frequently in the presence not of firmly maintained binaries but rather of the undecidable. We might even say that the 'question of the witch' is not a question susceptible of a permanent answer (if indeed there are any such questions) but rather has to do with transience, becoming, halting, temporary, liminal states: what might it be like, not to *be* a witch, but rather to experience a moment of 'witch-becoming', being able to think and feel with the intelligence and the senses of a witch?[1] Or is this something of which, actually, we all have experience, except that it must pass under the sign of repression, be unacknowledged in the daylight world? (see Warner 2014; Auerbach 1995).

My first text in the space of the witch is Jeanette Winterson's *The Daylight Gate* (2012). As well as being one of Winterson's most accomplished texts, it is also one of her shortest, and written in a terse, clipped, clear style. It responds to the true documents, whatever that might mean, of the notorious Lancaster witch trial of 1612 (also, of course, the topic of William Harrison Ainsworth's much earlier novel, *The Lancashire Witches*),[2] and by Winterson's own account it attempts to address several questions: principal among them is how it came to be the case that a wealthy independent woman, Alice Nutter, was arraigned and found guilty alongside many other women who were clearly destitute, without hope, and quite possibly mentally unwell (Winterson 2012: viii–ix).

The answer Winterson constructs is entirely plausible; but the wider issues which the novel throws up are not so easily addressed. It might be, for example, that some of those accused as witches might, when driven to the wall by persecution and without any prospect of just outcome, have found themselves driven to the only hope still available, namely that there might really be unconscious, unseen, supernatural powers that might come to rescue them *in extremis* and thus allow the space of the witch to come fully into being, as a recourse, as a shelter.

But what is especially fascinating about *The Daylight Gate* is the quality of doubt, of undecidability, which hovers over the entire text. At the very last, when Alice Nutter is about to be hanged, she is, in a sense, saved: she dies, certainly, but by what might appear to be her own design, through the agency of her pet falcon:

> The bird dropped through the air, wheeled, swooped, landed straight on Alice's arm. The crowd was screaming. No one dared approach her.
> Alice stared into the crowd for a second. Her hair was white. She was much changed. But in the crowd there was a face she recognised who recognised her. She smiled her old smile. She looked young again.

She stretched back her neck, exposing the long line of her throat. The falcon flapped his wings to keep himself steady as he dug his feet into her collarbone to make a perch. His head dived forwards in one swift movement. He severed her jugular vein.

(221–2)

This falcon has been an object of fear for some time; is it a witch's familiar rather than a real bird, and whatever it is, is it appropriate that a woman, albeit a rich and distinguished one, should so trespass on male territory, on an established space of power, as to keep and train a falcon?

Behind this lie further questions: "Her hair was white. . . . She looked young again" – throughout the novel there has been a hovering question as to where Alice Nutter's apparent sources of eternal youth come from – in earlier life, we are told, she had consorted with those great Elizabethan magical demons beloved of the Gothicists, the alchemist Dr John Dee and his associate Edward Kelley, and Kelley, we are told, had been her lover. But these questions, as is so often the case in the literature of the witch, are left unanswered. An example perhaps of that old Gothic trope, the 'unexplained supernatural'.

In moving on to my second text, Celia Rees's *Witch Child* (2000), I want to begin to attend to the peculiar connection between recent witch literature and the adolescent, especially, of course, the adolescent girl – there is a whole subgenre here, I have read some of it, and in many cases I wish I had not bothered (but then, obviously, I am not the target audience). But Rees's book has a distinct power, and conjures a witch-space, a *magissatopia*, of its own. It is again set in the seventeenth century, between England and America, as Mary tries to establish her identity against a background of puritan witch-hunting. She is a witch – she tells us so herself in the very first lines, "I am Mary. I am a witch" (11) – but is she? She has been brought up by her grandmother, and such an upbringing is, time and time again, the mark of the witch: her grandmother's name is not 'Nutter', but it does happen to be 'Nuttall' – but surely this must be, must it not, a mere coincidence. In any case, her grandmother is put to death as a witch, but Mary shows only slight signs of witchery: an affinity with native Americans, who see something in her not apparent to herself; and an ability to help in traumatic times of birthing.

This cannot save her. In scenes directly reminiscent of *The Crucible*, she is testified against by a group of hysterical young women, and only barely escapes with her life, which raises huge questions about readerly position. Are we to side with Mary, outcast, outlaw – and of course outlawry is the subtext of so many recent vampire tales, from Anne Rice to Poppy Z. Brite and the apparently endless Stephenie Meyer – or with the other young women, whose main concerns are with the 'normal' transition through the space of adolescence to adulthood, the attraction of boys, the expulsion of all 'othered' intimations of power? Mary is, or becomes, a herbalist: she seeks and finds knowledge of natural remedies, but to others this is a further sign of her suspect consanguinity with the native Americans, those who inhabit their own soil, evidence of a certain attraction to the places of the barbaric, and it is this evidence that condemns, places her – literally at times – in a neo-Gothic physical realm beyond the pale of civilization.

Yet we might say that these witch-signs are in fact the insignia of imagination, an imagination that must be rigorously repressed, as the puritan elders in the novel practise this same rigorous repression on themselves. The witch, then – that element of the self that we may refer to as the 'witch-self' – figures as the search for something beyond the established topography of culture, something both transcendent and transgressive; and it cannot be harboured within safe boundaries, it must be expelled. The witch as scapegoat: perhaps because she is too close to sacred female space, she represents a sanctuary which has no place within the modern. And so at the end, Mary says,

> I have taken refuge in Rebekah's borning room. Rebekah is near her time, very near. Martha says they will not dare to enter here. Sarah has brought me what I asked her for: food, boy's clothing, a blanket. I take the moccasins and the little leather pouch from my box and put it round my neck. My few precious things. All I have to show for my life so far lived. All I have to take with me to the wilderness. I must take my chances there. If I stay here, I hang for sure.

> (227–8)

It is in those modern classics of the supernatural, Terry Pratchett and J. K. Rowling, that we can find further versions of some of these ideas. Some of Pratchett's early work – I am thinking here particularly of *Wyrd Sisters* (1980) and *Witches Abroad* (1991) – deals extensively in the opposition between the wisdom of the wizard, incorporated in the spaces of Unseen University, and the learning of the witch, dis-corporated across places and histories. What the wizards possess is a kind of access to antiquity and tradition, but this has become hidebound, symbolized in an all too apt parody of the institution of 'higher learning', and in the even more hilarious and pointed figure of the Librarian, who has been transformed by some always previous, always ill-described act of magic into an orang-utan.

The witches in these books, however, represent another world, another *topos*, altogether. Reminiscent throughout of the three witches of *Macbeth*, they also represent three ages, stages and representations of witchcraft.[3] Granny Weatherwax, feared by villagers, aloof in her dealings with others, infinitely knowledgeable not only about herbal remedies but also, through her very own 'science' of 'headology', about human nature, is the witch as wise woman, terrifying and respected in equal measure. Nanny

Ogg is a different kind of witch: lubricious, full of sexual innuendo and given to over-eating and over-drinking, she signifies a different kind of female solidarity, the solidarity of childbirth, solicitude over errant husbands, the ability to rise above the vicissitudes of women's lives into a realm of Chaucerian ribaldry and jollity.[4] She is a one-woman hen party. And the third witch, the regrettably misnamed Magrat, is a parody of the maiden, all Glastonbury bells, beads and candles, hopelessly otherworldly as far as the older witches are concerned yet representing in some sense a more 'modern' witchcraft tradition.

As to Rowling, I have only space here to mention one crucial scene, which occurs in the final book, *Harry Potter and the Deathly Hallows*, where a final battle for power is played out between two versions of the witch.[5] What we might call the 'domestic', communal version is represented by Molly Weasley, wife to an abstracted and foolish (though lovable) husband, mother to seven (yes, of course, seven) boys, preoccupied with feeding her family and their friends, able to perform magic but apparently too busy most of the time with the mundane to bother with such frivolities. The other version of the witch is encapsulated in Bellatrix Lestrange – the witch as murderous, vengeful; angry with a psychotic fury that appears to know no bounds.[6] On the one hand the village wise woman, healer, supplier of goods both physical and spiritual, on the other the witch as source of fear, caster of curses, devastator of livestock. The witch can bless, and the witch can curse; it comes, of course, as no surprise who wins the battle (cf., for example, Sallis 2000).

In Neil Gaiman's rather more erudite *Stardust* (1998), we come across places of the witch and witchcraft in abundance; and in particular, there is again a group of three witches. They are nameless and old, and the plot is based around their search for rejuvenation. There are lone witches in literature – the Wicked Witch of the West, for example (Baum 1900) – and there are male witches – think of Tolkien's shadowy but tantalizing Witch-King of Angmar. But on the whole witches are female and multiple, and thus fit precisely into the category Jung defined as 'anima' (see Hillman 1979). But more than that; they can fit at times, especially in their pagan triplicity, with ancient representations of the terrifying, eating, castrating, threateningly fertile female: the Norns, the Furies, the harpies, the Graeae, the Gorgons – perhaps the list would be longer but for the overwhelming force of monolithic Greek and other patriarchies and their enduring power of displacement (see, for example, Graves 1948).

The force of the witch in *Stardust* derives from antiquity, but also from the weakness always inherent in the search for immortality. The witch-queen, eldest of the three sisters, sets out to replenish her sorority's supply of youth, but her story intersects with others: principally with a tale about succession – which of seven (yes, seven) brothers is to become the anointed ruler of the realm of Stormhold – and with a different tale of a young man, Tristran, who is charged by his beloved with finding for her a 'fallen star'. This fallen star, however, when Tristran finds it, turns out in fact to be a beautiful if rather alarming young woman, and the true inheritor of Stormhold is herself revealed as a woman, in fact as Tristran's mother.

This extended fable of the witch thus becomes another account of the three ages of woman – maiden, mother, crone – as it also becomes a story about liminal spaces, *magissatopias*, in particular those two countries which lie on either side of the 'wall' – on the one side the world of the everyday, the rather drab environs of village life, on the other the 'realms of faerie'. Yvaine, the fallen star, cannot return across the wall, because she would be transformed into the lump of rock which is all that is left, in the 'real' world, of 'star' material.

What, however, of the witch? Well, the motif of the witch in the novel bifurcates: on the one hand there is the witch-queen, possessed of enormous power (although insufficient to save herself and her sisters from ageing); on the other there is the figure known sometimes as Madame Semele and sometimes as Ditchwater Sal (her name varies precisely according to her *topos*, her location) who represents what we might by now call the 'everyday' form of witchcraft, a 'traveller' figure, complete with caravan, charms and spells, who reminds the reader above all of the gypsy. That gypsies and witches have always had a legendary affinity is perhaps a point that needs no reminder, especially in terms of their common history of abjection and exile from any space that might be considered to be their own; but what is significant in *Stardust* is the struggle between these two forms of the witch – the figure of power and the probable charlatan or chancer.

I want to turn now to a novel which is probably far more strange to the reader than the ones I have already discussed, David Lindsay's *The Witch*. If Lindsay is known at all, it is probably because of a book called *Voyage to Arcturus*, published in 1920, which is sometimes thought of as science fiction, although in truth it is a fantasy novel set in a remarkable profusion of strange places, heterotopias. He also published a book called *The Haunted Woman*, and both are characterized by two things: first, an extraordinarily powerful imagination; second, a writing style of such clogged and frequently ungrammatical density as to defy description. He was, one critic has remarked, the greatest writer in English to be unable to write English.

The Witch, you may or may not be pleased to hear, is even worse. The edition in which I have read it – it was not published during Lindsay's lifetime – was published in 1976, and the editor coyly remarks that he has tidied up the style here and there – to, I would say, little or no effect – though who can say? However: to the place of the witch. The first thing to say is that there is, in *The Witch*, no witch. Or rather, there may be: but as our hero is led by clues (which are to the reader incomprehensible) to pursue her, she continually retreats. As readers we even frequently doubt the status of the only brief glimpse of her to be found in the entire book, which is very near the beginning.

You will by now not be surprised to hear that what entrances me about this book – for I am entranced by it – is the spatial undecidability of the witch. She cannot be contained by boundaries; the evidence of her presence, or of her passing, is continually erased; it is unclear whether she takes a single form or many. She may merely be a figure for an only half-understood desire on the part of our hero; alternatively, or as well, she may be a figure for death, as the unattainable and constantly retreating female so frequently is in the ghost stories of, for example, Algernon Blackwood.

She casts no spells, we might say; yet the entire texture of the book is testament to an enveloping spell; and this spell takes a specific form, which is music. As again with Blackwood, in, say, *The Human Chord*, verbal language is insufficient; it could be argued that Lindsay's bizarre style is more willed than most critics have thought, and that it is designed specifically to repel meaning and demonstrate the feebleness of language when it comes to grasping higher truth (although in fairness, if that is the case, then one might ask why write at all?).

At any event, the witch in *The Witch* (if you see what I mean) is not there; she is a hole, a tear in the fabric of the everyday, a place that is not a place, a witch without witchcraft but with the power to form worlds, to relegate our customary view of events and history, as Gothic so often does, to a childish fantasy compared with the truer world which she represents and inhabits. I have to move on, after my brief mystical phase, to another excellent book which is not well enough known, *Witch Wood*, which is by John Buchan, a prolific popular writer, as you will know, but capable of a great deal more than that. And here, to an extent, we return to our witch-roots in the seventeenth century. That, of course, is simply what I am taking as my base for this chapter; the first witch in Western literary history is probably the biblical Witch of Endor, but because the word 'witch' was in this case supplied by the authorized version of the Bible, and this was commissioned by James I, otherwise famous for his terror of witchcraft, work on demonology and function as his very own witchfinder-general, one could argue that this takes us full circle – while underlining the significance of the fact that *Witch Wood* is, hardly surprisingly given that Buchan was himself a Scot, set in the specifically witch-haunted landscapes of Scotland.

It follows more or less directly in the tradition laid down so effectively by James Hogg in *Confessions of a Justified Sinner*, in that it deals in a rigid, high-minded but ultimately deeply oppressive form of Calvinist religion. To this it opposes, however, not the devil himself, as Hogg does in the form of Gil-Martin, but the apparently demonological practices of a group of villagers. The reality-status of these practices is left for the most part unclear; but the opposition itself is clear enough – between organized, institutionalized religion and the problematic survival of folk memories, the dances in the woods, the Dionysian rites that still survive in the dark places.

It is a book about haunting, about witchcraft, and about shape-changing. It is perhaps the shape-changing which I want to emphasize, for this strikes to the very heart of the legendry of the witch. For the witch, crucially, is not herself and can therefore be pinned down to no locality; she is the site of transformations. I have already mentioned the trope of witch's familiar, and it would take but a small step to see in this relation between the familiar and the unfamiliar the outlines of Freud's famous definition of the uncanny. Now you see her, now you don't. On the one hand, she is a 'familiar' element or aspect of community life, to be appealed to on matters requiring supernatural intervention, from individual health to the plague, from childbirth to the repelling of invaders; on the other, she is the utterly unfamiliar because she refuses to stay in one place, she refuses patriarchal categorization. Wherever the reasonable place, the space that can be categorized, might be, the witch is elsewhere: out of sight on the far shores of the fantastic.

The point is put particularly clearly in Paulo Coelho's *The Witch of Portobello*, which is centred on an idea of the 'worship of the Great Mother'. Whether Athena, also known as Sherine, the central figure, is actually part of this worship is a question forever deferred, since the entire book comprises different voices, different experiences of Athena, which never quite come together as a composite picture – spatially we might think of it as a form of cubist writing, perhaps. At any rate, one of these voices – a male one – tries to account for the phenomenon, which, he says, is 'hardly a new one':

> Whenever a religion tightens its rules, a significant number of people break away and go in search of more freedom in their search for spiritual contact. This happened during the Middle Ages when the Catholic Church did little more than impose taxes and build splendid monasteries and convents; the phenomenon known as 'witchcraft' was a reaction to this, and even though it was suppressed because of its revolutionary nature, it left behind it roots and traditions that have managed to survive over centuries.

Now, I don't want it to be supposed that I subscribe to Coelho's simplistic views on history, so clearly exemplified in *The Alchemist*, and after all on the following page he asserts that there is no female presence in Taoism despite the thousands of year in which Dao has welcomed and ordained female clerics, but this paragraph does serve, at least, to summarize one of the main lines of thought on the multiple locations of witchcraft.

Coelho summaries another one when he has another of his male characters – who are constantly, we notice, engaged in 'writing the woman' – say "I've always been convinced that women have a supernatural ability to know what's going on in a man's soul. They're all witches". This dismissive comment is, of course, par for the course: if a man can see into a woman's soul, then he has a gift – whether it be of magic, or love, or psychological acumen; if a woman can see into a man's soul, she is in 'the wrong place' – she is a witch.

But the so-called witch in *The Witch of Portobello*, although – or perhaps because – she is only seen through the eyes of others, is a character of interest. This is partly because she is an adopted child: born in Romania – yes, of course, to gypsies – then adopted into a Lebanese Christian family, from which she flees to London, then to Dubai – and so on. What this spatial rootlessness gives her is a need to 'fill in the gaps': this is most literally presented when she is learning Arabic calligraphy, and her teacher tells her that although her writing, her presentation of soul in letters, is improving remarkably, she has yet to give life and vividness to the gaps between letters and words. There is a gap in her past; and alongside the highly modern resonances here, we may also set historical and legendry uncertainty about the birth of witches, associated as this is with the intervention of the demonic, an unnatural transgression between realms.

It is probably as well to read these undecidabilities about the origin of witches as a characteristic reversion to the age-old uncertainty, resolved only by DNA testing, about paternity (when did you really last see your father?); and here we might think also, if there were space, about religious notions of immaculate conception – but I must move on, albeit in the light of some of these reflections, to my final text, Helen Oyeyemi's *White Is for Witching*. This is probably unique among the books I have mentioned in that in it we find ourselves frequently looking out through the eyes of the witch, whose name is Miranda.

But, of course, as in so many other cases it is not clear whether Miranda is a witch; it may be, for example, that the house in which she lives, the space she ambiguously occupies, is the real source of agency here. It is haunted by spirits from the past, in particular by the spirit of Miranda's great-grandmother, who shares (I put that in the present tense because in this house nobody is ever dead) the same eating disorder as Miranda – 'pica', a medical condition that leads to the consumption of chalk, pebbles, coal, anything which is non-nutritious. And indeed, we even see through the eyes – or windows – of the house at some points in the story.

Miranda's difficulties are also due to race, and they are due to what we might also refer to as body dysmorphic disorder; the witching referred to in the title and throughout the book might have nothing to do with Miranda's agency, or even that of the haunted house, but might instead be the effect of the impossibility of living within one's own skin:

> She tensed, and I cracked her open like a bad nut with a glutinous shell. She split, and cleanly, from head to toe. There was another girl inside her, the girl from the photograph, all long straight hair and

pretty pearlescence. This other girl wailed, "No, no, why did you do this? Put me back in". She gathered the halves of her shed skin and tried to fit them back together across herself.

What is the desire *of* the witch – not the desire which society implants on her suffering body, not the desire imputed to her through societal fear of the supernatural, but the desire *she* feels? The witch, it appears here, feeds on the unnatural; she consumes food which is not made for man. The witch can transform her own body, so that she becomes her own unfamiliar familiar. The witch has power over her associates (as does Miranda, in a fleeting, ephemeral kind of way). But the witch is also a victim. She is a victim of her own physical uncertainties; she is a victim of her outcast status, here emblematized principally in terms of race (Oyeyemi's black British self is somewhere here inside Miranda); she is a victim, in the end, of the baleful fate that awaits witches – probably dead, perhaps only confined behind an unbreakable wall which will not allow her to escape and return to a quotidian, living world, a place which will have nothing to do with witches, as it wishes nothing to do with the gendered or racialized other. It is, obviously, no accident that *White Is for Witching* is set in Dover.

I wish there were time here to refer to Toni Morrison's *Beloved*, which bears obvious comparison, but I am afraid there is not. Neither is there time to refer to Oyeyemi's Nigerian cultural ancestor, Amos Tutuola, with his tales of witchcraft in the Nigerian bush.[7] But just one or two closing remarks.

First, there are connections between witchcraft and the Gothic, and I worry that perhaps I have not made it sufficiently clear that the topology of witchcraft and the more conventional locations of the Gothic are intimately linked. They are, in two ways: first because there are plenty of witches, although some are known by another name, in the original Gothic – the figure of Matilda in Matthew Lewis' *The Monk* is the first to come to mind. But second, and more importantly, Gothic has always been a place to tell alternative histories, to find different, unfamiliar accounts of the world, and the witch, as liminal, alternative figure, is an apt location or metaphor for this alternative, unfamiliar view of the world where spaces of the fantastic continually loom and interlock.

I would want to add that there is no answer to the question of the witch, in part because the witch is a figure of transmutation and resurgence. Although it is true, as I have said, that there were male witches put to death during the terrible times of the trials, the vast majority were women, and most historians concur in seeing the phenomenon – hysterical, if you will, although the very term contains within itself an unfathomable gendered irony – as to do with anxiety about female knowledge and the ways in which this needed to be regarded as supernatural, which is, after all, but a short step from unnatural. It might therefore be that it is, forever, the 'season of the witch', in so many senses: because the witch is always 'in season', in the sense of being available to be hunted; because the witch has her own 'seasons' in the sense of periodic returns and recessions, as women's bodies do; because the witch will always recur, as the seasons do – although to pursue that path would take us into so many other cultures (and most recorded cultures have witches or some such phenomenon, some actuality of haunting, blessing, cursing: Chinese and Japanese fox fairies are just the first instance to come to mind).

'The witch is dead' – how comforting a thought that would be. Yet perhaps not: perhaps the idea of the witch is itself a succour of the deprived, the stricken, the powerless. But I cannot end without engaging with the most recent manifestations of so-called witchcraft in Britain, namely the accusations of witch practices levelled against small children by, among others, populations in the United Kingdom. What are we to make of this?

One must be brief. Accusations of witchcraft are made – always, and without exception – against the weak, the vulnerable, the confused. They are also, often, the outcome of an instability in religious certainty. But this returns us to what we might see as the main issue, which is about the witch's propensity to cast spells, to curse: perhaps the witch stands in for a wider wish to utter curses, to condemn – but we as ordinary citizens do not seem to have this power, and so will the witch arrive to redeem us from our impotence (which of course, to return momentarily to an earlier point, may be a form of adolescence); but then, of course, we will simultaneously need to continue to reject, to abject, to scapegoat the witch – witches, as unacknowledged parts of ourselves – in order to turn away from fears whose source may lie deeply in unresolved conflicts – about gender, about race, about power, about maturation – within our own customary, familiar acceptances. The witch needs a space of her own; but this space, while sometimes a place of succour or respite, is more usually a location of confinement, to do more with assurances of our own (temporary) safety than with her own.

Notes

1. The notion of 'witch-becoming' might refer us to the numerous examples of non-human becoming mentioned in Deleuze and Guattari (1987).
2. Cf., of course, William Harrison Ainsworth, *The Lancashire Witches* (1849).
3. Perhaps the world's most ancient witch, the Witch of Endor, appears in the Bible, in Samuel I, 28.
4. See Geoffrey Chaucer, 'The Wife of Bath's Tale', in *The Canterbury Tales* (C14th).
5. See my *Rapture: Literature, Addiction, Secrecy* (Eastbourne, 2009).
6. The crucial duel between Molly Weasley and Beatrix Lestrange occurs in the last book of the Harry Potter series, *Harry Potter and the Deathly Hallows* (2007).
7. See Amos Tutuola, e.g., *The Palm-Wine Drinkard* (1946) and *My Life in the Bush of Ghosts* (1954).

References

Ainsworth, W.H. (1849). *The Lancashire Witches*. London: Henry Colburn.

Auerbach, N. (1995). *Our Vampires, Ourselves*. Chicago: University of Chicago Press.

Baum, F. (1900). *The Wonderful Wizard of Oz*. New York: George M. Hill Company.

Deleuze, G., and Guattari, F. (1987). *A Thousand Plateaus: Capitalism and Schizophrenia*. Massumi, B. (trans.) Minneapolis: University of Minnesota Press.

Gaiman, N. (1998). *Stardust (Being a Romance Within the Realms of Faerie)*. New York: Vertigo.

Graves, R. (1948). *The White Goddess: A Historical Grammar of Poetic Myth*. London: Faber & Faber.

Hillman, J. (1979). *The Dream and the Underworld*. New York: Harper and Row.

Hutton, R. (1999). *The Triumph of the Moon: A History of Modern Pagan Witchcraft*. Oxford: Oxford University Press.

Macfarlane, A. (1970). *Witchcraft in Tudor and Stuart England*. London: Routledge.

Oyeyemi, H. (2009). *White is for Witching*. London: Picador.

Pratchett, T. (1980). *Wyrd Sisters*. London: Victor Gollancz.

Pratchett, T. (1991). *Witches Abroad*. London: Victor Gollancz.

Punter, D. (2009). *Rapture: Literature, Addiction, Secrecy*. Eastbourne: Sussex Academic Press.

Rees, C. (2000). *Witch Child*. London: Bloomsbury.

Rowling, J.K. (2007). *Harry Potter and the Deathly Hallows*. London: Bloomsbury.

Sallis, J. (2000). *Force of Imagination: The Sense of the Elemental*. Indianapolis: Indiana University Press.

Tutuola, A. (1946). *The Palm-Wine Drinkard*. London: Heinemann.

Tutuola, A. (1954). *My Life in the Bush of Ghosts*. London: Heinemann.

Warner, M. (2014). *Once upon a Time: A Short History of the Fairy Tale*. Oxford: Oxford University Press.

Winterson, J. (2012). *The Daylight Gate*. London: Bloomsbury.

2 Spaces of the Fantastic, the Fantastic of Spaces

(Psycho)Wandering the Urban Texture of London

C. Bruna Mancini

Crossing Boundaries and Haunting Thresholds: The Spaces of the Fantastic

What exactly is the fantastic? This question is still very much a topic of discussion. The long list of definitions that have appeared over time are often conflicting. The term has been characterized as an ambiguous category which refers to any form of magical, frightening, supernatural, or mysterious intervention, frequently colliding with other well-structured genres such as science-fiction, gothic, fantasy, and so on and so forth. The only recurrent element seems to reside in its antithesis to realistic fiction. In this sense it seems meaningful when Romolo Runcini defines it essentially in spatial terms, as crossing the threshold between real and unreal (Runcini and Mancini, 2009). This crucial crossing – from the known to the unknown, the full to the empty, the centre to the peripheries – is insecure, uncertain, dangerous, and defines the specific nature of the genre. Its characteristic ambiguity has often kept it on the margin thus overstepping every kind of limit or boundary. Indeed, this transgressive, uncanny, excessive genre often voraciously swallows others and incorporates them. It is enhanced by the persistent presence of fear and uncertainty and spawned an intriguing philosophical lucubration on life and death. Runcini affirms that the fantastic neglects the positive value of experience and memory. It relies on the vague, extemporaneous suggestions of the *rêverie*, on hesitations and fears in order to compete with the unknown. Therefore, the fantastic distances itself from the historical perspective and transforms the contextual references into visions and impressions perceived through an indefinite 'intellectual reality'. Runcini observes that only a clean break with experience and 'reality'[1] can give room to the action performed through one's personal determination and subjectivity.

Nonetheless, everyday life constitutes the authentic basis of the fantastic; in particular, its liminal, familiar and yet uncanny spaces, whenever a spark of irrationality bursts forth. In fact, the artistic and literary language of the fantastic is the most suitable to absorb these kind of spaces and transform the 'limit (of/in) situations' into a crazed phantasmagoria of an improper act of knowledge, or even better, an act without any experience. Károly Kerényi observed that in the past, in order to face this contingency, human beings used to ritualize it and insert it into the safe horizon of myth, thus the community had the time to assimilate slowly this new (unfamiliar) experience. Then by following personal inclinations stabilize the historical memory of the group. Nowadays, instead, with secularization, the division of labour, industrial and telematic development, and the so-called mass society, human beings can no longer interact directly within a natural context. This relationship is always mediated or re-mediated. In artistic/literary language, only the allure of the fantastic can evoke the defenceless, hesitant, loss of individuality of the self. Thus, the fantastic can free the reader from the normative bonds of haste and industriousness.

The fantastic focuses on the dialectics of the liminal, dark, frightful spaces of our everyday life and of ourselves. It is always permeating into the cracks and into the rifts of the real. It is present on the threshold between known and unknown, weird and daily, domestic and obscure, upside and downside, or the sudden upside down. It is a labyrinthine, both enigmatic, mysterious. It is a dangerous path in which it is extremely easy to lose one's direction and one's good sense, indeed, it is the immersion into the narrow, uncertain, insidious spaces of the rhizomatic existential dimension. It is a hermeneutical space that can be found only in language – as Paul Ricoeur would affirm. The logical sense is far from simply organizing and connecting the words of everyday life. What we call 'normality' transforms itself into a magma without any coherence. The fantastic envisions the temporal continuum through a partially fragmented lens altering the perspective and denying the deceiving 'serenity of the art'. In doing so, it furiously transcends 'reality', showing it as a true 'fall of the underworld'. The fantastic through the language of art and literature evokes a kind of 'return of the repressed' in which the image of the world (and its double, reflected in narrative texts) is an image in a distorted mirror.

Following Runcini's teachings, a sublime example of these literary 'spaces of the fantastic' is E. T. A. Hoffmann's famous short story, "The Sandman" (1815), which seems to cause a proper deep (narrative) crack in the realistic nineteenth-century German literature. It shows that, behind the usual backdrop of reality, some mysterious and uncanny whirlwinds spread out. It can be as a sort of enigmatic portal that can swallow up the characters as well as the readers and take them into an upside-down world. A world in which it is possible to face one's own alterity and to recognize in the surrounding universe a shadow of the most intimate human fears. They are frozen into the ambiguous space 'beyond the mirror', or fascinated by a drainage system between the pavement and the cobblestones in a dark street where the monster hides in order to destroy one's dreams. For example, from those first lines of Hoffmann's tale, written in epistolary form in order to recall and deconstruct a plausible atmosphere, Nathanael shows an obsession that sketches – like an x-ray – an everyday reality which is full of uncanny presences, dark perspectives, and lethal gazes. What used to be familiar looks more and more mysterious, more spectral, more unpleasant and despicable. A room transforms itself into a frightful cave. An old wardrobe turns out to be a dark cavern where a strange fire is burning. Home becomes the realm of transgression, of the forbidden, and of the bizarre.

Nathanael's initial fear becomes an obsession full of shocking interdictions when he is gripped by the terror that Coppelius or the Sandman could pull out his eyes and take them to feed to his own children. The reader is the double, the reflection of the protagonist and is dragged into Nathanael's vortex of fear. Evil peeps out from the breaches of the real, and insinuates itself into a dissolving, fragmented, metamorphic, nightmarish space. Thence, Hoffmann's tale becomes a fantastic spell in front of the mirror of reality.

Mapping the Fantastic Space of London

In *Space and the Postmodern Fantastic in Contemporary Literature* (Routledge, 2015), Patricia Garcia underlines that – at least before the publication of her own book – there has been no comprehensive model for analyzing space in relation to the Fantastic. Indeed, existing methodologies on space (Bachelard, Foucault, Moretti, Tuan, Massey, Hanson, Pratt) and on space in narrative (Hamon, Blanchot, Ronen, Soubeyroux, Álvarez Mendez) do exist, but they do not centre their interest on the Fantastic. Better still, the existing studies on the 'fantastic space' essentially focus on space as a metaphor, not on space as a physical dimension (re)created in the Fantastic texts. It is very possible that contemporary studies on space and spatiality could provide new paths, new itineraries, and new maps for the Study of the Fantastic. Robert J. Tally affirms that maps offer a representation of the space sketched in them and are never neutral or objective. They are a powerful interpretation of space. Maybe, that is why writers love maps and collect, create, describe, and dream about them (see also Hones, 2014). Maps are strange and wondrous things that reveal as much as they obscure. Asley Harrys and Jonathan Harrys observe that "Representations of space are involved in the very (re-)production of that space, meaning that maps have the power to influence the formation of territory, just as territory forms the inspiration for maps" (346). In his *Maps of the Imagination*, Peter Turchi writes that every writer is also a kind of a cartographer: "We organize information on maps in order to see our knowledge in a new way. As a result, maps suggest explanations; and while explanations reassure us, they also inspire us to ask more questions, consider other possibilities" (Turchi, 2004: 11). In "Mapping Narratives" (2014), Tally recalls that Joyce once stated that his goal in writing *Ulysses* was to give "a picture of Dublin complete that if the city one day suddenly disappeared from the earth, it could be reconstructed out of my book".[2]

After all a city like every other text not only tells history and but sums it up. As a matter of fact, in *The City as a Work of Art: London, Paris, Vienna* (1986) Donald J. Olsen considers the urban texture as a complex but legible document that can communicate precise perspectives about the values and the aspirations of its governors, its rulers, its builders, its citizens. The polysemy of its messages and its languages, the different codes used by its observers/citizens/walkers is why it is so complex for the not sequential reading. Therefore, the urban text is an endless hypertext, a monument/document that can stir up fear and wonder, joy and anxiety in its observers/decoders/citizens, but above all can be read as re-written in a literary and narrative form. As the boundary between reality and image is weak, labile, and ephemeral nowadays the real city looks more and more like the imaginary ones, overturning the terms of comparison. The urban texture becomes a linguistic/poetical text, the space of (the fantastic) narration. Quoting de Certeau, we could define it a *texturology*, very much similar to a rhizomatic network, and – as such – very complex to decode.

As John Gay had already forewarned in 1716, in his urban eclogue *Trivia, or, the Art of Walking the Streets of London*, in order to go through this dangerous labyrinthine urban texture the walker had to be an initiate of a superior and arcane art or cult. He had to be able to recognize its unknown signals, its dangerous paths, its untold stories, attentively moving like Theseus into the Knossos labyrinth. In the eighteenth century, London was the worldwide capital of finance and commerce, a shelter of exiles and crooks, a trading place where wares, money and peoples were exchanged on a daily basis. Everyone was chewed **out**, mangled, sold and brought into the big murky Babel of the Modern times. In very vivid language, Fernando Ferrara describes eighteenth-century London like a load of bleeding and rotten innards, sweating and stinking of the crap of indecent humanity. Like a muddle of worms, these scary inhabitants crowded the entrails and wielded knives, canes, hooks, rods in order to compete for every inch of soil and ready to beat up, hit, or stain the unwelcomed wayfarer (Ferrara, 1992). Besides Ferrara, also Charles Dickens, in an article entitled "Streetography", taken from *Household Words* (1851), described attentively the same typology of human fauna, affirming that to walk the streets of London was very dangerous, because of its criminality, its violence, its mystery. In his travel book entitled *English Hours*, published in 1905, Henry James defined London as a dreadful, hideous, cruel, mysterious, infernal city "where the natural fate of an obscure stranger would be to be trampled to death in Piccadilly and have his carcass thrown into the Thames".[3] For James, it has a smeared face and stony heart and is immeasurable, to the point that it is a monster whose embracing arms never meet. More than that, London is "a mighty ogress who devours human flesh", but she has a good alibi for that:

> It is mainly when you fall on your face before her that she gobbles you up. She heeds little what she takes, so long as she has her stint, and the smallest push to the right or the left will divert her wavering bulk from one form of prey to another. It is not to be denied that the heart tends to grow hard in her company; but she is a capital antidote to the morbid, and to live with her successfully is an education of the temper, a consecration of one's private philosophy. She gives one a surface for which in a rough world one can never be too thankful. She may take away reputations, but she forms character. She teaches her victims not to "mind", and the great danger for them is perhaps that they shall learn the lesson too well.

London – Jack the Ripper's bloody nest, Mr Hyde's playground, the only place where Poe's 'Man of the Crowd' could ever have felt at home – has always been the perfect (fantastic) maze in which to hide and seek mysteries, crimes, atrocities, unsaid and unknown disquieting enigmas. J. G. Ballard, the famous 'New Wave' science fiction writer, has described it as the surrealist canvas on which human psychopathologies could have been sketched.[4] It is a liminal, indefinite, oneiric, strange landscape where dreams and nightmares can meet and overturn, as it is the Pandora's box of our contemporaneity, uncannily predicting the future of London painted in the frightening colours of violence, racism, and inhumanity. In his post-Freudian worldview Ballard's London is fulfilled by multi-level car parks, shopping malls, elevated motorways, flyovers, drained swimming pools, isolated skyscrapers, and sinister gated communities. As he wrote in *High-rise* (1972), from the balconies, London's ragged skyline resembles "the disturbed encephalograph of an unresolved mental crisis" (9).

Michael Moorcock, another celebrated 'New Wave' writer, editor of the sf magazine *New Worlds*, describes the city as a porous urban hypertext in *Mother London* (1988) This epic novel that narrates 40 years of English history, from world conflicts to the 1980s, moving backwards and forwards in time, through the legends, the memories, the predictions, the empathy of the characters who inhabit the 'New Jerusalem of our times'. London becomes a maternal body with some evil dispositions. David Mummery, one of the main protagonists, is a journalist, a writer, and an "urban anthropologist". He is involved in writing the forgotten stories of London using his paranormal powers that allow him to read the thoughts of the city and its people. In his visions, Mummery perceives a 'fabulous flotsam' that transforms itself into metaphysical music:

> the city's inhabitants create an exquisitely complex geometry, a geography passing "*beyond the natural to become metaphysical*", only

describable in terms of music or abstract physics: nothing else makes sense of relationships between roads, rails, waterways, subways, sewers, tunnels, bridges, viaducts, cables, between every possible kind of intersection.

(7)

That '*going beyond*' what is considered natural, normal, or ordinary seems to be another typical feature of the fantastic genre that recalls the crossing of the threshold between real and unreal, known and unknown. Moreover, two other characters of Moorcock's novel, Joseph Kiss and Mary Gasalee, walk the streets of London tracing out its arcane pattern using their telepathic powers. The centuries gather into a complex cacophony that represents the true existence of the city:

Mummery found nothing alarming or mysterious about their condition, believing that most people chose to ignore the available information while certain cynics turned it to their advantage and became confidence tricksters, modern witch-doctors, publicists, predators of myriad varieties. Unable to block the wealth of information provided by a great city easily, he (David Mummery), she (Mary Gasalee) and Joseph Kiss were like powerful wireless receivers who must learn how to adjust their fine tuning to keep a required station.

(Moorcock, 30)

London's geography transforms itself into a psychogeography, or, the pseudo-science of occult symbols. It transforms into lost or erased spatial configurations, the semiology of London's cultural marginalia. In "Watching Your Step: the History and Practice of the Flâneur", Chris Jenks has written that psychogeography derives from

the subsequent 'mapping' of an unrouted route which, like primitive cartography, reveals not so much randomness and chance as spatial intentionality. It uncovers compulsive currents within the city along with unprescribed boundaries of exclusion and unconstructed gateways of opportunity. The city begins, without fantasy or exaggeration, to take on the characteristics of a *map of the mind*.

(Jenks, 154)

Psychowandering the Urban Networks: The Fantastic of/in London

In his Prologue to *Psychogeography* (2007), Will Self observes that:

Although we psychogeographers are all disciples of Guy Debord and those rollicking Situationists who tottered, soused, across the stage set of 1960s Paris, thereby hoping to tear down the scenery of the Society of Spectacle with their devilish *dérive*, there are still differences between us. While we all want to unpick this conundrum, the manner in which the contemporary world warps the relationship between psyche and place, the ways in which we go about the task, are various.

(11)

Self explains that some see psychogeography as concerned with the personality of place itself (like Peter Ackroyd and his 'phrenology' of London), while others prefer to pursue a 'deep topography', a detailed multilevel examination of select locales that impact upon the writer's own microscopic inner-eye (like Nick Papadimitrious). In fact, this occult art of walking the city of London officially dates back to the nineteenth century, when the urban flâneur Thomas de Quincey reimagined his surroundings through a veil of opium, juxtaposing the familiar and the alien, the seen and the perceivable. Almost exactly one century later Arthur Machen in *The London Adventure, or, The Art of Wandering* (1924), one of the most important texts in occult and literary geography, the narrator walks the city streets feeling a mysterious connection between past and present events, places and the people who inhabit them. A strange belief in miracles and wonders creates some eerie parallels between the narrator's experiences and those of sixth century monks. He affirms,

> I do my best to conquer this 'scientific' nonsense; and so, as I have noted, I try to reverence the signs, omens, messages that are delivered in queer ways and queer places, not in the least according to the plans laid down either by the theologians or the men of science.
>
> (14)

The 'Ars Magna of London' conceals a world of supernatural significance under the familiar surface of the urban streets, but the trained eye of the psycho wanderer can reveal the eternal behind the commonplace. Through Machen's 'London science', the writer/walker aims to utterly shun the familiar in favour of a deliberate attempt to lose himself through aimless wandering. As Merlin Coverley points out, Machen frees himself from all geographical or historical markers, and he remaps the city as he passes through it: "in establishing a trajectory away from the more well-trodden centre toward the overlooked suburban quarters of the city" (Coverley, 50). This crossing of every kind of habit and/or pre-established order definitely recalls the ex-centricity of the fantastic, with its dangerous transgressions, its fearful uncertainties, its uncanny hesitations that constitute the main features of the genre.

In *Walking Backwards: or, The Magical Art of Psychedelic Psychogeography* (2018) Greg Humphries and Julian Vayne observe that in the mid-twentieth century the Situationists formalized the wanderings of the *flâneur* into a political act, naming it psychogeography, which means: "The study of the specific effects of the geographical environment, consciously organized or not, on the emotions and behaviour of individuals" (Coverley, 93). From the outset, the Situationist International sought to distance itself from the primarily artistic preoccupations of the Lettrists in favour of a revolutionary political agenda (see Ford 2004). Hence, what was a playful avant-garde movement with a clear debt to the Surrealists became a radical political organization keen to overthrow and replace the predominantly bourgeois nature of Western society. To this end, the Situationists pursued a theoretical and practical activity of constructing situations. Thus, they used their bodies to carve new paths through space, intending to sculpt it anew. In "A Road of One's Own", published in the *Times Literary Supplement* (7 October 2005), Robert MacFarlane sketched a sort of beginner's guide to psychogeography:

> Unfold a street map of London, place a glass, rim down, anywhere on the map, and draw round its edge. Pick up the map, go out in the city, and walk the circle, keeping as close as you can to the curve. Record the experience as you go, in whatever medium you favour: film, photograph, manuscript, tape. Catch the textual run-off of the streets; the graffiti, the branded letter, the snatches of conversation. Cut for sign. Log the data-stream. Be alert to the happenstance of metaphors, watch for visual rhymes, coincidences, analogies, family resemblances, the changing moods of the street. Complete the circle, and the record ends. Walking makes for content; footage for footage.[5]

The map of London becomes a kind of Ouija board a porous portal towards Freud's the Uncanny. It is a fantastic text to decode in order to apprehend and to get in contact deeply with one's urban environment and oneself. In the book entitled *Psychogeography* (2010) Merlin Coverley clarifies that in the 1950s Guy Debord – member of the Letterist Group, a forerunner of the Situationist International – often repeated that the term describes, "the study of the specific effects of the geographical environment, consciously organised or not, on the emotions and behaviour of individuals" (10). In this sense, walking becomes an act of transgression, of subversion, provocation and trickery, a political opposition to authority as well as to the London governance (as in the works of contemporary London Psychogeographers such as Iain Sinclair, Peter Ackroyd, and Stewart Home). Walking is especially an act of transgression if we think that nowadays the simple act of walking is contrary to the spirit of the contemporary city with its promotion of swift circulation, celebrating the praise of speed. Walking requires a more personal relationship with the urban space, which establishes new routes and new perspectives, and which explores those marginal and forgotten areas often overlooked by city's inhabitants. In Coverley's words, psychogeography represents "the point where psychology and geography intersects" (13), in search of new ways of apprehending our urban environment and overcoming the processes of 'banalization'. The city is perceived as a site of mystery with the (psycho)walker seeking to reveal the true an occult nature that lies beneath the flux of the everyday:

> The act of urban wandering, the spirit of political radicalism, allied to a playful sense of subversion and governed by an inquiry into the methods by which we can transform our relationship with the urban environment. This entire project is then further coloured by an engagement with the occult and is one that is as preoccupied with excavating the past as it is with recording the present.
>
> (Coverley, 14)

In short, the urban (psycho)wandering is an imaginative reworking of the city, evoking the otherworldly sense of spirit of place through unexpected insights and juxtapositions created by aimless drifting, or *dèrive* – a new way of experiencing familiar and yet unexpected surroundings.

Arthur Watkins's *Theory of Ley Lines* is another key element of this eccentric, liminal, fantastic perspective. Watkins, known as the prophet for New Age ideas, was a sales rep for a local brewery. At the age of 65, while travelling across the Herefordshire countryside he perceived that the surrounding familiar landscape was covered by a vast prehistoric network of straight tracks, aligned through the hills, beacons, mounds, moats and other landmarks. As he wrote in *The Old Straight Track* (1925), the alignment across miles of country of a great number of objects, or sites of objects, of prehistoric antiquity in scores and hundreds "are either facts beyond the possibility of accidental coincidence or they are not" (Watkins, XX). His theory intersects with psychogeography as he takes into consideration the existence of urban leys. In fact, he affirms that: "There are curious facts linking up orientation with the ley system illustrated by some London Churches" (133). This point of view proposes an occult pattern encompassing Nicholas Hawksmoor's six remaining London churches. Hawksmoor was an English architect and an active freemason who lived between the seventeenth and the eighteenth centuries. In *From the Shadows* this architect becomes rather a cult figure with his churches that rear up above their surroundings like fossilized beasts (Hopkins, 2015). In late twentieth-century literature his architecture was that transformed by a magician, an orchestrator of occult symbolism. Iain Sinclair and Peter Ackroyd, in particular, have woven respectively a novel around Hawksmoor's buildings, seen as the site of the fantastic, in which ley lines and psychogeography converge.

The Fantastic Psychogeography of Hawksmoor's London Churches

In *The Old Straight Track*, an esoteric book centred on dowsing and geomancy, Alfred Watkins wrote that: "There are curious facts linking up orientation with the ley system illustrated by some London churches" (Watkins, 133). He refers to a strange 'force' or 'power' whose nature remains unclear, a visionary English tradition starting with de Quincey and Blake, among the others, that celebrates the *genius loci* in both the otherworldliness of the English countryside and the labyrinthine complexity of London. In this sense, such a tradition intersects and oversteps Debord's perspective, according to which the city had to be rebuilt upon a magical awareness of the fantastic that surrounds us, a new method of apprehending our environment. The political theorist and activist Ivan Chtcheglov affirmed that:

> All cities are geological; you cannot take three steps without encountering ghosts bearing all the prestige of their legends. We move within a closed landscape whose landmarks constantly draws up toward the past. Certain *shifting* angles, certain *receding* perspectives, allow us to glimpse original conceptions of space, but this vision remains fragmentary. It must be sought in the magical locales of fairy tales and surrealist writings: castles, endless walls, little forgotten bars, mammoth caverns, casino mirrors.
>
> (Knabb, 1–2)

According to Chtcheglov, 'banalization' was the mental disease that had swept the planet. The cure for such a malaise could have been a new way to envisage the urban environment, in which architecture reflects an emotional/intimate engagement with its inhabitants. In this perspective, the 'psychogeographer' is a kind of skilled chemist who is able both to identify and to distil the varied ambiances of the urban environment through the mandate of a new science called 'psychogeography'. In Debord's words, it concerns "the study of the precise laws and specific effects of the geographical environment, consciously organized or not, on the emotions and behaviour of individuals" (Knabb, 5). Therefore, Debord sees psychogeography as the point where psychology and geography collide. The emotional and behavioural impact of urban space upon individual consciousness had to be carefully monitored and recorded in order to promote the construction of a new urban environment that reflects the inner responses of its inhabitants. The emotional zones of the city had to be determined by following the aimless stroll or *dérive*, with the aim of forming and performing a new cartography. As Debord wrote in "Introduction to a Critique of Urban Geography" (1955):

> The production of psychogeographical maps, or even the introduction of alterations such as more or less arbitrarily transposing maps of two different regions, can contribute to clarifying certain wanderings that express not subordination to randomness but complete *insubordination* to habitual influences.
>
> (Knabb, 7)

Coverley underlines that nowadays psychogeography remains alert to the increasing banalization and commodification of the urban environment and "continues to provide a political response to the perceived failures of urban governance" (Coverley, 111). Of course, the playful, plagiaristic and political activities of the Situationists and their avant-garde forebearers continue to be expressed through the psychogeographical groups, but the best results can be found in its narrative/literary versions, in particular, in the fictional "Londons" depicted by some psychogeographical authors such as Stewart Home, J. G. Ballard, Patrick Keiller, Iain Sinclair, Peter Ackroyd, just to mention the more well-known names. In *Lights Out of the Territory* (1997), Sinclair writes that:

> Walking is the best way to explore and exploit the city; the changes, shifts, breaks in the cloud helmet, movement of light on water. Drifting purposefully in the recommended mode, tramping asphalted earth in alert reverie, allowing the fiction of an underlying pattern to reveal itself.
>
> (4)

His complex 'London Project' – which incorporates poems, novels, documentaries and films – had the aim of coping with mythology and the matter of London, following his own belief in the power of a transformative bond between walking and (every kind of) writing. As a matter of fact, in his *Liquid City* (1997) he writes of:

> Strategic walks (. . .) as a method of interrogating fellow pilgrims. Walks as portraits. Walks as prophecy. Walks as rage. Walks as seduction. Walks for the purpose of working out the plot. (. . .) Walks that release delirious chemicals in the brain as they link random sights. (. . .) Savagely mute walks that provoke language.
>
> (15)

Iain Sinclair's *Lud Heat*

In his prose-poem *Lud Heat. A Book of the Dead Hamlets* (1975), Sinclair proposes the occult/uncanny alignment of Hawksmoor's London churches arguing that some 'lines of forces' can be traced among them in order to reveal a mysterious secret, the hidden relationship among the city's financial, political, and religious institutions. He suggests that:

> A triangle is formed between Christ Church, St George-in-the-East and St. Anne, Limehouse. These are centres of power for those territories; sentinel, sphinx-form, slack dynamos abandoned as the culture they supported goes into retreat. The power remains latent, the

frustration mounts on a current of animal magnetism, and victims are still claimed.

St George, Bloomsbury, St Alfege, and Greenwich make up the major pentacle-star. The five card is reversed, beggars in snow pass under the lit church window; the judgement is "disorder, chaos, ruin, discord, profligacy". These churches guard or mark, rest upon, two major sources of occult power. The British Museum and Greenwich Observatory – the locked cellar of words, the labyrinth of all recorded knowledge, the repository of stolen fires and symbols, excavated god-forms – and measurement, star-knowledge, time calculations, Maze Hill, the bank of light that faces the Isle of Dogs. So many spectres operate along these fringes.

(16–17)

The old maps present a skyline dominated by these churches. Nicholas Hawksmoor's churches soon invade the consciousness, giving shape to a 'geography of fear and mystery': white stones erected on a fen of undisclosed horrors. Hawksmoor, the surveyor, walked over the ground, drew up the plans, made wooden models in order to rewrite the city. His churches are incredible grafts, risky quotations, key symbols that remain secret. The author observes that there is the sub-system of five obelisks: St. Luke's, Old Street, and St. John's, Horsleydown. They form an equilateral triangle, raised over the water, with London's true obelisk, Cleopatra's Needle. Moreover, along the long chain of Hawksmoor churches (Figure 2.1), Sinclair notes five minor obelisks in the fenced area beyond Blake's burial slab:

The Old Street obelisk is aligned beyond the boundary wall: the point of force is discovered. We also come across a lichen diagram, the quadrivium, recognised later in that walk, the conflux of four roads beyond St George's-in the East.

(17–18)

Marking the total plan of Hawksmoor's churches on the map, it is possible to try to decode its meanings. In fact, for what we know of Hawksmoor – the skilful mathematician, geographer, geometrician, passionate psychogeographer, and walker – it is plausible to imagine that he did work a code into the buildings; each building and all the buildings taken together "knotted across the city, yield a further word" (19), Sinclair observes. They are totems, drawn by the energy of London. The churches are a system of energies, or a unity of connection within the urban texture. Each of them is "an enclosure of force, a trap, a sight-block, a raised place with an unacknowledged influence on events enacted within their name-lines" (19). Metaphors inflate. Obviously, the Tower is central, a fixed point: "The lesser vertebrae support the wings of the beast. The web

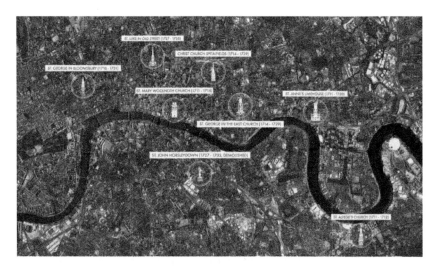

Figure 2.1 Map of Hawksmoor's Churches

is printed on the city and disguised with multiple superimpositions" (18). The possibilities are multiple and fascinating:

> We can still follow one direct line of escape: Christ Church – Bunhill Fields – St Luke's – the Penton Mound and Suicide Ponds – Parliament Hill. The returning arrow is equally interesting: St George's, Bloomsbury – Cleopatra's Needle – Blake's Lambeth. And the connecting rod. The straight line from Hercules Road to Christ Church passes, of course, through St Mary Woolnoth, Hawksmoor's pulpit of slave sermons, attacks on the blood trade. Christ Church is in alignment with St George's in-the-East and St Alfege's. St George's in-the-East and St Luke's are equidistant from Christ Church, etc., – This is another whole work.
>
> (18)

Sinclair's delightful and yet uncanny blend of paranoia, occult imagination and London history places him within a tradition of London visionaries and urban (psycho) wanderers, authors, and explorers of the fantastic such as Blake, Stevenson, Machen, Ballard, Moorcock. Sinclair's connected buildings are "generators" of an uncanny kind of energy as they were built on lines where murders, ritual killings, mysteries, unknown and incomprehensible events of the hidden and lost city occurred.

Sinclair invokes the theory of the ley lines proposed by Watkins, and revives the occult and old visions of London, updating the classic image of the *flâneur* into the figure of the stalker, with his walking made with a thesis or an intent, a stroller who sweats, inspects and knows where he is going, but not why or how. Merlin Coverley observes that:

> Sinclair's peculiar form of historical and geographical research displays none of the rigour of psychogeographical theory and is overlaid by a mixture of autobiography and literary eclecticism. But beneath this allusive surface, lies a political engagement and a clear anger directed against the legacy of Thatcherite redevelopment.
>
> (121)

Under the surface of this fantastic text, that haunts and grips like an assassin's hands, always lies our society with its occurrences, its desires, its fears, its mistakes. It is undoubtedly an eerie reflection of what we are and the way we live, investigating within the folds of our reality. In fact, Moorcock defined Sinclair a revenant, an archivist of the marginal, a genuine wizard capable of tracing patterns and designs only barely perceptible to most people and able to reveal them to us (Figure 2.2).

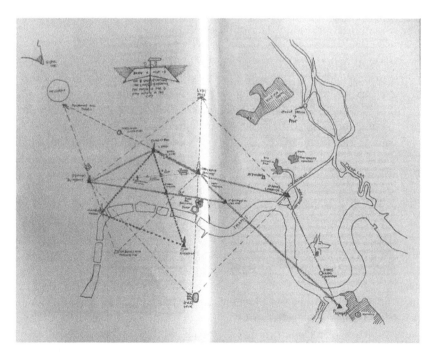

Figure 2.2 Sinclair's Map of King Lud

London is a rhizomatic texture to navigate, to explore, to dive into in order to recognize oneself and one's own reality. Coverley writes that "London's topography is reconstituted through a superimposition of local and literary history, autobiographical elements and poetic preoccupations, to create an idiosyncratic and highly personal vision of the city" (121–2). Hawksmoor's churches represent Ariadne's thread, a personal and initiatic path into and beyond London streets. And it is meaningful that the same occult symbolism and sense of history espoused by Sinclair is echoed by Peter Ackroyd in his novel *Hawksmoor* (1985), where Sinclair's earlier speculations are extended in Ackroyd's idiosyncratic theory of temporal and spatial correspondences within London. As we know, Peter Ackroyd is one of the most recognized biographers of London,[6] in which he recognizes some zones within the urban text(ure) that display some clear resonances with past events, activities, and inhabitants. For example, in *Hawksmoor*, Ackroyd's detective muses upon the tendency of murders and their victims to return repeatedly through the centuries to similar places, as if they were drawn there by some evil force: "Certain streets or patches of ground provoked a malevolence which generally seemed to be quite without motive" (116).

Peter Ackroyd's *Hawksmoor*

Ackroyd's novel tells two stories in alternating chapters. The odd-numbered chapters are set in London between 1711 and 1715 and are written in the first person, as a kind of "confession" or "true account" of the events narrated in accordance with the narrative conventions of the period, while the even-numbered ones are set in Margaret Thatcher's London and told by an apparently objective third-person narrator who seems to assume the perspective of the victims themselves. In the earlier narrative, the architect Nicholas Dyer relates how he murders young boys to offer them up as sacrifices in churches that the city of London has commissioned him to erect as beacons of a rational, humane religion. In the later narrative, Nicholas Hawksmoor is a detective commissioned by Scotland Yard to investigate seven inexplicable recent murders committed at the churches built by Nicholas Hawksmoor in the eighteenth century. The watchful reader can recognize the strict connection of this character with the historical figure of Hawksmoor, who was Wren's collaborator in the rebuilding and expansion of London after the Great Fire. Indeed, the detective Nicholas Hawksmoor has a time-transcending *Doppelgänger*-relationship with the eighteenth-century murderer Dyer, who is modelled after the historical architect Nicholas Hawksmoor himself. A series of infinite reflections characterizes the narrated events. As Martin Rosenstock affirmed in an essay of 2013: "The detective is in pursuit of himself; in an allegorical sense, Western culture is searching for those of its traits it had to slough off in the process of its modern constitution" (132).

Moreover, the novel seems to interweave and to compare science and occultism, reality and imagination, morality and geniality into the complex urban texture of London that is the principal protagonist of the two correlated stories. In fact, it represents a perfect example of postmodern historiographic metafiction, of the Gothic, and of the Fantastic.

As Will Self observes, Ackroyd's aim is ambitious:

> to expose the linear character of time as described by conventional narratives – whether real or invented – for the fabrication that it is, and to propel his readers into a zone of full temporal simultaneity. Read *Hawksmoor* intently, read it as a divine might his breviary, or an adept his arcane text, and it will work its magic on you – you will become that wanderer beside St Mary Woolnoth, gripped by a transgenerational ague.
>
> (VI)

Thus, also the reader(s) and the assassin/narrator Dyer end by coinciding. Ackroyd has fully acknowledged the influence of Sinclair's *Lud Heat* on his novel. Will Self writes that it is also possible to find the notion of Hawksmoor's forms performing a murderous function: "the pyramids, towers and spires of his churches provoking blood sacrifices such as the Ratcliffe Highway murders to loving limned by De Quincey in *On Murder as One of the Fine Arts*" (VI). Nicholas Dyer's journal clearly recalls both Pepy's and Defoe's writing, full of Frenchified suffixes and irregular orthography, and testifies his repulsion and his lure towards the London risen upon the plague pits and the ashes of the Great Fire. Following an almost endless process of self-reflection, since the beginning Dyer's design and Ackroyd's novel seem to mirror one another, and celebrate "the art of Shaddowes" because: "(i)t is only the Darknesse that can give trew Forme to our Work and trew Perspective to our Fabrick" (2). As David Ashford writes in an essay in the Literary London Journal in 2014, the churches of the Freemason Hawksmoor are explicitly identified with contemporaneous transformations in literary form that would ultimately result in the novel:

> I have finished six Designes of my last Church, fastned with Pinns on the Walls of my Closet so that the Images surround me and I am once more at Peece. In the first I have the Detail of the Ground Plot, which is like a Prologue in a Story; in the second there is all the Plan in a small form, like the disposition of Figures in a Narrative; the third Draught shews the Elevation, which is like the Symbol or The of a Narrative, and the fourth displays the Upright of the Front, which is like to the main part of the Story; in the fifth there are designed the many and irregular Doors, Stairways and Passages like so many ambiguous Expressions, Tropes, Dialogues and

Metaphoricall speeches; in the sixth there is the Upright of the Portico and the Tower which will strike the Mind with Magnificence, as in the Conclusion of a Book.

(Ackroyd, 205)

Throughout this piece of fantastic narrative and its paths (also the physical ones performed inside the urban hypertext of the city) it is possible to investigate the hidden stories of London and its inhabitants. Both the killer and the solution of the mystery lie hidden away in the unconscious memory of the detective Hawksmoor and in the bowels of the city itself, built "upon the Dead" (4). David Richter observes that in *Hawksmoor* Ackroyd conveys the baleful influence of monstrosities realized inside the urban texture and he inextricably connects them with the novel structure and its postmodern fight against the English conventional aesthetics that has been reified into a codified tradition; after all:

> when Dyer is not murdering innocents to lay their corpses in the foundations of his Satanic churches, he is engaging in a running debate, a *querelle des anciens et des modems* – against a series of rationalistic opponents, who include fictional characters along with real ones like John Vanbrugh and Christopher.

(Richter, 112)

As the reader goes on, he/she finds more and more

> shocking reduplications of names, events, actions, even identical sentences uttered by characters who live two centuries apart, until we are forced to conclude that, in the novel, nothing progresses in time, that the same events repeat themselves endlessly, and that the same people live and die only in order to be born and to live the same events again and again, eternally caught in what appears to be the ever-revolving wheel of life and death.

(Onega Jaén, 33)

In detail, Hawksmoor and Dyer are simultaneously complementary and opposite, a kind of 'repetition-with-difference' that recalls Beckett's tramps, ghostly figures in suspension and in decay waiting for another day or century to come. The interchangeability between the two characters and among all his/their victims underline a circularity that is also echoed at the structural and symbolic levels. Their nest is a very mysterious and uncanny London, standing out against an official appearance of rationalism and coherence. Onega Jaén underlines,

> The acknowledgement of the existence of this *mundus tenebrous* is the first step in the direction of true knowledge, one capable of

unravelling the labyrinthine course of its occult mysteries, which are open only to those versed in the Scientia Umbrarum, the occult science developed out of Neolithic, Hermetic, Cabalistic and Gnomic elements.

(Onega Jaén, 37)

In the Preface, Dyer is clearly presented as an architect and as a magus who works to access the true knowledge of the occult. He is the Master-Mason[7] able to activate and to proceed through a diagrammatic map inspired by the Method of Loci, or Memory Palace, spoken of in the *Rhetorica ad Herennium*. Obviously, he is scared by the weight of such a dreadful magic/knowledge and fears to be assaulted by ghosts and spirits. Anyway, together with Mirabilis and the members of the Black Step Lane occult society, he thinks that the only way to escape the desperate destiny of humanity is to realize the *Anthropos*, the cosmic man, a kind of a godly figure who would permit the return to heaven. In the end, the two characters of Dyer and Hawksmoor speak in one voice. They seem to achieve the ultimate transformation and to fuse into another mysterious and uncanny being, maybe the *Anthropos*, left begging on the threshold of eternity. This explains Dyer's obsession with creating a geometric pattern with his churches, capable of reflecting the "Proportion of the Seven Orders" through calculation of "the positions and influences of the Celestial bodies and the Heavenly Orbs" (5). As also Onega Jaén observes, when Dyer projects a certain pattern with his seven London churches, he is submitting to his will the seven planetary gods who control the intermediate spheres between god and the world:

It is in the light of this theory of reincarnation that the duplication of characters and the repetitions of situation and actions acquire overall meaning, as it helps explain the otherwise baffling existence of Hawksmoor: Dyer, who must experience all kinds of human situations in order to achieve his long sought-for essential transformation, has to be both murderer and victim, but also criminal and criminal hunter.

(Onega Jaén, 41)

The great chain of repetitions and re-incarnations finds its umpteenth reflection in a palimpsestic London seen as "the Capitol of Darkness", through the fantastic pattern designed by Dyer with his churches, but also as the threshold or portal for other kinds of spatialities.[8]

Alex Link writes that Ackroyd's novel:

posits a London replete with forgotten places that repress the excess traditionally apparent in the popular and in the feminine, and that offer the possibility of social relations unmediated by modern capitalism or national history. When these places re-emerge in the uncanny, they open a space for popular voices, and they realign the urban subject's relation to urban history by fracturing its apparent seamlessness.

(Link, 516)

In this perspective, Links affirms that the novel employs a heretofore unacknowledged 'third term' and abstract[9] spatiality that gives voice to the repressed, the excess and the abjection in the form of the feminine, the popular, the poor, the body, the corpse. The uncanniness of Dyer's (and Hawsmoor's) churches feeds the local knowledge that produce the timelessness of the popular – as Link emphasizes. In Ackroyd's novel, initially Dyer's churches are built as instruments driving an urban illusion of 'opacity', thus declaring them the perfect realization of Wren's rationalism. Only later they re-emerge as uncanny, counter-rational, fantastic places: a return of the repressed that takes advantage of "the disjunctions in urban spatiality generated by competing discourses of power" (Link, 521). In short, the transformation of these churches moves them to the edge of the dynamics of capital:

They become instead a response to capitalist abstract spatialities in the form of sites of uncanny, repressed cultural values: indigenous English cultural history, the legacies of paganism and Catholicism, and a sense of a historical continuity that is at once inescapable and irrecoverable. (. . .) *Hawksmoor* suggests at least the following three things: first, that the organization of urban spaces is driven by inherently masculinist processes of abjection; second, that the unruly play of the popular opens urban spaces through the grotesque, fore-grounding the uncanny materiality of London's monumental signifiers and raising the uneasy possibility that historical progress is an illusion; and third, that the complexity of urban codes opens a space for a multiplicity of possible urban histories that are at once textual constructs.

(Link, 521–2)

It is easy to agree with Link when we move inside the London imagined by Ackroyd, seen as the place of abjection, excess, repression and difference. Wren's rational city harbours an indefinite number of pale, hidden, dangerous, mysterious sites in which it is possible to disappear. In Dyer's vision, through the descent into a deep pit he can enable one to see the brightness of the stars at noon. In this sense, also his churches may represent the obscure sites of potential resistance, erected to give the world a (maybe transgressive) coherence. Paraphrasing de Certeau, Steve Pile observes that, "the child's desire to control the mother plays out as a desire to control space: that is, to render space visible, transparent and readable" (Pile, 228). Thus, Dyer's churches may seem an abject response to the feminized "Nest of Death and Contagion" (47) Dyer sees in the stinking labyrinthine streets of London. They are a sort of disquieting pyramids rising "above the Mire and Stink of this City" (203) just in order to govern it. On the other hand, Hawksmoor has the duty to make sense – in the sense of putting together the pieces, the fragments, the carcasses – of the dismembered story he is investigating. The body of the city – like the female one – appears as a corpse on a dissecting table "seen without God and outside science" (Kristeva, 4) that represents the utmost abjection. The erection of Dyer's churches represents the celebration of knowledge upon a weak soil, filled with curses and corpses. In the complex system of an occult belief and of the Satanic community led by Mirabilis, the churches are the monument that document the evils of the British Metropolis and celebrate the return of otherness. At the end, during the late twentieth century, Christ Church is like a ghost amid a strong re-inscription of the urban space, filled with trucks, trains, graffiti, advertising, and so on and so forth. The murders have the power to rewrite, reassert or re-motivate the urban labyrinth of London through the voices, the bodies, the uncanny presence of the dead and everything lies unsaid, repressed, forgotten, below the surface of appearance, or between the margins of the known world.

As Will Self observes, for Ackroyd the *derive* is circumambulations through time as well as place:

> a widening gyre that exposes the very timelessness of this two-millennia-old city. (. . .) From the miserable trauma of Dyer's childhood, to the dazed and crazed tramp wandering the high road, to the frowsty landladies pleading for a little company, to the couples humping in the churchyards, to the children abandoned in the tunnels, this is a prose that (. . .) surges off the page to invade and then derange your senses.
>
> (IX)

Like Sinclair, Peter Ackroyd is obsessed with the repressed history of the contemporary landscape: "a coherent project that is both gripping in, and gripped by, its fascination with particular territories, driven by its concern with the rival claims staked by those who would both make and tell the history of those territories" (Mengham, 56). The city is a text(ure) that is endlessly recomposed, rewritten, inscribed on, fantastically reactivated. Ackroyd clearly believes in the transhistorical power of *genius loci*, the underlying forces operating within certain places and areas in London due to which these have managed to retain their particular spirit and atmosphere across centuries until the present day. His characters' circumambulations are primarily meant to visualize the spirit of the city, its imagination and perceptiveness: "the intricate, subtle and often contradictory relationship between personal and official histories within the city as an aggregate of commonly shared experience" (Chalupský, 12). In a truly psychogeographic manner, they can push the readers to receive the immensity of countless obscure stimuli through a series of epiphanies which may allow them to glance the at the city in its complexity, diversity, and hidden mysteries, because its 'unofficial', occult stories are even more important than the 'official' one.

Notes

1. After all, as Baudrillard wrote in *Simulacra and Simulation* (1994), our reality has lost all contact with the real world. Reality has begun to imitate the model which precedes and determines the real world. The map precedes the territory; the procession of simulacra engenders the territory. It is a question of substituting the signs of the real for the real. Thus, simulacra are copies that depict things either that had no original, or that no longer have an original, and substitute for reality.
2. See Frank Budgen, *James Joyce and the Making of Ulysses, and Other Writings*, ed. Clive Hart (Oxford: Oxford University Press, 1989), 69.
3. The text is downloadable: www.gutenberg.org/files/58938/58938-h/58938-h. htm#Page_1.
4. See my previous essays on "Imagined/Remembered Londons" (2004), "Neural Spaces in J. G. Ballard's *Vermilion Sands*" (2017), the first chapter of *Spazi del femminile* (2020), and the book edited with M. T. Chialant and C. B. Mancini, *Declinazioni del fantastico* (2020).
5. www.the-*tls*.co.uk/articles/private/a-road-of-ones-own/. See also Baker 2003.
6. In 2000 Peter Ackroyd published his *London: The Biography*. Martin Rosenstock observes: "For over three decades now, Peter Ackroyd has been with near obsession charting the geography and history of the city that in so many ways constituted an epicentre of this transition. London features in the majority of his works, sometimes as backdrop, more often as a shaping force in the lives of the text's characters, and occasionally as its overt theme" (131).
7. As the historian Vaughan Hart observes, despite the early eighteenth-century's appeal to reason, this was also the period of rapid growth of freemasonry as an institution, whose attraction lay in its apparent mystery, ritual, secrecy, and quest for hidden truth.
8. In an essay on William Blake, Ackroyd defines the occult as a potential site for the localization or the tactical creation of "some kind of reality beyond the world of the manufactory and the workhouse" (Ackroyd, 361).
9. For Lefebvre abstract space is space whose political inscription tends to be naturalized through the discursive mechanisms of power; (social) space is a (social) product and it behooves the analyst to inquire how "this fact (is) concealed" (Lefebvre, 27). See also: Bachelard, *The Power of Space* (2014).

Bibliography

Ackroyd P., 1985, *Hawksmoor*, London, Hamish Hamilton.

———, 2000, *London: The Biography*, London, Chatto & Windus.

———, 2012, *Lud Heat: A Book of the Dead Hamlets*, Cheltenham, Skylight Press.

Atkins M., I. Sinclair, 1997, *Liquid City*, London, Reaktion Books.

Bachelard G., 2014, *The Poetics of Space*, London, Penguin.

Baker B., 2003, "Maps of London Underground: Iain Sinclair and Michael Moorcock's Psychogeography of the City", *Literary London: Interdisciplinary Studies in the Representation of London*, www.literarylondon.org/london-journal/march2003/baker.html.

Baudrillard J., 1988, "Simulacra and Simulation", in *Selected Writings*, ed. Mark Poster, Stanford, Stanford University Press, pp. 166–84.

Bauman Z., 2003, *Wasted Lives: Modernity and Its Outcasts*, Cambridge, Polity Press.

Bhabha H., 1994, *The Location of Culture*, London and New York, Routledge.

Chialant M. T., C. B. Mancini (eds) 2020, *Declinazioni del Fantastico. La prospettiva critica di Romolo Runcini e l'opera di Edgar Allan Poe*, Napoli, Liguori.

Coverly M., 2010, *Psychogeography*, Herts, Pocket Essentials.

Debord G., 1992, *The Society of the Spectacle*, London, Rebel Press.

De Certeau M., 1984, "Walking in the City", in *The Practice of Everyday Life*, Berkeley, Los Angeles, and London, University of California Press, pp. 91–113.

De Quincey T., 1997, *Confessions of an English Opium-Eater*, London, Penguin.

Farnetti M. (ed), 1995, *Geografia, storia e poetiche del fantastico*, Firenze, Olschki.

Ferrara F. (ed), 1992, *Momenti della Città di Londra dalle origini a oggi*, Napoli, Istituto Universitario Orientale.

Ford S., *The Situationist International. A User's Guide*, London, Black Dog.

Foucault M., 2006, *Madness and Civilization*, London, Vintage Books.

———, 2001, *The Order of Things: The Archaeology of the Human Sciences*, London, Routledge.

———, 2007, *Security, Territory, Population*, Palgrave MacMillan.

Garcia P., 2015, *Space and the Postmodern Fantastic in Contemporary Literature*, London and New York, Routledge.

Gay J., 2016, *Trivia, or, the Art of Walking the Streets of London*, Penguin.

Hoffmann E. T. A., 1815, *The Sandman*, transl. Peter Wortsman, London, Penguin.

Home S., 1997, *The House of Nine Squares: Letters on Neoism, Psychogeography and Epistological Trepidation*, London, Invisible Books.

Hones S., 2014, *Literary Geographies. Narrative Space in Let The Great World Spin*, London, Palgrave MacMillan.

Hopkins O., 2015, *From the Shadows: The Architecture and Afterlife of Nicholas Hawksmoor*, London, Reaktion Books.

Humphries G., J. Vayne, 2018, *Wlaking Backwards, or, The Magical Art of Psychedelic Psychogeography*, Norwich, The Universe Machine.

James H., 1905, *English Hours*, www.gutenberg.org/ebooks/58938.

Kerényi K., 1950, *Labyrinth-Studien* (trad. di Leda Spiller, *Nel labirinto*, a cura di Corrado Bologna, Boringhieri, Torino 1983).

Kitchin R., J. Gleeson, M. Dodge, 2012, "Unfolding Mapping Practices: A New Epistemology for Cartography", *Transactions of the Institute of British Geographies*, vol. 38, no. 3, pp. 480–96.

Knabb K. (ed), 1981, *Situationist International Anthology*, Berkeley CA, Bureau of Public Secrets.

Lefebvre H., 1991, *The Production of Space*, Trans. by D. Nicholson-Smith, Oxford, Blackwell.

Link A., 2004, "'The Capitol of Darknesse': Gothic Spatialities in the London of Peter Ackroyd's", *Contemporary Literature*, vol. 45, no. 3 (Autumn), pp. 516–37.

Machen A., 1924, *The London Adventure, or the Art of Wandering*, London, Martin Secker.

Mancini C. B., 2004, "Imagined/Remembered Londons", *Literary London Journal*, vol. 2, no. 2, http://literarylondon.org/the-literary-london-journal/archive-of-the-literary-london-journal/issue-2-2/imaginedremembered-londons/.

——, 2017, "Neural Spaces in J. G. Ballard's *Vermilion Sands*", *Literary Geographies*, vol. 3, no. 2, www.literarygeographies.net/index.php/LitGeogs/article/view/21.

——, 2020, *Spazi del femminile nelle letterature e culture di lingua inglese fra Settecento e Ottocento*, Milano, Mimesis.

Moorcock M., 1997, *Mother London* (1988), Bath, The Bath Press.

Olsen D. J., 1987, *La città come opera d'arte: Londra, Parigi, Vienna*, Milano, Serra e Riva.

Onega Jaén S., 1991, "Pattern and Magic in *Hawksmoor*", *Atlantis*, vol. 12, no. 2 (noviembre), pp. 31–43.

Poe E. A., 1951, "The Man of the Crowd" (1840), in *The Complete Poems and Stories of Edgar Allan Poe*, with an Introduction and Explanatory notes by Arthur Hobson Quinn, New York, A. Knopf, vol. I, pp. 308–14.

Richter D., 1989, "Murder in Jest: Serila Killing in the Post-Modern Detective Story", *The Journal of Narrative Technique*, vol. 19, no. 1 (Winter), pp. 106–15.

Runcini R., 2012, *Abissi del reale. Per un'estetica dell'eccentrico*, Chieti, Solfanelli.

——, 2007, *Enigmi del fantastico*, Chieti, Solfanelli.

Runcini R., C. B. Mancini (eds) 2009, *Universi del fantastico: per una definizione di genere*, Napoli, Edizioni Scientifiche Italiane.

Self W., 2007, *Psychogeography*, with pictures by R. Steadman, London- Oxford – New York – New Dehli – Sydney, Bloomsbury.

Sinclair I., 2003, *Lights Out for the Territory*, London, Penguin.

Tally R. T. (ed), 2014, *Literary Geographies. Spatiality, Representation, and Narrative*, Cambridge, Polity Press.

Turchi P., 2004, *Maps of the Imagination: The Writer as a Cartographer*. San Antonio, TX: Trinity University Press.

Watkins A., 1925, *The Old Straight Track*, London, Methuen,

3 The Literary Motif of the Devil Architect

Where Built Space Meets the Fantastic

Patricia García[1]

"For the commission to do a great building, I would have sold my soul like Faust. Now I had found my Mephistopheles. He seemed no less engaging than Goethe's" (Speer, 1970: 31). These words were uttered by Albert Speer, Nazi architect and member of Hitler's inner circles. During his period as the Nazi Party's chief architect, Speer was in charge of designing buildings that projected the megalomania of the Third Reich. At the Nuremberg trials, from which he emerged as one of the few to be acquitted, Speer pleaded that his connection with Nazism had been motivated by utilitarian principles (see Forsgreen, 2012). This utilitarianism is captured in the preceding quote, in which Speer merges the act of constructing capital buildings with the fictional motif of the pact with the devil. This fusion of the architectural with the diabolic is the theme of this chapter, with a specific focus on the motif of the Devil architect in legends and in literary texts of the fantastic.

The first section presents a theoretical overview showing how the dimension of space has largely been reduced to serving as a neutral setting of the fantastic and how various biographies of the Devil pay little attention to the category of built space. The analysis is then structured into two focus areas. The first of these is of a historical-anthropological nature and explores the origins of the Devil architect in medieval folklore, highlighting the parallels in European legends. The second section offers an analysis of different variations of this motif in literatures of the fantastic from the twentieth and twenty-first centuries, drawing on texts by American horror writers H. P. Lovecraft, Shirley Jackson, Argentinean Jorge Luis Borges, and Peruvian Fernando Iwasaki, among others.

Space and the Fantastic

The relationship between the diabolic and material space has a long history. Architectural studies have focused on buildings that symbolize political tyranny or misrule (Kirk, 2008) or on constructions that violate human rights, such as concentration camps (Jaskot, 2000). Some have researched the intersectional symbiosis between space and the monstrous that stems from the metonymic relationship between architectural space and the human body (Frescari, 1991; Vidler, 1992). However, very few works have been devoted to the mythological figure of the Devil or to his imprint on built structures. A review of the key biographies dedicated to the Devil (Graves, [1924] 2000; Stanford, 1996; Kelly, 2006; Centini, 2012; Almond, 2014) and of canonical teratology studies, such as those by Dale Bailey (1999) and Stephen T. Asma (2009), exposes the fact that architectural spaces, to date, played little part in studies on the supernatural. While the Devil has been analyzed from a multitude of angles, including those of sin, sexuality, medicine, heresy, and exorcisms, there are few mentions of a devilish relationship with architecture. There are some exceptions: Peter Stanford's biography refers in a brief paragraph to the bridges and dams whose medieval legends are attributed to the Devil deeds (1996: 102). The Aarne-Thompson-Uther Index, a referential classification system of legends and fairy tales, assigns a stand-alone category to the Devil Bridge (category 1191) and *The Encyclopedia of Demons and Demonology* also dedicates a brief entry to the "Devil's Bridge" (Guiley, 2009: 65–6) without developing the transnational literary representations of this motif.

This dearth of studies is representative of the scant attention that has been paid to spatiality in studies on the fantastic. Space has not traditionally been conceived in narratology as an element with agency in the text. Whereas human characters, animals with anthropomorphic characteristics, and animated objects are attributed with the ability to influence the plot, space is not expected to function in this way: "Character is a text- or media-based figure in a storyworld, usually human or human-like" (Jannidis, 2012: 2; see also Prince, 1982: 71 and Bal, 2006: 12). An illustrative example is Tzvetan Todorov's canonical study on the fantastic, in which he refers to Witold Ostrowsky's scheme of reality as the basis for his theory (Figure 3.1):

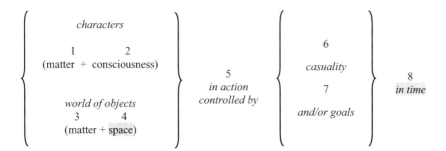

Figure 3.1 Witold Ostrowsky "The Fantastic and the Realistic in Literature: Suggestions on How to Define and Analyse Fantastic Fiction" (in Todorov 1975: 102, shading added)

Todorov's understanding of the fantastic regards space as nothing more than a situational dimension. Whereas everything unfolds in time, space is reduced to a container that hosts characters and objects. The same logic can be applied to the relationship between the diabolic and architecture. Space has been approached in, for example, endless studies on the haunted house as the setting for the supernatural (Vidler, 1992: 17–44; Bailey, 1999; Weinstock, 2014: 317–21), or as a reflection of the protagonists' psyche (see as an example "Le cauchemar comme espace maudit", Bozzetto 2001: 236–72) but not as the diabolic element as such.

How is the diabolic manifested in architectural form? Who builds it? What are the attributes of the builder? Is there a symbiosis between builder and built form? These questions can be fruitfully explored through the figure of the "Devil architect". This motif, which recurs across legends in Europe and is also present in texts of the fantastic, unifies three familiar elements of fantastic narratives: the motif of a cursed space, the theme of creation as a divine activity and the pact with the Devil in order to exceed human capabilities.

Origins of the Devil Architect in Folklore

Anthropological studies by Joseph Rykwert (1988), Otto Friedrich Boll-now (2011), and Myriam White-Le Goff (2014) offer some perspectives on human rituals that were developed with the aim of controlling the supernatural. Of the mechanisms designed to create the illusion of keeping the unexplainable under control, two types of approach stand out: those that frame the supernatural within spatial boundaries and thus build a separate space for it or those that give the supernatural the shape of a defined creature (for example monster, devil or *genius loci*, as discussed later).

Two examples, from very different eras, illustrate the first type of approach: the Roman *Mundus* and the Winchester Mansion. The *Mundus*, a ditch excavated by the Romans during the construction of new cities, was an opening into hell. As Rykwert explains, three times a year the lid of the *Mundus* was lifted open in a ceremony designed to reconcile the world of the living with the world of the dead. The rest of the year, the *Mundus* was kept covered, thus keeping the supernatural away from the human world (Rykwert, 1988: 59).

The Winchester Mansion (today Winchester Mystery House) in San José (California) is a further model of an architectural form that has been instrumentalized to control the supernatural. Legend has it that its owner, Sarah L. Winchester, widow of the famous weapon manufacturer, believed herself to be cursed for the deaths brought about as a result of her husband's business. She lived obsessed by the idea of being haunted by ghosts. To avoid this, she dedicated her life to building an enormous mansion that would tame and distract those spirits. In 1884 she purchased a farmhouse of about eight rooms; when she died in 1922, the building consisted of more than 160. The sprawling, eccentric architecture of this mansion reflected Sarah Winchester's obsession. The interior incorporated physically impossible spaces, such as stairs that led nowhere, so that spirits would be confused and misguided in their efforts to haunt her (see Schuyt *et al.* 1980: 196–9).

The second type of anthropological attempt to control the supernatural is illustrated by the figure of the *genius loci*, or spirit of the place, characteristic of pre-Christian pagan traditions. These deities varied according to geographical area and possessed the power to cause both good and evil. The locals would venerate them through rituals and offerings to gain their protection, secure good crops and avoid droughts, famines, and other natural disasters. The symbolic value of such deities was ambivalent: they had the power to protect as well as to punish. Humans had to live among these polyvalent spirits. Therefore, the spatial conception in these cases was more one of spaces being cohabited by humans and the supernatural than that of spaces doomed by magic forces.

This spatial paradigm was to change as Christianity developed. The convenient dualism (Stanford, 1996: 103) between the divine and the diabolic that permeated the Medieval Ages was personified in concrete figures: God and the Devil. Saint Augustine's interpretation of the Bible was key in assigning agency to the figure of the Devil as the incarnation of evil. Augustine's understanding of evil as the lack of good was intended to reconcile the conflict between reason and faith that had been the cause of so much worry to the Church Fathers and to later Medieval scholasticism. The representations of evil acquired traits that then made their way into the collective imaginary: the Devil as the greatest rival of God, the one who perverts the human being and who brings sin to the Garden of Eden. This belief consolidates religious dualistic thought by separating good from evil through the representative forms of God and the Devil (Bailey, 2013: 69).

As Christianity grew in influence, the control of culture and faith also extended to how this culture and faith were practiced in space. The multidenominational folklore beliefs of the *genius loci* were dangerous. Superstitions, characterized by magical aspects and personified in a vast diversity of pagan deities, were an obstacle to the unifying mission of Christianity. As a strategy, these pagan deities began to be associated with the Devil, in order to dismantle, dominate, and homogenize local beliefs. Those magic spaces previously inhabited by the *genius loci* increasingly became places considered as being cursed or possessed. Therefore, the idea of haunted, diabolic spaces or buildings made by a morally reprehensible being spread across Europe, reflecting the need to moralize and stigmatize pagan spatiality. The Devil became synonymous with all local deities that were in competition with the Christian

Figure 3.2 J. M. W. Turner, *Little Devil's Bridge over the Reuss* (Switzerland), 1809, Metropolitan Museum of Art, Public Domain

doctrine. A great number of legends associated with evil architectural structures attest to this change, such as "Devil's staircases" as found in the Finnish town of Porvoo, "Devil's cathedrals" such as the one in Cologne, and "Devil's bridges", a construction to which the Devil architect appears to have been particularly fond, with examples found across Europe, including in Eume (Galicia), Martorell (Catalonia), Segovia and Mediano (Huesca) in Spain, the Pont Valentré in Cahors (France), the Ponte della Maddalena and the Ponte del Diavolo in Lanzo Torinese (Italy), Dyavolski most in Ardino (Bulgaria), and the Devil's bridges in Kirkby Lonsdale (England), Aberystwyth (Wales), Einsiedeln and Reuss (Switzerland, Figure 3.2).

The Legends of the Devil Architect

What is it that links the Devil with particular buildings? Stanford (1996: 102) explains that some pagan gods, such as Thor, were portrayed as giants who created or lived in gigantic constructions. This allowed communities of the Middle Ages to rationalize the exceptional dimensions and complexity of certain existing built structures, in particular those of Roman origin. These legends become increasingly associated with the leitmotif of evil and thus the possessive term "the Devil's" was introduced to the names of bridges, staircases, cathedrals, and dams.

There is an alternative explanation for this vast array of buildings allegedly made by the Devil. Pedro Azara reminds us in his study on myth and architecture (2005: 29–40) that in its etymological and mythical origin architecture is a divine activity: the architect (*arché* – origin and *tektoon/tekne* – technique – construction – craft) is s/he who has the ability to create from a formless origin a space crafted for the human being to inhabit. Azara analyzes three common traits of the different constructing deities in myths: the original architect provides shelter from bad weather, external threats, the monstrous, and the unknown. S/he humanizes chaos and, most importantly, s/he succeeds in constructing a livable space, fulfilling the function of "removing humans from their human, barbaric condition" (Azara, 2005: 194, translation is my own). This is why foundational myths attribute a divine aura to the architect.

If architecture is an activity related and restricted to the divine, it should be no surprise that in the building of certain "monstrous" structures the devil is portrayed in medieval imaginaries as God's rival. Human creation is an activity close to the divine, as represented in other motifs such as that of the doomed artist. Therefore, to have been able to create certain constructions believed to be beyond human capabilities (too big, too complex, built in strange and dangerous locations, with unusual features), the builder must have sealed a pact with the God's enemy: the Devil.

The legends of the Devil's architectural creations contain clear common elements. The starting point of these legends generally takes the form of a challenge. In exchange for his help with the bridge-building project, the Devil obtains the guarantee that he can take possession of the first being to cross the bridge once it is finished, expecting this to be the protagonist with whom he has struck the deal. In many versions, the protagonist manages to trick the Devil by sending an animal down the bridge instead. This is how, according to the legend, the Devil is outsmarted by the human, the bridge stays, and order is restored in the village or town.

The legends of the Devil's bridge in the Spanish localities of Eume, Segovia, and Martorell feature a villager who needs to cross the river, to get water and to gather livestock. The Devil appears to the villager – who in many versions is an old woman – and proposes a solution to this arduous task: he will build a bridge for her overnight.

- [The Devil] I can see that the mishap you just suffered has rendered you desperate, and I come to offer my services: do you want to cross the river without delay, on foot and safely?

    (*Ponte de Eume*, Mellado, 1849: II, 35–6)

And one day, when she was going to get water, she cried out in desperation:

- I would give my soul to the Devil to have this hill made flatter.

- If you keep your word, I will soon make a bridge for you and it will ease the path for you.

> (*El Puente del Diablo, Puente de Segovia*,
> Camarena and Chevalier, 2003: 251)

———

- Is there anyone capable of building a bridge for this poor old lady who cannot collect water each day without becoming wet through?

> (*El Puente del Diablo [Martorell]*, Ausona 2004: 152
> [all translations are my own])[2]

In other versions, a pact is struck with a frustrated architect, who has been commissioned to build an extremely beautiful building. The completion of this task exceeds his capabilities and, in desperation, he strikes a pact with the Devil. An illustrative example is included in *Bulletin de la société des gens de lettres*, a Parisian periodical which in December 1851 published the story of *Le diable architecte*. The two legends featuring in this compilation describe some of the Devil's terrestrial excursions, as he intervenes in the construction of the cathedrals of Aachen and Cologne. The city of Aachen is looking for means by which to finish the cathedral when the Devil interrupts a session of the City Council. His physical appearance (an "impertinent stranger" with "hair as red as the flames from Hell"/"impertinent étranger", "cheveux rouges comme les flammes de l'enfer", Deslys, 1851: 316) and the manner in which he unexpectedly enters the room (of which all doors and windows are closed) give him away as Beelzebub. He identifies himself as contemptuous of churches but as a lover of arts and offers his help in exchange for the first soul that enters the cathedral upon completion. The economic desperation that prompts the City Council to accept this pact is rendered explicit:

- [The Devil] You are the penniless ones.
- [The Council] And you?
- [The Devil] Me, I am the one with the money.

> (Deslys, 1851: 16)[3]

The legend tells how the Devil's funds enabled the cathedral in Aachen to be completed but how for a while the new cathedral remained empty as nobody dared enter it. Seeking to trick the Devil, the Council sent a wolf instead of a human as the first being to cross the threshold of the cathedral. Upon realizing the trick, the Devil slammed the front door of the cathedral in a rage and in doing so severed his thumb. Some versions of the tale say that this fingerprint can still be observed today. In his collection of legends *Le Rhin* (1842), Victor Hugo refers to the legendary construction of this cathedral and adds that the Devil kicked the door so vigorously that a crack in the main door is visible to this day.

The legend of Cologne's cathedral became one of the most famous in popular culture and is still used in tourist promotion. That this iconic building, now designated a UNESCO World Heritage site, took such a long time to complete also inspired legends involving the Devil. In this case, the challenge involved was not financial but aesthetic. The Archbishop Conrad of Hochstaden wanted an architect who would be "up to task of making the dream a reality" ("à la hauteur de l'oevre rêvée", Deslys, 1851: 317). The protagonist, Wilhelm, a young man seeking to prove his genius, was the ill-fated architect who struck a pact with the Devil in order to accomplish this impossibly beautiful architectural work. Upon discovering that he had been tricked, the Devil stopped the construction works, making the completion of this exceptionally intricate architectural work impossible.

The aforementioned legends of Devil's bridges and cathedrals contain a discourse on the diabolic and the monstrous that can be appreciated on three levels:

> Aesthetic monstrosity, as with the cathedral of Cologne. The aesthetic characteristics conceived of by the Devil for such buildings exceed standard norms. These are excessively beautiful designs that no human hand could execute. After the Devil is tricked, his work of art cannot be completed by human hand: "No lines, no human combinations did succeed in reaching a harmony with the diabolic work. The unfortunate architect had to work day and night, blasphemed against the Devil and God, and ended his life damning his soul. After one month, he died trying".
>
> (Deslys, 1851: 319)[4]

> Physical monstrosity: the building requires engineering skill that exceeds human capacity. Some of the Devil's bridges were the highest, widest or most technically challenging in their regions, situated in complex geographical locations and with intricate arches. In some cases these bridges are suspended between mountains or waterfalls. Their inexplicable existence seemed to defy the laws of physics, which is why the motif of the diabolical pact comes into play.
>
> Moral monstrosity: the Devil finishes what the architect cannot or does not dare finish. He helps him overcome these human limitations for a price. The Devil's involvement allowed for the moralisation of these spaces and was also used to explain the great number of fatal accidents during their construction: it was a divine punishment for commissioning such diabolic structures.

The emphasis on the aesthetic, physical, or moral themes and motifs can vary across legends and literary texts, as analyzed in the next section. This difference of emphasis allows for the identification of different clusters of texts of the fantastic that present common features in the relationship between architecture and the diabolic.

Evil Architecture and the Architect of Evil in Literature of the Fantastic

Classic texts such as "The Nameless City" (H.P. Lovecraft, [1921] 2005), *The Haunting of Hill House* (Shirley Jackson, [1959] 1999) and other lesser-known stories, such as "La escalera de Sarto" ("Sarto's staircase", 1980) by Spanish author Ricardo Doménech and *The House Next Door* (2006) by American writer Ann R. Siddons, contain similar portrayals of the figure of the evil builder. In this group of texts the moral discourse associated with the evil architectural structure is highlighted. The architect (either voluntarily, as in the stories by Lovecraft and by Doménech, or involuntarily, as in Jackson's haunted house) works as a carrier of evil. He transmits this evil through his architectural constructions.[5]

The opening scene of "The Nameless City" introduces an explorer who enters a site that no other human has ever seen and that no other person dares approach. The traits of this city are only gradually disclosed to the reader, which contributes to the suspense in the story. The city that is revealed to the explorer in these initial scenes gives an insight into the architects who built it. The characteristics of the reptiles who designed the city are evoked in the descriptions of the different – and diabolic – architectural elements the narrator encounters as he advances in his search. These reptiles have built a space that both mirrors them and suits them to perfection.

Just like its inhabitants, the city is aesthetically monstrous. "Crumbling and inarticulate" (2005: 30), "too regular to be natural" (33), its indefinable age, size, and "changes of direction and of steepness" (34) characterize this grotesque site. The narrator realizes that this is not a space built for the human and by the human: "Not even the physical horror of my position in that cramped corridor [. . .] could match the lethal dread I felt at the abysmal antiquity of the scene and its soul" (39).

The diabolic is embedded in more than the physical structure of the city. This site eludes human codification: it is inexplicable, unnamable, and its ancient and labyrinthine design exists outside the laws of the spatial and temporal: "There is no legend so old as to give it a name" (30). The city is also morally condemned because it is the incarnation of evil, and as such it needs to remain buried, forgotten, and unfound ("antique and sinister secrets that no man should see, and no man else had ever dared to see" [30]).

Shirley Jackson's Gothic novel *The Haunting of Hill House* ([1959] 1999) uses similar mechanisms in presenting a fictional diabolic space. Hill House is haunted but there is no haunter; no ghost or fantastic creature is mentioned at any stage (cf. Finné, 2006: 12). Jackson dedicates extensive passages to the description of the physical features of this mansion and to the evil influence that the building's peculiar form exercises upon those who inhabit it. The distortion of "natural" form is recurrently employed in the text to portray how this structure diverges from architectural symmetry and harmony. Hugh Crain, its architect, has projected a "manic juxtaposition" of shapes and angles that render it "a masterpiece of architectural misdirection" (1999: 34–6). He has created a place "unfit for human habitation" (70). The character of the architect Crain, however, is only vaguely developed and has little agency. He is rather presented as an involuntary emissary of evil, because the true builder of this house is not human. Hill House is a diabolic product, "flying together into its own powerful pattern under the hands of its builders": "the evil is the house itself" (82). There is a passage in the novel that makes an explicit reference to the eccentricity and madness inherent in the Winchester Mansion: "old Hugh Crain expected that someday Hill House might become a showplace, like the Winchester House in California" (105).[6]

A further example of the motif of evil space is found in the novel *The House Next Door* (2006) by American writer Ann R. Siddons. Set in a residential neighbourhood in an ordinary North American suburban area, this apparently unremarkable house has the power to corrupt those who own it. As in Hill House, the architect character is presented as being possessed by evil:

> "It's not just in the house", I said, "it's in him first. In Kim. That's where it starts. It was born in him. He's a carrier, some kind of terrible carrier, and he doesn't even know it. It will be in everything he ever builds for as long as he lives, and he'll never know it".
>
> (Siddons, 2006: 350)

No monster inhabits this building and it is rather the whole structure that is evil; therefore, of central relevance is the perverse effect the house has on its inhabitants and the power it has to pervert the morals of a seemingly perfect neighbourhood community.

In the short story "La escalera de Sarto" (1980), the Spanish author Ricardo Doménech presents similar motifs and places a particular emphasis on the mundaneness of such diabolic constructions. The main character is a young art scholar who is obsessed with the origin, function, and shape of a certain staircase that has an unusual architectural form. The young man embarks upon a quest to understand this strange construction. When he finally finds the answer, he ascends the staircase in order to demonstrate his hypothesis empirically. His prediction was correct: it is a staircase of no return and thus he is never seen again. This staircase defies the laws of physics; on these steps one can only go upwards. The stairs are a bewildering architectural exception: "its architectural originality was evident at first glance" ("su originalidad arquitectónica se podía comprobar a simple vista", 1980: 31, translation my own). It needs to be kept hidden, or "neutralised" ("neutralizar", 35). The narrator tells us that the monks who guarded this staircase had covered up parts of it so that it would remain undiscovered. Some of the incoherent and absurd features of the staircase point to the fact that this is not a human construction: there were "paths that ascended and descended and ascended again, and they cut and converged, like a labyrinth, on top of each other" ("caminos que ascendían y descendían y volvían a ascender, y que tan pronto se cortaban como convergían, laberínticamente, unos en otros", 35). As with Lovecraft's evil city, this staircase eludes the human frame of time and any foreseeable human function: "it seemed that it had always been there" ("daba la impresión de que estaba allí desde siempre") (33); "it disregarded reality and utilitarianism" ("un desprecio de la realidad y de lo utilitario", 1980: 33). The protagonist comes to the conclusion that this "Devil's staircase" ("escalera del Diablo", 32) was built by a "strange and powerful creator" ("extraña y poderosa personalidad creadora", 33) who crafted this "diabolic invention", ("un diabólico invento", 35).

Argentinian writer Jorge Luis Borges invents a different type of evil space in his short story "El inmortal" ("The Immortal", [1947] 2007). Parallels with "The Nameless City" can be traced but in this case the supernatural architecture is portrayed without a moralizing discourse and without intimations of evil. The narrator of this tale does not condemn the City of the Immortals. While this site is portrayed as "superhuman" ([1947] 2007: 108), it is not diabolic. The original planners of this site are not devils but immortal beings, coming from "barbarous regions, where the earth is mother of monsters"; that these barbarous regions "could shelter in their interior a famous city seemed inconceivable to all of us" (107). The "enormous antiquity" (110) of this city renders it outside the temporal human frame: "I felt that it was older than mankind, than the earth" (110). Its structure has neither a logic perceptible to the human mind ("intellectual horror", "the interminable", "the atrocious", "the complexely senseless", 110) nor an identifiable purpose. Borges illustrates this by contrasting the city structure with the idea of the labyrinth. While the labyrinth has at least a recognizable shape and function, the City of the Immortals does not: "A labyrinth is a structure compounded to confuse men; its architecture, rich in symmetries, is subordinated to that end. In the palace I imperfectly explored, the architecture lacked any such finality" (110). The City of Immortals is a subversion of the concept of architecture as divine activity designed to protect the human, as encountered earlier in this chapter. The narrator expresses this idea in three consecutive reflections:

"This palace is a fabrication of the gods", I thought at the beginning. I explored the uninhabited interiors and corrected myself: "The gods who built it have died". I noted its peculiarities and said: "The gods who built it were mad".

(110)

Finally, there is a group of contemporary texts that stand out for their subversive use of the motifs identified in the traditional legends of the Devil architect. In the short stories "El proyecto" ("The project", Ángel Olgoso, 2009), "Dejen salir" ("Exit" or "Let me out", José Ferrer-Bermejo, 1982), "El nacimiento en el desván" ("The birth in the attic", José María Merino, 1982), "La cueva" ("The cave", by Fernando Iwasaki 2004), and "Voluntary Committal" (Joe Hill, 2005) the motif of architecture as supernatural element is once again central to the plot. However, there are significant differences between these texts and the previously analyzed stories. Firstly, in these texts the architect of monstrous structures has human attributes. Evil, the superhuman and pacts with the Devil are no longer present. In "El proyecto", for example, the architect is an ordinary boy who for his end-of-year project creates a miniature world that unexpectedly comes to life. In "La cueva", the builder of the supernatural is a child playing with bed sheets. He makes the sheets into a cave-shape, enters the sheet-cave and never returns. In "El nacimiento en el desván", the protagonist, who is passionate about miniature models, constructs a faithful replica of his town. This replica is so accurate that whatever happens in and to it has a direct impact on the real town of which it is a copy. In "Dejen salir", the person responsible for the construction of the labyrinthine metro station in Madrid is an engineer. The narrator is kept hostage by this structure, which – whatever turn he takes, always returns him to his starting point in a Möbius-type effect.

The act of creating a monstrous space is made banal in these stories. Not only is the discourse on Evil absent but the creation of a fantastic architectural piece is presented as accidental: an ordinary and casual act. The architect frequently loses control of the work he has created, as the following excerpts show:

He stepped back from this unexpected discovery and the surprise turned to fear – a cold fear that knotted up inside him – with a greater panoramic view of the village he could see that all the figurines moved.

(Merino, "El nacimiento en el desván", 1982: 19, translation my own)

Against all logic, random processes began with the splitting of unplanned atoms, and a wild breath of life began to spread inexorably.

(Olgoso, "El proyecto", 2009: 22, translation my own)[7]

The other significant modification in these texts is that although the creation is less ostentatious and more mundane (a school project, a metro station), the implications are far reaching. The architect is a creator of worlds; he builds new realities that swallow him up, as in "La cueva" and "Voluntary Commital". He even creates spaces that end up replacing the reality they imitate, like in "El nacimiento en el desván". Some texts render explicit the biblical connotation of creation as a divine act. For example in "El proyecto", the child models "a small clay ball [. . .]. It had taken the child six days to create that world" ("una pequeña bola de arcilla que había modelado cuidadosamente [. . .]. El niño, con orgullo de artífice [. . .]. Al niño le había llevado seis días crear aquel mundo", Olgoso, 2009: 22–3).

The microstory "El dominio" ("The domain", 2004) by Peruvian writer Fernando Iwasaki experiments with a more radical variation of the motif of the Devil architect by introducing touches of humour. Iwasaki proposes a change of context – contemporary and mundane – in which to situate the pact. The story is built around the semantic polyvalence of the term "domain". The protagonist buys the internet domain of "el infierno" (hell) www.infierno.com. When the Devil learns of this, he contacts the protagonist and offers him a pact: a great sum of money in exchange for both his domain and the protagonist's soul. The pact is described in the terms of a financial transaction in a corporate, neoliberal context: the protagonist becomes a client of the Devil. The enforcement of the pact is communicated by email, sent from Hell. The tone recalls the polite formulas of standard customer service correspondence: "Dear client, according to our files, your soul has been added to our database. With kind regards" ("Estimado cliente, de acuerdo con nuestros archivos su alma ya forma parte de nuestra base de datos. Reciba un cordial saludo", Iwasaki, 2004: 109). This pact with the Devil architect, in this case over an intangible domain, has a clear moral dimension in a contemporary, capitalist context. Hell is a database; the domain of Evil is the Internet and the Devil its CEO. In this last example, the materiality of the Devil's bridges and cathedrals disintegrates. The agency exercised by built space in the earlier legends is transferred to the digital world. This reveals the versatility of the motif of the Devil architect across different historical periods: his tempting offers extend their reach into the virtual spaces in which we are currently immersed.

***

This chapter sought to bring to the fore the motif of the Devil architect, from its origins in medieval legends of Devil's bridges to its different variations in twentieth and twenty-first literature of the fantastic. As the analysis shows, there are significant common structural and symbolic elements within the corpus. It could be argued, therefore, that this motif operates as a distinctive element within the many Devil fictions that exist and is thus deserving of a separate subcategory. The Devil architect merges different approaches to aesthetic, physical and moral monstrosity. As a leitmotif across texts in different cultures, languages, and historical periods, the Devil architect allows for the exploration of the dynamics between built space, builder, and the fantastic. Ultimately, the Devil architect and its diabolic architectures subvert the function, meaning, and power of the figure of the architect in its most primitive sense: s/he who builds a world – aesthetically, physically, morally – suitable for the human to live in.

Notes

1. This article is a revised, extended, and translated version of "El diablo arquitecto: orígenes y evolución de un motivo literario", in David Roas (ed.) *El monstruo fantástico: visiones y perspectivas*. Madrid: Áluvión, 2016, pp. 103–119.
2. Veo que estáis desesperada por el contratiempo que acabáis de sufrir, y vengo a ofreceros mis servicios: ¿queréis pasar al momento el río a pie enjuto y sin el menor riesgo? (*Ponte de Eume*)//
   Y un día, yendo a por agua, de desesperada que estaba, dijo:

   - Si me se allanaría la cuesta, le entregaba el alma al diablo. [. . .]

   - Si te atienes a tu palabra, pronto te haré un puente y te se allanará el camino. (*El Puente del Diablo, Puente de Segovia*)//

   - ¿Quién sería capaz de construir un puente para esta pobre anciana que tiene que mojarse para ir por agua? (*El Puente del Diablo*, Martorell)

3. Vous êtes ceux qui n'ont pas le sou! . . .

   - Et vous?

   - Moi, je suis celui qui a de l'argent.

4. "Aucunes lignes, aucunes combinaisons humaines ne parvinrent à s'harmoniser avec l'œuvre diabolique. Le malheureux architecte eut beau travailler jour et nuit, blasphémer tour à tour le diable et Dieu, tuer sa vie en damnant son âme. Au bout d'un mois, il mourut à la peine".
5. I refer to the architect throughout using the male pronoun because, unfortunately, this fictional character is male in all the examples found. This in itself certainly would justify a gender reading of this motif in future research.
6. Among the many books and films that the Winchester mansion has inspired, one of the most recent of these, the novel *Las madres negras* (*The Black Mothers*, 2018) by Spanish author Patricia Esteban Erlés, is worth noting. The story is set in the Santa Vela convent, which previously belonged to Larah Corven. Her character is based upon the Winchester widow. After her husband dies in a tragic gun accident, she obsessed with the belief that the souls of all those killed by a Winchester rifle haunt her. This obsession leads her to build a remote mansion, designed to protect her from these spirits, who are now distracted by the numerous rooms and staircases that have been added to the building. The house in this novel is given a voice and describes itself in the third chapter: "Lavaderos, más dormitorios y peldaños burlones y puertas tapiadas. Había que engañarlos a todos, y eran tantos" ("Laundry rooms, more bedrooms and misleading stairways and walled doors. They all had to be fooled, and there was so many of them", Esteban Erlés, *Las madres negras*, 2018: 36, translation my own).

7. "Retrocedió ante el inesperado descubrimiento y la sorpresa se convirtió en miedo – un miedo frío que se le enredaba con fuerza en el cuerpo – cuando su mirada abarcó una panorámica mayor del pueblo: porque todas las figuras se movían".// "Contra toda lógica, procesos azarosos comenzaron por escindir átomos imprevistos y el hálito de la vida, desbocado, se extendió desmesuradamente".

Bibliography

Almond, P. C. *The Devil: A New Biography*. New York: I.B. Tauris, 2014.

Asma, S. T. *On Monsters: An Unnatural History of Our Worst Fears*. Oxford: Oxford U.P., 2009.

Ausona, R. de. *Leyendas española*. Madrid: Rialp, 2004.

Azara, P. *Castillos en el aire. Mito y arquitectura en Occidente*. Barcelona: Gustavo Gili, 2005.

Bailey, D. *American Nightmares: The Haunted House Formula in American Popular Fiction*. Bowling Green: Bowling Green State University Popular Press, 1999.

Bailey, M. D. *Fearful Spirits, Reasoned Follies: The Boundaries of Superstition in Late Medieval Europe*. Ithaca and London: Cornell Univesity Press, 2013.

Bal, M. *A Mieke Bal Reader*. Chicago; London: University of Chicago Press, 2006.

Bollnow, O.F. *Human Space*. London: Hyphen, 2011.

Borges, J. L. "The Immortal". In *Labyrinths: Selected Stories & Other Writings*. New York: New Directions, [1947] 2007.

Bozzetto, R. *Le Fantastique dans tous ses états*. Aix-en-Provence: Presses universitaires de Provence, 2001.

Camarena, J.; Chevalier, M. *Catálogo tipológico del cuento folklórico español*. Alcalá: Ed. del Centro de Estudios Cervantinos, 2003.

Centini, M. *El ángel caído: el diablo en la religión, la historia, el arte, el folclore y la sociedad en general*. Barcelona: De Vecchi, 2012.

Deslys, C. "Le diable architecte". *Bulletin de la société des gens de lettres* (Dec. 1851), no. 12, 315–19.

Doménech, R. "La escalera de Sarto". In *La pirámide de Kheops*. Madrid: E.M.E.S.A., 1980.

Esteban Erlés, P. *Las madres negras*. Barcelona: Galaxia Gutenberg, 2018.

Ferrer-Bermejo, J. "Dejen salir". In *Incidente en Atocha*. Madrid: Alfaguara, 1982.

Finné, J. *Panorama de la littérature fantastique américaine*. Liège: Éditions du Céfal, 2006.

Forsgreen, R. "The Architecture of Evil". *The New Atlantis* (2012), no. 36, 44–62.

Frescari, M. *Monsters of Architecture*. New York: Rowman & Littlefield Publishers, 1991.

Graves, K. *The Biography of Satan*. Chicago: Research Associates School Times Publications, [1924] 2000.

Guiley, R. E. *The Encyclopedia of Demons and Demonology*. New York: Facts on File, 2009.

Hill, J. "Voluntary Committtal". In *20th Century Ghosts*. London: Gollancz, 2005.

Hugo, V. *Le Rhin*. Paris: Hetzel, 1842.

Iwasaki, F. "La cueva". In *Ajuar funerario*. Madrid: Páginas de Espuma, 2004.

———. "El dominio". In *Ajuar funerario*. Madrid: Páginas de Espuma, 2004.

Jackson, S. *The Haunting of Hill House*. London: Robinson, [1959] 1999.

Jannidis, F. "Character". In Hühn, Peter et al. (eds.): *The Living Handbook of Narratology*. Hamburg: Hamburg University Press, 2012. Available in: www.lhn.uni-hamburg.de/article/character [Accessed 08/09/2019].

Jaskot, P. B. *The Architecture of Oppression. The SS, Forced Labor and the Nazi Monumental Building Economy*. New York, London: Routledge, 2000.

Kelly, A. *Satan: A Biography*. Cambridge: Cambridge U.P., 2006.

Kirk, T. "Monumental Monstrosity, Monstrous Monumentality". *Perspecta* (2008), vol. 40, 6–15.

Lovecraft, H. P. "The Nameless City". In *Through the Gates of the Silver Key*. London: Penguin Books, [1921] 2005.

Mellado, F. *Recuerdos de un viaje por España. Tomo II*. 1849. Available in: www.descubreleyendas.es/Info/Consultas.aspx?IdLeyenda=194 [Accessed 08/09/2019].

Merino, J. M. "El nacimiento en el desván". In *Cuentos del reino secreto*. Madrid: Alfaguara, 1982.

Olgoso, A. "El proyecto". In *La máquina de languidecer*. Madrid: Páginas de Espuma, 2009.

Prince, G. *Narratology: The Form and Functioning of Narrative*. Berlin; New York, Mouton, 1982.

Rykwert, J. *The Idea of a Town: The Anthropology of Urban Form in Rome, Italy and the Ancient World*. Princeton: Princeton University Press, 1988.

Schuyt, M. et al. *Fantastic Architecture: Personal and Eccentric Visions*. New York: H.N. Abrams, 1980.

Siddons, A. R. *The House Next Door*. London: Collins, 2006.

Speer, A. *Inside the Third Reich: Memoirs*. New York: Touchstone, 1970.

Stanford, P. *The Devil, A Biography*. London: Arrow Books, 1996.

Todorov, T. *The Fantastic: A Structural Approach to a Literary Genre*. New York: Cornell University Press, 1975.

Vidler, A. *The Architectural Uncanny: Essays in the Modern Unhomely*. Cambridge, MA; London: MIT Press, 1992.

Weinstock, J. *Ashgate Encyclopedia of Literary and Cinematic Monsters*. Brookfield: Ashgate Publishing Company, 2014.

White-Le Goff, M. (dir.) *Merveilleux et Spiritualité*. Paris: Presses de l'université Paris-Sorbonne, 2014.

4   Time and Space in Fantastic Theory and Fiction of Charles Nodier's *Trilby*

Matthew Gibson

Introduction: The Development of Nodier's Ideas

Charles Nodier (1780–1844) is a somewhat forgotten literary figure in France, whose impact on Romanticism and the Frénétique and Fantastique Genres is nevertheless fundamental to the direction of the literature of that country. Born into a lower middle-class family in Besançon, Eastern France, and son of a Jacobin mason who became the town's mayor (Henry-Rosier 23), he interested himself early with both literature and the progressive science of entomology, mocking his father's Jacobin beliefs (63), while never formally adopting a consistent political line. His youth was spent in a variety of positions, including a period from 1812–13 as Librarian in Napoleon's Illyrian republic.

After the fall of Napoleon in 1815, he quickly established himself under the new auspices of the monarchy, and became librarian at L'Arsenal, where he created a salon which included Delacroix. It was at this time that he came to prominence at last as a major man of letters, but also as someone who embraced the new trends in literature from Britain and Germany, which had been repressed during the reign of the Voltairean-minded Napoleon, and began the trajectory towards developing the fantastique in literature. His first novel of this period, *Jean Sbogar* ([1818] 1987) reprises the experience of his time in Illyria, or Dalmatia, when he had been librarian at Laybach. In it a Breton woman, Antonia, finds herself with her older sister on the coast of Dalmatia, when the brigand Jean Sbogar is pillaging the country, a young man whom she only meets in moments between sleeping and waking or "la folie", on one such occasion the brigand declaring her "mon épouse devant dieu" (Nodier *Jean Sbogar*, 90). Later she befriends a young man in Venice with Jacobin ideals called Lothario and falls in love (150), but is then captured by Sbogar and imprisoned in Dalmatia, undergoing many liminal experiences, including a nightmarish wedding in the basement of the castle where she is kept (192). Once freed she sees Sbogar led to the guillotine and names him as Lothario before dying on the spot. The novel incorporates features of the Radcliffean novel, as Brian Rogers noted, but crucially as moments of "folie", and in the description of "oneiric castles" with an elastic sense of depth where Antonia can explore symbolically "the meeting of desires and fears which she has never revealed to herself in a conscious manner" ["la rencontre de désirs ou de craintes qu'elle ne s'est jamais révélés d'une manière consciente"] (Rogers 36) – desire and fear unite in a proto-Freudian way.

In 1819, Nodier adapted Byron's (really Polidori's) *The Vampyre* into a play with a Scottish setting, and published another novelistic adaptation by Cyprien Bérard, called *Lord Ruthven*, in 1820, for which he wrote a preface extolling the virtues of the "romantique," equating it with the "roman", as a form that can bend classical unities (Bérard, I, iii).

Nodier was yet to write the important sequence of essays and fictions which culminated in his work "Du Fantastique en Littérature" in 1830. However, in 1821 he coined the term "frénétique" in a review of the German writer Christian Spiess, in which he defined it as designating a literature which deviates too much from the laws of nature and includes too much of the macabre for classical sensibilities (Nodier *Spiess*, 77, 81, 83). As Glinoer notes, this was an attempt to salvage Romanticism in the eyes of conservative classicists by distancing it from its more extreme variants (Glinoer 68). Despite this "olive branch" he produced one of his most purely fantastic and gruesome works the same year, *Smarra*, which involves a dream within a dream, where the Thessalian youth Lucius falls asleep and is trapped by the witch Méroe, who beheads Lucius and allows the stryge Smarra to attack his heart (Nodier *Smarra*, 92). The work is based both on local, Dalmatian superstitions about the Stryge (a half-owl, half-human figure that attacks the heart) and a story similar to Apuleius's *The Golden Ass*, whose stories he believed to have suffused the folklore of that region. A year later, Nodier published *Trilby, ou le Lutin d'Argail* [Argyle] (1822), a work inspired by the mania for Scotland that derived from Scott and Ossian. In it we read the tale of a fisherman's wife, who falls in love with a form of incubus fairy or goblin: a descendant of the aristocratic Macfarlanes of her area and relative of St Columba, in what constitutes a self-conscious contrast between contemporary Catholicism and ancient fairy faiths.

In the years afterwards Nodier wrote more on his developing theory of the fantastic, explaining his intentions in using a form of writing that explored dream, the supernatural and magic. In his introduction to Amédée Pichot's essay on Lord Byron he sees the "marvelous" as a necessary antidote to rationalism and materialism, in an age which has been "betrayed by a keen and cruel philosophy" ["trahi par une philosophie avide et cruelle"] (Pichot 6) by both the Enlightenment and the Catholic Church. In his much later work, "Du Fantastique en littérature", he sees literature as being cyclical in history and as occurring in three stages. This begins with the material and sensational, which he now characterized differently as the age of wonder (such as in the *Arabian Nights*); then this is replaced by the age of the spiritual, when philosophers divine the secret abstract laws of the world, and paradoxically cease to see properly (leading to realism); and finally there comes the age of the Fantastic, in which a generation that has begun to despair of science and reason begins to question nature anew and see it with their eyes, eschewing scientific dogma, creating the form of the fantastic (Nodier *Fantastique*, 9–10).

Later stories and memoirs like "La Fée aux miettes" ([1832] 1846) and "Inès de las Sierras" (published 1837) definitely exemplify the ideas on the Fantastic as a form which Nodier generated during this time, but both "Smarra" – which is purely a dream – and "Trilby" – which is more a work of the pure fantastic – were written when his ideas were still forming. In the rest of this chapter, therefore, I shall be concentrating on "Trilby" and trying to examine firstly, what is the purpose of dream and the supernatural in the tale, and secondly in what ways does Nodier use the form of the fantastic to challenge the unities of time and space, and for what purpose. This is important not least because although various scholars like Scanu, Rogers, and Lowe-Dupas have observed the fantastic as it develops in Nodier's thought with a view to examining its ontological and scientific purpose, except for Rogers none have observed Nodier's Fantastic fiction by analyzing how it alters the experience of space and time for the characters, and what the significance of this might be. In this sense also we shall be exploring how we can judge this most unusual tale against the discussion of the various chronotopes promulgated by Bakhtin, and how Nodier effectively interfuses them in an entirely new way.

The Compression and Expansion of Space

"Trilby" is set in Western Scotland, presumably in a time not quite the present, but not quite historic either. The fairies ("lutins") and goblin-like creatures ("follets") of Argyll reside in the houses of fishermen, and prey on their dreams and superstitions, despite being wooed back by the aristocrats to whom they are related by birth (Nodier *Trilby*, 28–9). One, Trilby, resides in the house of the young couple Dougal and Jeannies, and enters the dreams of the fisherman's beautiful wife, usually around dawn or sunset (36–7). Often he arrives in the form of a small child, looking after her and keeping her from trouble, in a way somewhat akin to the sylphs of *The Rape of the Lock* by Pope. Although he only enters Jeannies's thoughts in the passage between sleeping and waking (37–8), and is a source of delight for her, Jeannies nevertheless foolishly complains to her husband about him, declaring that he may be the same demon who is harassing Dougal by making his nets become tangled in the weeds. Dougal calls the 100-year-old hermit Ronald to exorcise the goblin/fairy. The monk drives the fairy out (42).

Although exorcised from the house, Trilby returns to haunt Jeannies's dreams in the form of a handsome young man, who nevertheless appears sad (58), and so they join others from the community to make a pilgrimage to the monastery for St Columba's day, a group including Jeannies's jealous rival Clady, and they progress to the monastery of "Balva" (Balvaig) in the region of "Calender" (Callander). After a visit to the ruined Chapel of Glenfallach (75), they enter a decaying monastery with a gallery full of pictures of the earlier clan of Macfarlanes (83), most of whom had been benefactors, but whose later descendants are accused of betraying their allegiances and becoming enemies of the monastery. One veiled painting far off attracts Jeannies's interest (87), as Ronald the hermit details how the fairies try to lead men into sin (92), and that they have caused two deaths at a funeral not long before in the "caveau mortuaire" (97), meaning that they should be shown no pity and cursed. As Ronald urges the pilgrims to join a ritual denunciation of the fairies, Jeannies unveils the painting at the end of the gallery and sees in the old picture Trilby himself in the incarnation of the disgraced John Trilby Macfarlane, and runs to the altar and tomb of St Columba – also the patron saint of forlorn lovers and a relative of Trilby – and whispers the words "love" and "pity" at the statue's feet (110–11). She asks the saint whether she is right not to curse Trilby, and a shaft of light reveals a smile on the saint's face (116–17).

We next move to a later time in winter, when the fishermen are off on the Clyde, and Jeannies, still obsessed with Trilby, is rowing along the Loch Long to where in earlier times the giant Arthur, cast out due to the walls built by fearful humans around Edinburgh (separating him from the cave-nymph whom he loved) had amassed an enormous stone retreat there with the remains of his palace ([126] thus now the mountain Ben-Arthur). In former times an Irish monk had asked him to make the water peaceful for the fishermen after the giant had been terrorizing them through storms for years (130). After the ensuing freeze and abatement of the giant's anger, and effective exorcism, the monk had come and founded the monastery of Balva with some Anchorites (131–2). Emerging from a period of sleep, Jeannies helps a shipwrecked old man to safety (137), only for him to reveal himself as Trilby after she confesses her betrayal, and sees him doff his disguise to confess his slave-like love to her (147–8). She nevertheless still refuses him, and once the fairy is back on the shore, he is exorcised anew by Dougal and Ronald and trapped in a birch tree, causing Jeannies to kill herself.

Nodier's own preface to the tale, which he declares is rooted in the work of Ossian and Sir Walter Scott, justifies its eccentricities as a necessary return to the beliefs of the cradle ("berceau") and furthermore to the beliefs and literature of primitive people, citing Hesiod as one of his forerunners. He also defines it as "Romantique", and admits the potential deficiencies of this new form, but still defends his decision to write such a piece. He does not, as in later essays, proselytize for the overturn or augmentation of science through the Fantastic, but does argue for the necessity of returning to a more primitive form in order to rejuvenate oneself at a certain period of one's life: "it is so natural a need for all men to *recradle* themselves, as Schiller says, in the dreams of their springtime" ["c'est besoin si naturel à tous les hommes de se *rebercer*, comme dit Schiller, dans les rêves de leurs printemps"] "a period of life when the soul, already tired, rejuvenates itself once more in the pleasant conquests of space and of time" ["une epoque de la vie, où l'ame déjà fatigue se rajeunit encore dans les agréables conquêtes sur l'espace et sur le temps" (xv)]. As shall be shown, in breaking classical ideas of literature, the *conte* challenges the geometric and positivistic understanding of space as much as it potentially challenges the belief that the supernatural is impossible, or that spirits cannot be reborn.

The story is probably the first truly Fantastic short story which Nodier wrote, more so than either *Jean Sbogar*, which has elements of reverie and what Rogers calls "oneiric" castles or labyrinths ["labyrinthes oniriques"] that combine dream with reality (Rogers 28), or *Smarra*, whose macabre supernaturalism is framed by the dream of Lorenzo. Here we see an example of what Neil Cornwell calls the "pure fantastic" (Cornwell 82–3), like Hoffmann's "The Mines of Falun" or "Ritter Glück", since we can never be sure whether the fairies are real or simply the villagers' and monks' own superstitions (in Laurence Porter's opinion, the supernatural events are all simply the result of neurosis (Porter 41)). The purpose of using dream, madness, and oneiric spaces to explore the "moi profonde" identified by Rogers in *Jean Sbogar* is, according to that critic, to transcend time and space and allow the self to investigate the schism between attraction and revulsion to the same object (Rogers 37), in a way that of course anticipates the exploration of the id by Freud. Here it can be seen as a distinction between Jeannies's public identity and private, if not repressed, desires (she who inexplicably denounces the fairy who gives her so much pleasure), but with the added sense of probing the history of the Catholic church and correcting it. This is made particularly clear in the scene in the decaying monastery when the pilgrims are all called upon to execrate the fairies and curse them, while Jeannies herself unveils the painting to see in the form of John Trilby Macfarlane her own phantom beloved, the fairy Trilby, before running plaintively to the altar and statue of Saint Columba. Columba, as Trilby's relative, represents the true spirit of Christianity before it turned into the restrictive Augustinian dogma of Ronald, and was clearly not antithetical to the fairies who can change shape and fly through space and time. Likewise Trilby's ability to move through time in the fantastic reveries of Jeannies – whether in paintings or in dreams – is both a device for juxtaposing the present state of the ruined abbey and its decayed belief, and the proper, magical anteced-ents of the faith in Scotland, but also may well foresee Nodier's own wholly non-Augustinian adoption of palingenesis in 1832. In this view Nodier understands the material world as being infused with a creative essence which will allow it to continue mutating, eventually creating a higher being than men, or un "être compréhensif" that can understand things which are impossible for contemporary man to understand, and for whom the mystery of resurrection after death, scotched by the materialists, can be understood (Nodier *Palingénésie*, 90, 95, 96–98).

The portrayal of time in the abbey's painting gallery draws obvious comparison with Bakhtin's depiction of the Castle Chronotope in both the Gothic and Historical Novel, as one which involves, through the incorporation of legends in an otherwise realist setting, a special conflated historical time, which suffuses the sense of space with the felt presence of history. According to Bakhtin,

> Legends and traditions animate every corner of the castle and its environs through their constant reminders of past events. It is this quality that gives rise to the specific kind of narrative inherent in castles and that is then worked out in Gothic novels.
>
> (Bakhtin 245–6)

The narrative of Trilby certainly partakes of this chronotope in the sense that the abbey provides legends that explain the contemporary events and affect them at the festival of Saint Columba.

However, if we apply the chronotope further in this novella, we will notice that it is transferred to nature itself through a form of metaphorical comparison. On her journey to the abbey, Jeannies is massively disoriented by the sense of space in the forests through which both she and Dougal walk:

> In these decadent days of Autumn there is something inexplicable added to the solemnity of all feelings. Each step of time then impresses itself on the fields which denude themselves, or on the foreheads of the trees which turn yellow: a new sign of expiration ever more serious and impressive. There can be heard from the bottom of the wood a sort of menacing murmur which is made from the cry of dry branches, from the brushing of leaves that fall, from the confused lament of beasts of prey when the foreglimpse of a harsh winter disturbs their young, from murmurs, sighs, groans, sometimes similar to human voices which astonish the ear and grip the heart. Even in the refuge of temples the traveller does not escape the sensations which pursue them. The vaults of old churches give out the same noises as the depths of old forests, when the foot of the passing solitary interrogates the resounding echoes of the nave, and when the air outside slips between the badly joined boards or attacks the lead of the shattered window-panes, adds weird harmonies to the muted sound of its step.
>
> [Chaque pas que fait le temps imprime alors sur les champs qui se dépouillent, ou au front des arbres qui jaunissent, un nouveau signe de caducité plus grave et plus imposant. On entend sortir du fond

des bois une sorte de rumeur menaçante qui se compose du cri des
branches sèches, du frôlement des feuilles qui tombent, de la plainte
confuse des bêtes de proie que la prévoyance d'un hiver rigoureux
alarme sur leurs petits, de rumeurs, de soupirs, de gémissements,
quelquefois semblables à des voix humaines, qui étonnent l'oreille et
saisissent le coeur. Le voyageur n'échappe pas même à l'abri des tem-
ples aux sensations qui le poursuivent. Les voûtes des vieilles églises
rendent les mêmes bruits que les profondeurs des vieilles forêts, quand
le pied du passant solitaire interroge les échos sonores de la nef, et
que l'air extérieur qui se glisse entre les ais mal joints ou qui agite
le plomb des vitraux rompus, marie des accords bizarres au sourd
retentissement de sa marche.]

(72–3)

In this passage the Autumn forest is portrayed as a symbol of solemnity
caused by the obvious markings of time, consisting of signs of the continual arrival of death and increase of decay, with each mark of that decay
in the trees indicating the "expiring" (transience) that is progressively
more perturbing, and of sounds that are tinged with pathetic fallacy. In
this we can see elements of what Bakhtin would later call the Agricultural Idyll Chronotope, which repeats the cyclical time of the ancients,
and is based in regional communities who work with the land (Bakhtin
128) – a chronotope which is also found in the novels of Radcliffe. However, the narrator further compares the Autumn forest with the vaults of
churches, whose sudden echoes and sonority are similar to its own reso-
nant qualities, and which are, like the forest to which they are compared,
again awarded a faint pathetic fallacy in this description. This metaphorical comparison anticipates the arrival in Balva, and can be taken as an
example, in Bakhtinian terms, of the Castle Chronotope (indeed just after
this description we see the pilgrims arrive at the ruined Chappelle de
Glenfallach). As Nele Bemong writes, ruined castles (and Balva is also
in ruin) are used in the Agricultural Idyll Chronotope to reinforce the
superiority of nature to human constructions (Bemong 173), which latter
cannot self-renew with time. However, if we also take the tale as being an
example of the Castle Chronotope, then this metaphorical comparison
would seem to be an important prelude to the critique of modern Catholicism, by relating the features of the haunted castle/church to the forest
itself, so that the modern Catholic church is portrayed as having rejected
the spiritual antecedents of Scotland's past, despite Saint Columba's own
connection to the fairies who abound in nature.

Coming finally to the view fir trees of Balva, the pilgrims see the scene
enlarge in front of them, like the realization of a three-dimensional,
extended view of the monastery from what at first appears to be a picture-
like or "pittoresque" division of the monastery's green demesne from the
rest of the landscape (77):

Above its barren backyard, and as if leaning on the apex of a per-
pendicular rock from where they seemed to be rushing towards
the abyss, the old towers of the monastery could be seen blacken-
ing, and in the distance the wings of half-collapsed buildings were
developing.

   [Au-dessus de son revers aride, et comme penchées à la pointe d'un
roc perpendiculaire d'où elles semblaient se précipiter vers l'abîme,
on voyait noircir les vieilles tours du monastère, et se développer, au
loin, les ailes des bâtiments à demi écroulés.]

(77)

The passage here suggests the temporal revelation of the scene of the
monastery to the eyes of the pilgrims, as though they are slowly grasping
the deep-focus features of the scene, despite the towers initially seeming
to be leaning against a rock (clearly an example of *trompe l'oeil*), and
bringing the parts into focus. Like the earlier description of the forest's
decay in Autumn, there seems to be a temporal element here, with the
towers appearing to be in rapid decline to their destruction. However,
the movement from two-dimensionality to three-dimensionality in space
and depth is the most important part of the impression of the scenery in
relation to the rest of the episode, as the reader is further informed of the
impressive immensity of the picture gallery in the abbey from Jeannies's
perspective when she finally witnesses it (84).

   The picture gallery, which exhibits the abbey's historical benefactors, is
an obvious feature of the Castle Chronotope, which Bakhtin observes in
the work of Scott and of Radcliffe, since it compresses historical time in
its legendary depictions of the MacFarlanes, whose descendants (the fairies) are now a part of the continuing narrative. However, the portrayal
of space takes on new and interesting overtones once Ronald recalls how
the fairies had interfered with a burial some days earlier in the "caveau
mortuaire" beneath them, when coffins had appeared to whine and moan
because of the fairies infesting it, and darkness had entered the crypt,
creating an unusual sense of unseen, but felt, depth:

> The torches of the acolytes, said Ronald, threw some spare, fugi-
> tive flickers which scattered, dancing in blue and slender rays, like
> the magic fires of sorcerers, and then rose up and lost themselves
> in the black recesses of the vestibules and the chapels. Finally, the
> immortal lamp of the saint of saints – I saw it flicker, dim, and die.
> Die! The deep night, the complete night, in the church, in the choir,
> in the tabernacle! The night was fallen for the first time on the Lord's
> sacrament! The night so humid, so dark, so powerful everywhere;
> frightening, horrible beneath the dome of our basilisks where eternal
> day is promised to us! Our forsaken monks lost themselves in the
> immensity of the temple, made larger by the depth of the night.

[Les torches des acolytes, dit Ronald, lançaient à peine quelques flammèches fugitives qui s'éloignaient, se rapprochaient, dansaient en rayons bleus et grêles, comme les feux magiques des sorcières, et puis montaient et se perdaient dans les recoins noirs des vestibules et des chapelles. Enfin, la lampe immortelle du saint des saints . . . – je la vis s'agiter, s'obscurcir et mourir. – mourir! La nuit profonde, la nuit tout entière, dans l'église, dans le choeur, dans le tabernacle! La nuit descendue pour la première fois sur le sacrement du seigneur! La nuit si humide, si obscure, si redoutable partout; effrayante, horrible sous le dôme de nos basiliques où est promis le jour éternel! . . . – nos moines éperdus s'égaraient dans l'immensité du temple, agrandi encore par la profondeur de la nuit.]

(98–9)

This passage presents the obvious horror of a haunted vault – in Laurence Porter's view simply the monks' repressed desires and fears coming to haunt them rather than real ghosts and their tormenting fairies (Porter 41) – but more intriguingly an enlarged sense of space, as the "depth of the night" and the ghostly sounds creating hysteria actually increase the space itself. The castle space of the Castle Chronotope, which Bakhtin understands as indicating historical time in a space/place that comes to fruition in the narrative, and which space Rogers, in defining the oneiric castles of Nodier, interprets as creating a sense of depthlessness where dream becomes apparent to the waking mind (Rogers 37), here actually enlarges its own space, although not necessarily its material being, with the suffusion of past time through the fairies and the ghosts (and – alternatively – the monks' own fears). This itself indicates the ability of either the supernatural or of imagined anxiety to bely space in the material world, unmasking the possibility of its unreality.

After returning to the village and going out on the lake in her bark, Jeannies herself begins to lose the ordinary sense of perspective, and ability even to cognize the contours of nature. The effect of space upon the perceiver on this occasion is one which, at first glance, appears to approach Kant's sublime of magnitude, first through the confusing vapours off the stream,[1] but then in the more general confusion created by the sense of magnitude in the mountains themselves:

She was again contemplating with an emotion, which renewed itself every day without weakening, this crowd of summits that appear to be seamless, jostling against each other, enmeshed, or else only to be detached through the unexpected effects of light, above all in that season when the silvery silk of mosses [sphinxes], the dark marbling of granite, and the pearly shells of the rocky reef, disappear under the monotonous veil of snow.

[Elle contemplait encore avec une émotion qui se renouvelait tous les jours sans s'affaiblir cette foule de sommets qui se poursuivent, qui se pressent, qui se confondent, ou ne se détachent les uns des autres que par des effets inattendus de lumière, surtout dans la saison où disparaissent sous le voile monotone des neiges, et la soie argentée des sphaignes, et la marbrure foncée des granits, les écailles nacrées des récifs.]

(124)

The landscape is a vast space, but the major effect revealed, after an initial description of the vagueness of colours and contours off the lake, is one in which the actual perspective of three dimensions disappears (the narrator later refers to it as a "tableau" (125), as though in picturesque tradition): not only that, they can only be "detached" as visual objects through effects that are "inattendus", unexpected, and not through the subject's direct act of cognition, this two-dimensionality being passively accepted by Jeannies. The description is given just before the account of the Giant Ben-Arthur, supposedly cursed by the fairies, who in pre-Christian times had created his own mountain of stone and troubled the fishermen, before being exorcised by an Irish monk.

I would argue that this impression is less an example of the sublime of magnitude described by Kant, and more an example of Jeannies's own sense of space being restricted to two dimensions, and thus to the limitations of her perspective. If one considers that this compression of dimension and thus of space occurs as her mind begins to approach madness and moves from liminal spaces like dreams and daydreams to the direct confrontation with Trilby in the bark, it can again be understood as indicating an example of her mind taking on the attributes of the Fantastic itself, but also more directly as an example of the unreal nature of physical space. The uncanny quality of this is also reinforced through the temporal nature of the apprehension, since the optical illusion is something that is repeated every day, as though it is an unchanging, recurring experience in which the subject fails to create the sense of depth through familiarity.

Such a collapsing of dimension is definitely at odds with one of the most famous works of the French Enlightenment, Diderot's *Lettre sur les Aveugles*, which argued that the technique of counting by touch was the purest way of observing material and spatial reality, since it could not be distorted so easily as sight (92–4). Diderot's rejection of sight as a means of discerning truth is incorporated into his atheistical and arch-materialist view of nature (Diderot 125–6). While we cannot impose the future on the past, if we nevertheless look forward to *Du Fantastique en Littérature* ([1830] 1989), we notice that Nodier there characterized the second age, that of the spiritual, as an age in which man gave himself over to the "unseen", and thus paradoxically created a materialist, unquestioning literature, and that the Fantastic, which threatened these unseen laws through the insertion of the irrational, occurs when we once more begin to see properly as in the first age of wonder and sensory impression (Nodier, *fantastique*, 9–10). This early presentation of Jean-nies's perception demonstrates the power of human perspective to make a mockery of the givenness of three-dimensional space, just as the scene in the abbey had effectively enlarged the sense of space through dark-ness. As a theory of seeing it is more in keeping with Berkeley's *New Theory of Vision* ([1709] 1963) than Newton's *Optics*, since the former had argued that "we do not see the Magnitude of Objects immediately by sight" but rather from inference through experience (Berkeley 41). Thus the Gothic elements of the tale, which incorporate in Bakhtinian terms the Castle and the Agricultural Idyll Chronotopes of Bakhtin and their necessary inclusion of historical time and cyclical time in particular, local spaces, also incorporate a genuine perspectival mockery of space in the impressions of the characters which, it can be argued, prefigures Nodier's later dependence on raw sensation as a means of divining truth in the Fantastic, and is every bit as much a part of the tale's skepticism towards post-Enlightenment science as are the fairies and supernatural creatures themselves.

The Chronotopes of "Trilby"

The question might occur, however, as to why Nodier includes this close attention to both *trompe l'oeil* and the expansion or contraction of space in his work – a feature that is more foregrounded than the flexing of time, despite the reference to reverie and the potential muddling of con-secutive experience in some of the passages through iteration. If we look at the text in purely Bakhtinian terms, and apply Bakhtin's rigorous for-malist definitions of genre, we can see that Nodier's tale conflates older with newer forms of the Chronotope, and that it is this mixing of the old with the new which facilitates and even necessitates the perceptual adjust-ments of time and space that we find in the characters' observations. It is, of course, well known that the first Gothic novel, by Walpole, prefaced its second edition with a declaration of the author's intent "to blend the two types of romance, the ancient and the moderns". The first, according to Walpole, was "all imagination and improbability", while in the second "nature is always intended to be, and sometimes has been, copied with success" (Walpole 10). If we look at these distinctions against the graph created by Bakhtin's rigorous, formalist definitions of chronotopes, we will see that Nodier perhaps extends this blending more than any of the better known "Gothic" writers in this putative Fantastic novella, since he has blended the further "modern" type of Gothic romance that Walpole and Radcliffe themselves created when fusing ancient and modern, with the structures and the belief systems of even more ancient genres.

Certainly, as has already been shown, the Castle Chronotope is evident through the suffusion of historical time in the features of the abbey, with its picture gallery of eminent figures related to the fairy, although in this *conte* the chronotope is metaphorically extended to nature itself. The use of the ruined abbey also indicates features of the Agricultural Idyll Chronotope, a work which celebrates the cyclical time of the seasons and is furthermore situated in a community in a very particular location. While cyclical time was for Bakhtin a feature of some of the most ancient literature, it was a type of time that appeared in much later chronotopes, in a way that inhered more closely with the psyches of the characters. It can be found in works like *Gray's Elegy* (228) and then in romantic and regional novels of the eighteenth to nineteenth centuries. In these oeuvres the individual often expresses themself through their rejection of the idyll and its renewing nature and rituals, only to return to it (as in the Rousseau model), or else the individual attempts to immerse themselves in the healing power of nature and primitive rituals (as in Chateaubriand's *René* (231)). In *Trilby* the Agricultural Idyll Chronotope is certainly manifest in the depiction of a fisherman's society and the local habitation of Western Scotland, and the clear movement of the seasons from summer through to autumn and to winter, which measure Jeannies's own psychological descent into madness. Furthermore, as Nele Bemong has written, the castle as ruin is often a feature of the Agricultural Idyll, as it affirms the durability of nature ([Bemong 173] an obvious feature being the "ivy-mantled tower" in Gray's "Elegy"), and the ruined abbey of Balva certainly conforms to this feature of the chronotope. The Castle and Idyll Chronotopes, so evident in the works of Radcliffe, whose characters find harmony and relief in the local, rustic habitations where they live or travel, but who are threatened and terrified by the embedded histories of the castles or monasteries where they are imprisoned, are thus also evident in *Trilby* as well, which has taken many features from Radcliffe's *roman noir*.[2]

However, the structure of the story, its events and the attitudes of the characters is wildly different to Radcliffe's *roman*, not least in the universal acceptance of the supernatural by all except the implied reader, and the main character's rejection of the terror felt by the other characters towards the supernatural. This is because, in a Bakhtinian sense, the novel draws from other earlier chronotopes, including the "Greek Romance", the "Adventure Romance of Everyday Life", "Folklore time", and the "Chivalric Romance Chronotope". The first type, an example of which is *Leucippe and Clitophon*, and which were written from the second to the sixth centuries CE, usually involve two characters falling in love, only to be thwarted by constant events outside their control, then undergoing a set of haphazard, sudden happenings with revelations and encounters over many continents in what are always exotic and alien worlds (101). In it time is "empty", since nothing ever really changes in the characters themselves: only the events they experience are isolated, exotic, and all disconnected to each other. The second, of which the only examples are by Apuleius (*The Golden Ass*) and Petronius (*Satyricon*), has the same set of sudden, unexpected events (what Bakhtin calls "adventure time" (97)) in exotic, dislocated places, but features physical and psychic metamorphosis of the main character, in keeping with the influence of folklore, and takes the character through a path of punishment and redemption (114–15). Furthermore, the path is one measured physically by the space of the road they travel (120), and the events of the "everyday" consist in the exploration of the seamier and more corrupt side of life. Such a chronotope transforms the moral nature of the character, with Lucius becoming a priest and a rhetorician at the end, and is definitely an important precursor of the later, post-classical picaresque novel. Folkloric time – present in several chronotopes – is one which celebrates the past as a Golden Age at the expense of the present and future (148), and uses size and physical stature to represent a character's strength and stature morally (150), its fantastic elements being a "realistic fantastic" (150) – one that is physically manifest rather than otherworldly. The Chivalric Romance chronotope has the same sense of sudden and haphazard adventure in its temporal unfolding as does the earlier Greek Romance, except that here the miraculous is expected rather than a shock (152), as Knights come into constant encounters with magical events. Furthermore, according to Bakhtin, this is the first chronotope to break the very objective portrayal of time of the classical era, including dreams and with them "the particular distortions of temporal perspectives characteristic of dreams", and thus "exhibits a *subjective playing with time*" (154, 155).

In reexamining *Trilby* in the light of these earlier chronotopes, there are apparent features which conform to these earlier types, and which may help to explain its Fantastic genre in Bakhtinian terms. First of all, the tale does involve events that seem to occur suddenly to the main protagonist as in the Greek Romance chronotope, such as the arrival of Ronald to the house (which Laurence Porter sees as fortuitous and not explained in the plot (Porter 37)), and the sudden arrival of the old man in Loch Long – although this may be more due to the perspective of Jeannies. In relation to the "Adventure Romance of Everyday Life" we can see two elements which are similar, namely the use of metamorphosis: both in the frequent metempsychosis of *Trilby* himself, whether real or imagined, and in the change of Jeannies as she descends into madness and suicide. There is the further fact that Jeannies's psychological change, which could be seen as one from guilt to a failed chance of redemption before Trilby, is measured through the roads and trips she takes: to Balva and then to Loch Long, although they are not, as in the earlier adventure romances, in an entirely exotic landscape (rather a familiar one), nor is it one single trip, as she makes several in the Agricultural Idyll space whence she comes. The tale also draws upon folkloric time, not simply in its use of metamorphosis but in the presentation of the old as golden, the present as degraded, with the contemporary Catholic church trying to repress its spiritual antecedents – although the tendency in the various folkloric chronotopes to use physical stature to represent both power and moral stature is ambivalent in this conte, since while the mythical Giant Arthur created part of the scenery as a mountain, Trilby himself can assume any size and any bodily form, his moral and spiritual stature never changing. Nevertheless, the playing with perspective does suggest an ability to transcend space in a way which is pre-modern. Finally, like the Chivalric romance, the magical adventures and events are expected by the characters, even if not desired by any except Jeannies herself, and the experience of dream allows the main character to subvert the speed of time as an objective, measurable continuum, Jeannies's dreams of Trilby being passages of greater length, and the recurrent experience of the mountain view from her bark presenting no perceptual progression in her psyche at all.

However, even in the Chivalric Romance chronotope as described by Bakhtin we do not see quite the same perceptual changes of space in so post-enlightenment a form as we do in *Trilby*. If we return to Walpole's statement and stand back from Bakhtin's definitions we can see why. For the fantastic work *Trilby*, despite its antecedents in the Radcliffe novel or *roman noir*, does not so much blend the "ancient" romance with the "moderns", but actually blends the *roman noir* itself and its magical intimations but rational expectations – the hesitation of Todorov – with the folkloric elements of metamorphosis, expected magical occurrences and a primitivist understanding of size, which we find in some of the genres (chronotopes) of the ancient world. Thus the Todorovian hesitation between a rational and supernatural explanation only occurs for the implied reader (Todorov 29), not the superstitious fishermen, their minds still governed by folklore and the marvellous. Likewise, space does not possess fixed, positivistic dimensions, but can expand or contract with the characters' untutored experience. However, in the *conte* this has to be presented in terms that acknowledge the denial of perspective from the position of post-Enlightenment science – in keeping with the rational expectations of the *roman noir*, or Radcliffe novel, that is still informed fundamentally by the "laws of nature" (Todorov 29). The return to a more folkloric understanding of nature in a rational age necessitates this flexing and bending of space, and is indeed the very basis of what Nodier later sees as the age of the Fantastic, when writers, bored and unconvinced by science, return to naïve sensation in order to expand their knowledge (Nodier, *fantastique*, 35). The positivist dimensionality of Diderot – whose writing Nodier greatly admired – is further rejected.

In conclusion, *Trilby* is a work which anticipates Nodier's later definition of the fantastic by challenging the perspective and objectivity of space, and to a lesser degree time, much as do its supernatural elements. *Trilby* makes use of both the Castle Chronotope described by Bakhtin and the Agricultural Idyll Chronotope in order to suggest cyclical time, but blends this with the folkloric elements of earlier Chronotopes, effectively infusing the already developed *roman noir* with influences from classical and medieval literature. Such a blending necessitates the actual flexing of space in a post-Enlightenment narrative in order to convey the perspective of an earlier time. This perspective returns sensation to that of an earlier period in human history, which anticipates Nodier's discussion of the fantastic, and also his belief in palingenesis as a form of creative evolution.

Notes

1. Immanuel Kant, *Critique of Judgement*, trans. James Creed Meredith (Infomotions LLC, 2000), 55–9. Kant initially discovers this inability of the imagination to find an end in descriptions of the Pyramids and St Peters, and the effect they have on the apprehender, but moves to discussing "magnitude" in nature as well.
2. The *roman noir* was effectively the translation, and further adaptation, of English gothic novels in France from the beginning of the revolution onwards (see Hale 24–8).

Bibliography

Bakhtin, M. M., *The Dialogic Imagination: Four Essays*, trans. Caryl Emerson and Michael Holquist, ed. Michael Holquist (Austin: Texas University Press, 1983).

Bemong, Nele, "Internal Chronotope Genre Structures: The Nineteenth-Century Historical Novel in the Context of the Belgian Literary Polysystem," in Nele Bemong et al. (eds), *Bakhtin's Theory of the Literary Chronotope: Reflections, Applications, Perspectives* (Gent: University Press, 2010), 159–78.

Bérard, Cyprien, *Lord Ruthven, ou les vampires* [with a Preface by Charles Nodier] (Paris: Ladvocat, 1820).

Berkeley, George, *An Essay Towards a New Theory of Vision* and Other Writings, repr. (London: Dent [Everyman's Library], [1709] 1963).

Cornwell, Neil, *The Literary Fantastic* (New York: Harvester Wheatsheaf, 1990).

Diderot, Denis, *Lettre sur les aveugles, à l'usage de ceux qui voyent* (Londres: Diderot, 1749).

Glinoer, Antony, *La Littérature frénétique* (Paris: Presses universitaires de France, coll. "Les littéraires", 2009).

Hale, Terry, "Translation in Distress: The Construction of the Gothic," in Avril Horner (ed.), *European Gothic: A Spirited Exchange, 1760–90* (Manchester: Manchester University Press, 2002), 17–38, 24–8.

Nodier, Charles, "Critique littéraire: le Petit Pierre, traduit de l'allemand de SPIESS (à paraître chez l'Avocat, au Palais-Royal)," *Annales de la littérature et des arts*, 16ème Livraison (1821).

Nodier, Charles, "De la Palingénésie et de la résurrection", in *Revue de Paris*, Août 1832 (41:8), 81–107.

Nodier, Charles, *Du fantastique en littérature* (Paris: Chimères, [1830] 1989).

Nodier, Charles, *Jean Sbogar*, ed. Jean Sgard (Paris: Librairie Honoré Champion, Editeur, [1818] 1987).

Nodier, Charles, "La Fée aux miettes," in *Contes de Charles Nodier* (Paris: J. Hetzel, [1832] 1846).

Nodier, Charles, "Smarra, ou les démons de la nuit," in *Contes du pays des rêves* (Paris: Club des Librairies de France, 1957).

Nodier, Charles, *Trilby, ou le Lutin d'Argail, nouvelle ecossaise*, 2nd ed (Paris: Ladvocat, 1822).

Pichot, Amédée, *Essai sur le genie et le caractère de Lord Byron*, précédé d'une notice préliminaire par M. Charles Nodier (Paris: Ladvocat, Librairie, Palais-Royal, 1824).

Porter, Laurence, *The Literary Dream in French Romanticism* (Detroit: Wayne State University Press, 1979).

Rogers, Brian, *Charles Nodier et la Tentation de la Folie* (Geneva-Paris: Editions Slatkine, 1985).

Scanu, Ada Myriam, *Charles Nodier: Du Fantastique en littérature*, Séminaire d'Histoire Littéraire: la naissance du fantastique en Europe – Histoire et Théorie (2004). www.rilune.org.

Walpole, Horace, *The Castle of Otranto*, ed. Nick Groom, 3rd ed (Oxford: Oxford University Press, 2014).

5   Border Imagery in Victorian 'Supernatural' Short Stories

The Portrait

Maria Teresa Chialant

The topography of the modern fantastic suggests a preoccupation with problems of vision and visibility for it is structured around a spectral imagery; it is remarkable how many fantasies introduce mirrors, glasses, reflections, portraits, eyes [. . .] to effect a transformation of the familiar into the unfamiliar.

(Jackson 1981, 43)

If we were to draw a topography of the Fantastic in late eighteenth- and nineteenth-century English fiction, we should think of a series of physical structures that are not only the settings in which a story unfolds but also function as recurrent themes and metaphors. Moving from the Gothic romance to Victorian supernatural fiction, some important transformations in the spatial architecture of the Fantastic occur; one is in the gradual demise of images of closure in favour of apertures "which open into another region found in the spaces of the familiar and the known" (Jackson, 44). Between the Romantic period and the mid- and late-Victorian Age, a transition takes place from the claustrophobic enclaves of *The Castle of Otranto* and *The Monk* – with their crypts, vaults, and castles – and the labyrinthine plots of *Melmoth the Wanderer* and *Frankenstein* – with the tale-within-tale structure – to various types of boundaries and optic imagery.

In some Victorian short stories, alongside manifest border images such as doors, walls and windows, frames, and portraits stand out as thresholds between the visible and the invisible worlds: objects whose liminal dimension marks the tension between the rational and the irrational, the real and the unreal, that is typical of the fantastic mode. The frame of the portrait (either a painting or a photograph) has the function of literally delimiting the space of the fantastic, as it encapsulates the ghost within its edges. The figure the portrait represents *is* the ghost, in the etymological sense of the word, that is, an apparition, a spectre, a supernatural being, but is also a projection of the beholder's fears and desires.

Literary pictures are quite recurrent in Victorian fiction. In the present chapter I propose a reading of three texts whose plots unfold around a portrait: J. Sheridan Le Fanu's "Schalken the Painter" ([1839] 1964), Margaret Oliphant's "The Portrait" ([1885] 2000), and Thomas Hardy's "An Imaginative Woman" ([1894/1996] 2008). Although these short stories may be considered 'minor' works when compared to Poe's "The Oval Portrait", Pater's "Sebastian van Storck", and Wilde's *The Picture of Dorian Gray*, they are significant examples of a narrative space belonging to the Fantastic, where a magic exchange "between a life-imbued portrait and its astonished viewer" occurs; "[t]his bidirectional exchange in Victorian fiction is the site of contestations of power in matters psychological, sexual, social, and artistic that would not be formally theorized until well into the twentieth century", writes Deborah Manion (2010, 2), who adopts, in her book, psychoanalytic and narratological methodologies, particularly those relevant to feminist and queer image theory. Partly sharing this critical stance, my analysis will probe the material representation of the individual portrayed in the painting or photograph, as well as the dynamics between the viewer of the portrait and the figure within it.

As regards our texts, I wish, firstly, to point out their authors' cultural identities; they are British writers who belong to three distinct national contexts, Irish, Scottish, and English: LeFanu (1814–73) was born in Dublin, Oliphant (1828–97) in Wallyford, near Edinburgh, and Hardy (1840–1928) at Higher Bockhampton, near Dorchester. Their origins inevitably connect them to different literary traditions, while the historical moments in which their stories were produced may account for their different approaches to the fantastic mode: Le Fanu's writings, which are an expression of Victorian Gothic, were strongly influenced by Irish folklore, and Oliphant, whose work is inscribed in the magical-religious modality typical of late-Victorian fantasies (e.g. George MacDonald), "retained a strong sense of her Scottish inheritance" (Calder 2000, viii). Hardy, a modern writer with an interest in the psychological complexities of the mind, distanced himself from the English ghost story tradition to explore the ambiguities of human personality and the inexplicable workings of chance.

J. S. Le Fanu, "Schalken the Painter"

An important aspect in the evolution of the nineteenth-century ghost story is the shift from the effect of physical terror produced by cruel acts and wicked characters to the psychological fear experienced through more complicated narrative solutions. This is the case with Le Fanu's supernatural stories, in which we find narratives that take place in a distanced spatial and temporal dimension, and psychically disturbed individuals, isolated from the outer world owing to their obsessions (Carter 1987, 84). The protagonist of these stories often "opens his mind in such a way as to become subject to haunting by a figure which is unmistakably part of his own self" (Punter 1980, 232). Some of Le Fanu's ghost stories present the figure of the "metaphysical doctor", a master of the occult who tries to reconcile the supernatural with nineteenth-century scientific progress, as it happens in "Green Tea" and in "The Familiar", both considered the best of the five texts included in the collection *In a Glass Darkly* ([1872] 1999), of which "Carmilla" is probably the better known.

"Schalken the Painter" (originally entitled "Strange Event in the Life of Schalken the Painter") is one of the 12 tales which first appeared in *Dublin University Magazine* between 1838 and 1840, and were then collected under the posthumous title, provided by Alfred Percival Graves, of *The Purcell Papers*, published in three volumes in 1880.[1] In these texts, the author conceals himself under two distinct figures: a narrator, the eighteenth-century Catholic priest Father Purcell, who is a collector of Irish folklore and the 'compiler' of the 12 stories; and an editor, Purcell's anonymous friend and literary executor, who selects those stories which appear to him as the most appropriate to a Protestant audience – the same audience of the *Dublin University Magazine* that Le Fanu addressed. The presence of a Catholic narrator and a Protestant editor, both situated in a temporally distanced epoch, has several functions: it creates the effect of a 'historical romance', recalls the 'framing' device of the Gothic tradition, and hints at the issue of 'reconciliation' of Catholics and Protestants which was very strongly felt in late-1830s Ireland (Sage 2004, 12). The "resurrection and revenancy" narrative motifs link the stories of *The Purcell Papers* thematically and provide the collection with a sort of structural frame: "The other aspect of framing which needs to be pointed out is the notion of *aesthetic* framing, coming from the painting" – an aspect that directly concerns "Schalken the Painter", which is structured by "a layering of representational forms" (22, 24).

The story begins with the narrator's description of a painting. Its "fearful story" had been told him by his great grandfather, who, in turn, had learnt it from Schalken himself, "and from him too he ultimately received the picture itself as a bequest" (Le Fanu 1964, 30). From the start, Father Purcell underlines the indissoluble connection between the story and the picture: the latter, minutely described, seems to be the pretext for the story that illustrates "its subject":

> The picture represents the interior of what might be a chamber in some antique religious building; and its foreground is occupied by a female figure, in a species of white robe, part of which is arranged so as to form a veil. This dress, however, is not that of any religious order. In her hand the figure bears a lamp, by which alone her figure and face are illuminated; and her features wear such an arch smile, as well becomes a pretty woman when practising some prankish roguery; in the background, and, excepting where the dim red light of an expiring fire serves to define the form, in total shadow, stands the

figure of a man dressed in the old Flemish fashion, in an attitude of alarm, his hand being placed upon the hilt of his sword, which he appears to be in the act of drawing.

(29)

This passage is followed by the narrator's assurance – according to the Gothic romance tradition – of the reliability of his account: "[t]here is in that strange picture, something that stamps it as the representation of a reality. And such in truth it is, for it faithfully records a remarkable and mysterious occurrence" (*ibidem*).

The female figure in the portrait is Rose Velderkaust, the seventeen-year-old niece of the painter Gerard Douw; his apprentice Godfrey Schalken is secretly in love with the girl, but, although she loves him back, he cannot yet propose to her owing to his lack of financial prospects. The narrative element that triggers the "remarkable and mysterious occurrence" is a sort of Faustian contract between Schalken and the devil, unexpectedly evoked by the painter's oath: "Curse the subject! [. . .] curse the Picture, the devils, the saint –" (31). To this curse the devil himself seems to answer in the guise of a mysterious man, who suddenly appears in Schalken's studio, introducing himself as Minheer Vanderhausen of Rotterdam, and imperiously asking to meet Douw the next evening. The stranger, exhibiting an extraordinary wealth and boasting of an immense reputation and power, asks the older painter for the hand of his ward; Douw, although treated with arrogance by Vanderhausen, accepts the latter's request to marry Rose. In spite of the girl's sense of repulsion for this mysterious suitor, the contract of marriage is fulfilled. Thus, through Schalken's unintentional complicity and owing to Douw's greed, the "bargain" (36) is defined and Rose is 'sold' to Vanderhausen. At this point the stranger, revealing his true diabolic nature through an awful physical countenance and a weird power, lures his spouse away from his guardian's and Schalken's protection. This figure is described by a crescendo of terms that define him as not human:

> the entire character of the face was sensual, malignant, and even satanic [. . .]. There was something indescribably odd, even horrible, about all his motion, something undefinable, that was unnatural, unhuman; [. . .] there was a death-like stillness in his whole person.
>
> (39)

All these peculiarities, together with his ability to appear and disappear suddenly, connote him as a creature belonging to the world of the dead. When, some time later, Rose tries to escape and take refuge in his ward's house, Vanderhausen manages to carry her off again. Since then,

> [n]o trace of Rose was ever after found. [. . .] But an incident occurred, which, though it will not be received by our rational readers in lieu

of evidence, produced nevertheless a strong and a lasting impression upon the mind of Shalken.

(45)

The "incident" takes place, years later, with the reappearance of Rose in a church in Rotterdam, where Schalken has been called by his father's death; here he sees her under the guise of "a female form, clothed in a kind of light robe of white, part of which was so disposed as to form a veil, and in her hand she carried a lamp" (45–6). After having guided him through winding stairs and narrow passages, the veiled woman leads him into an old-fashioned Dutch apartment, richly furnished, where stood a four-post bed, with black curtains around it, until she "disclosed to the horror-stricken painter, sitting bolt upright in the bed, the livid and demonic form of Vanderhausen" (46). At this monstrous sight, Shalken falls senseless upon the floor, until he wakes up, next morning, beside a large coffin; but after that "incident" – a vision, a nightmare, a hallucination? – he "left behind him a curious evidence of the impression which it wrought upon his fancy, in a painting executed shortly after the event I have narrated" (*ibidem*).

Thus, the narrative ends with the picture described in the beginning. The originality of the story lies in its closure, with the return to the frame of the text:

> [t]he painting is the pretext for the story we read: it frames it, starting and finishing it, in that sense. But the fiction purports to tell us of the origin of the painting: it drives us towards what it represents. The fiction also frames the painting. The painting represents 'one scene' of the story it is part of, and that 'scene' is an uncanny one.
>
> (Sage, 24)

The human figures and the objects surrounding them are situated as though the scene took place on a stage; and, in fact, there is a viewer of this sort of performance, Schalken himself, who had (actually or supposedly?) watched the scene in its making. The role played by the observer in Le Fanu's ghost stories is underlined by E. F. Bleiler – "to him alone it occurred that the personality of the beholder could be just as important and perhaps just as supernatural as the manifestation itself" (1964, vii) – and, with reference to this particular story, by James Walton: "In the climactic scene Schalken is reduced to a mere passive spectator, whose gaze is drawn by Rose, the light-bearer (foreground), to the figure (background) of her seducer: patriarchal, erect, undead" (2007, 14).

This tale has been positively evaluated by several critics. Among them, Jack Sullivan, who writes that "La Fanu handled both the necrophilia and the supernaturalism in the tale with a new anti-Gothic restraint" (1980, 11), and W. L. McCormack, according to whom this is, in many ways, "the most successful of the *Purcell Papers*, being less crudely death-focussed than its companions" ([1980] 1997, 75–6). The element of wonder is certainly one of its strongest points. At the end of the narrative, the reader is left with a doubt about the actual veracity of the events in the church; after all, Schalken, being an artist, is endowed with a strong imagination which can create fantastic worlds of its own: the subject of the painting may be either the faithful reproduction of what he had witnessed in the church, or a thorough invention. But also Rose's "mysterious fate must always remain matter of speculation" (Le Fanu 46), thus corroborating the most typical feature of the fantastic mode: Todorov's hesitation, Brassière's uncertainty. In the end, the function of the portrait, in this text, is that of leaving the reader with a sensation of ambiguity about the whole story.

Margaret Oliphant, "The Portrait"

In nineteenth-century fantastic literature, the portrait is most frequently a narrative device adopted in order to convey the presence of a ghost to the reader. This may happen through the return of the dead, as we have seen in Le Fanu's story in which the traditional Gothic features of the resurrected body are meant to provoke the reader's fear and anxiety; or by the saving vision of the visitation of the dead in the world of the living, as in Oliphant's "The Portrait", where the supernatural event fulfills a consolatory and redemptive function.

"The Portrait" ([1885] 2000) belongs to a group of tales entitled by their author as *Stories of the Seen and the Unseen*, which had appeared separately in *Blackwood's Magazine*, to which Oliphant contributed throughout her life and career:[2] "[a]ll of them have a serious purpose, which is to measure the great gap between the 'seen' world around us and the 'unseen', where the dead have gone" (Williams 1986, 126). The very title of the collection underlines the liminal dimension of these narratives in more than one sense: it situates them between the world of the living and the world of the dead; it indirectly suggests that the narrative mode of these stories is between the realistic and the fantastic; it hints at their religious content, but, almost in spite of their author's intentions, it also has psychological implications.

The dimension of the in-between is also confirmed by the spatial structures of these texts. In most of them, the spirits of the dead signal their presence on such borders as doors, windows, gates, walls, and other physical or metaphorical barriers; these images trace the edges of the empty spaces in which the supernatural event takes place, and bridge the gap between the known and the unknown. Only a few individuals are able to perceive or cross the uncertain boundaries between the visible and the invisible worlds: to make connections between different worlds requires "a particular kind of light, a particular ability to see.

In Oliphant's view, these abilities have a moral and spiritual, rather than intellectual, source" (Calder, xiv) – but not only that. *Stories of the Seen and the Unseen* tell the contemporary reader something more than they did to the late-Victorian one: the invisible is not only the world of the dead but also something that our culture does not want to see and conceals to common sensorial perceptions: that is, what Freud has taught us to acknowledge as the repressed. In the attempt "to make visible what is culturally invisible and which written out as negation and as death, the fantastic introduces the absence" (Jackson, 69).

In "The Open Door" and "The Library Window", probably the best tales of the collection, architectural structures are endowed with uncanny implications and, owing to their shape, recall the frame of a portrait: all of them are threshold images (the door, the window, the frame) which mark the perimeter of the fantastic and the boundary between the 'full' space inhabited by the living and the 'empty' space of the dead. The portrait in the eponymous short story occupies that empty space and becomes not only a place of reconciliation between the living and the dead, but also the meeting point of the said and the unsaid.

As in "The Open Door" and "The Library Window", problems of an oedipal nature underlie the supernatural phenomenon experienced by the protagonist and narrator of "The Portrait", Philip Canning. At the very beginning of the story, he remarks that, after his mother's death at his birth, he had grown up "in the gravity and silence of a house without women" (Oliphant [1885] 2000, 275), who are, in fact, excluded from his life (with the exception of a housekeeper and some maids), although he recognizes them "as part of the economy of nature" (276). Having removed his mother's figure from his consciousness – he has never asked his father about her – he is bound dramatically to feel this absence. He shares the family mansion with his father, Mr Canning, who is a wealthy landowner, cold and austere, who, with age, has become more and more greedy and behaves as an absolute monarch, a true patriarch within and outside his home. Through this peculiar family structure, Oliphant seems inclined to explore "the spiritual sterility of the male ethos by alternately removing and replacing feminine influence in a young man's life" (Jay 1995, 168).

In this psychological situation there occurs a particular event in Philip's existence: he pleads with his father on behalf of one of his insolvent tenants, a poor woman who could not pay her rent. His son's compassion prompts Mr Canning to mention his wife – "You've become a little like your mother, Phil –" (Oliphant, 284) – thus changing the narrative's direction and introducing the portrait motif. The father asks his son to go into the drawing room, where he shows him a painting:

> It was the full-length portrait of a very young woman – I might say a girl, scarcely twenty – in a white dress, made in a very simple old fashion, though I was too little accustomed to female costume to

be able to fix the date. It might have been a hundred years old, or twenty, for aught I knew. The face had an expression of youth, candour, and simplicity more than any face I had ever seen. – [. . .] It was not, perhaps, beautiful in the highest sense of the word. The girl must have been too young, too slight, too little developed for actual beauty; but a face which so invited love and confidence I never saw.

(286)

The woman's almost childish countenance provokes an uncanny effect on Philip: *das Unheimliche* presents itself in the guise of a female figure who he learns to be that of his dead mother, although she is too young to be such: while she looks more like a sister or a daughter to Philip, she appears as a granddaughter rather than a wife to Mr Canning. The strange mixture of displaced family relationships evoked by the portrait, or, rather, the projection of both men's somewhat 'inappropriate' feelings onto the figure in the portrait, situates this part of the story in an area of discourse that we could define of repressed sexuality. Owing to the oedipal fantasies it sparks off in Philip, the portrait becomes a sort of fetish for him, a sacred object with a life of its own: "The picture was full-length, and we had hung it low, so that she might have been stepping into the room, and was little above my own level as I stood and looked at her again" (291).

The mother's image stepping out of the picture to enter into the room is the first embodiment of the spectre in the narrative, a mysterious presence Philip falls prey to. He begins to fantasize about "the newcomer" in the house (295), and one night, when he feels particularly dejected and wishes to go to the drawing-room and visit her, a "strange occurrence" (*ibidem*) takes place. As the narrator hears the disturbing sound of a door opening and shutting, he starts suffering from a deep turmoil and physical disturbance which he describes through a series of powerful metaphors, the last of which may also refer to the woman of the portrait, who is, in the narrator's imagination, kept prisoner within the picture's frame: "It was like a maddened living creature making the wildest efforts to get free" (296). The episodes of possession, which, in medical terms, could be described as panic attacks, take place, in a crescendo of agitation and disquiet, on three different occasions; these strange experiences are at last acknowledged by Philip as symptoms of the "visitation" – the last term being first used by him in front of the portrait, which is now worshipped like a sacred relic in a shrine (304).

After the third meeting with the spectre, a further marvellous phenomenon occurs: "a woman, a girl, a black-shrouded figure, with a thick veil over her face" (306–7) appears in the hall; she is like a double or projection of the painted woman in the portrait. When Mr Canning sees her, he cries out, uttering his dead wife's name: "'Agnes!' then [he] fell back like a sudden ruin, upon himself, into his chair" (309). His shock is provoked by the striking resemblance between the two women: the young Agnes, being the elder one's relative, unawares plays the role of the other's messenger, the instrument of a supernatural visitation. Philip recognizes, in this girl clothed in black, the same figure dressed in white that inhabits the portrait; thus, the dead mother comes to a new life by way of her "representative" (310), the young Agnes who, as it was predictable, marries Philip in the end. "This summoned doppelgänger serves as the new, permanent vessel of the elder Agnes's spirit, having escaped the confines of the ostensibly dead canvas", comments Deborah Manion (2010, 80). By playing the multiple roles of mother, daughter and wife, this woman becomes a powerful figure who brings the beneficial influence of a feminine presence into Mr Canning's house. Her power is not due to a supernatural intervention, though, but to the force of love: Philip's wish to get in touch with his mother, and his need to bring compassion and generosity into his father's house. The story's ending is wholly consistent with the author's deep Christian faith.

Through the spatial image of the portrait, there takes place a juxtaposition of, and an exchange between, the two female figures in temporal terms: the past and present of real life (the elder Agnes and the younger one) meet through the fictitious image of the portrait, opening the way to the future Agnes as Philip's wife. In psychoanalytical terms,

> The mother has used her son's oedipal vulnerability to make him challenge his father, fulfill her physical needs as both receptacle of energy and agent of her plans, and deliver her to the living world again, right where she had left off: as a new wife.
>
> (Manion, 93)

The narrator's unconsciously 'incestuous' relationship with the figure in the portrait reveals itself quite openly at the end of the narrative, when he says that the picture on the wall is supposed by strangers to be "that of my wife; and I have always been glad that it should be so supposed" (311).

Thomas Hardy, "An Imaginative Woman"

The photograph of a young and unhappy poet is the material space around which the plot of "An Imaginative Woman" (whose original title was "A Woman of Imagination") unfolds. The story, written in 1893, first published in the *Pall Mall Magazine* for April 1894 in a slightly bowdlerized version but with Hardy's permission, was originally included in the 1896 edition of *Wessex Tales*, and then transferred to *Life's Little Ironies* in the 1912 Wessex Edition. It was apparently based on "a psychological fantasy" Hardy found in August Weismann's *Essays on Heredity* (1889), which he is known to have read in 1890 (Manford [1996] 2008, 232).

The setting is a seaside town where William Marchmill, his wife Ella, and their three children are spending their holidays; here, they find lodgings usually occupied by the poet Robert Trewe, who moves out to allow the Marchmills to rent them. The protagonist of the story (the "imaginative woman" of the title) and her husband could not be more different from each other: he is a small-arms manufacturer whose "likes and inclinations" are considered by his wife "sordid and material", while she is "a votary of the muse", whose tastes and likings are regarded by him as "somewhat silly"; he is a rather prosaic man, while Ella is described as "nervous and sanguine", "[a]n impressionable palpitating creature" (Hardy [1894/1996] 2008, 7), who lets off "her delicate and ethereal emotions in imaginative occupations, day-dreams, and night-sighs" (8). An attractive and intelligent woman, she tries to overcome her frustrations as a wife by cultivating her literary ambitions, which are temporarily satisfied by the publication of some of her poems – "a congenial channel in which to let flow her painfully embayed emotions" (11) – under the pseudonym John Ivy. Some of her verses – which generally come out "in various obscure magazines" (*ibidem*) – happen to be published in the same page of a journal in which another, and more renowned poet's compositions appear; by a mere 'chance', he is the same Robert Trewe whose lodgings the Marchmills are occupying. Ella, who is an enthusiastic admirer of his poems, manages to draw more information about him from the boarding-house landlady, Mrs Hooper, somewhat encouraged by the latter's not quite innocent complicity. Ella begins to fantasize about the young poet; she starts reading his books, wearing his mackintosh found in a closet, and lying in his bed, until she gets from the householder his photograph, usually kept hidden behind another one in the ornamental frame on the bedroom's mantelpiece:

> It was a striking countenance to look upon. The poet wore a luxuriant black moustache and imperial, and a slouched hat which shaded the forehead. The large dark eyes described by the landlady showed an unlimited capacity for misery: they looked out from beneath well-shaped brows as if they were reading the universe in the microcosm of the confronter's face, and were not altogether overjoyed at what the spectacle portended. [. . .] As she gazed long at the portrait she fell into thought, till her eyes filled with tears, and she touched the cardboard with her lips. Then she laughed with a nervous lightness, and wiped her eyes.
>
> (18–19)

This event marks a turning point in the narrative: Ella develops a morbid attraction to Trewe, and the photograph becomes a sort of fetish for her; she sets it up on its edge upon the bed's coverlet, and contemplates it at night, while reading the verses he had scribbled in pencil on the wall-paper behind the curtains at the head of his bed – the same one she sleeps in. Ella indulges in erotic day-dreaming: "And now her hair was dragging where his arm had lain when he secured the fugitive fancies: she was sleeping on a poet's lips, immersed in the very essence of him, permeated by his spirit as by an ether" (20). Once, while she is absorbed in her reveries, her husband suddenly enters the bedroom and she quickly slips the photograph under her pillow. The man, after refusing her hint that he should sleep in another room – a passage in the original manuscript that was omitted from *The Pall Mall Magazine* publication (Manford, 233) – unexpectedly kisses her and says: "I wanted to be with you to-night" (Hardy, 20), the implication being they make love and she gets pregnant.

In the meantime, after her three unsuccessful attempts to meet Trewe, news arrives of his suicide, together with a letter he had written to a friend. A crucial letter, in diegetic terms, as it reveals that the young man had put an end to his life not so much out of frustration because of the severe criticism his last poem "Lyrics to a Woman Unknown" had received, but as a consequence of his utter solitude and lack of love – the love of a mother, or a sister, or a female friend:

> I have long dreamt of such an unattainable creature, as you know; and she, this undiscoverable, elusive one, inspired my last volume; the imaginary woman alone; for in spite of what has been said in some quarters there is no real woman behind the title.
>
> (27)

The consonance between the "imaginary woman" the unfortunate poet mentions in his letter and the "imaginative woman" protagonist of the story is an important element of Hardy's design, as is the narrator's early claim that "by an odd conjunction she found herself in the room of Robert Trewe" (12). This is not surprising, as every reader knows the role chance plays in Hardy's work. In this case, the suggestion is that Robert Trewe and Ella Marchmill were soul mates who would have made a perfect match if only they could have met. In this allusion to their being kindred spirits, too unlucky to have the opportunity to live happily ever after, we find the author's well-known pessimism and dramatic irony.

The story is tinged with irony throughout. In quite realistic terms, the (cynical?) narrator gives a rational explanation for Ella's infatuation with the poet which demystifies that sort of magic aura around these two: the infatuation was inevitable because

> [t]o be sure, she was surrounded noon and night by his customary environment, which literally whispered of him to her at every moment; but he was a man she had never seen: and that all that moved her was the instinct to specialize a waiting emotion on the first fit thing that came to hand, did not, of course, suggest itself to Ella.
>
> (14)

Moreover, the relationship with her husband survived only in the form of friendship, "[a]nd being a woman of very living ardours that required sustenance of some sort, they were beginning to feed on this chancing material, which was, indeed, of a quality far better than Chance usually offers" (14–15).

Chance seems to work, here, at a more uncanny level. Two years after Ella's death (as a consequence of the stress of childbirth), her husband, on the point of getting married a second time, happens to discover a lock of hair in an envelope, with the photograph of the deceased poet and a date written on the back. The likeness between the little boy and Trewe is stunning:

> By a known but inexplicable trick of Nature there were undoubt-edly strong traces of resemblance to the man Ella had never seen; the dreamy and peculiar expression of the poet's face sat, as the transmit-ted idea, upon the child's, and the hair was of the same hue.
>
> (32)[3]

William Marchmill, who till then had been tolerant of his wife's behav-iour which he considered as a typically feminine romantic indulgence, is now certain of her unfaithfulness and rejects the child as not his own: "Get away, you poor little brat! You are nothing to me!" (*ibidem*).

The portrait is, then, at the centre of the story, as being at the core of that "inexplicable trick of Nature". The inference here is that Ella, having kept the photograph under her pillow while having sex with her husband, and having fixed her gaze on it during her pregnancy, has somewhat intro-jected his image into her psyche to the point of transmitting the man's features to her child. Another explanation for this visionary circumstance is that the poet, although only indirectly 'present' in Ella's bed, 'influences' the couple's sexual intercourse in conceiving their child – an interpretation that is consistent with the overall symbolic and structural centrality of the visual paradigm in this story (Ettorre 2012, 16–17). Moreover, Trewe's photograph shows his large dark eyes "[looking] out from beneath well-shaped brows as if they were reading the universe in the microcosm of the confronter's face" (Hardy: 18), thus implying a reciprocity of the gaze: "This notion of *mutual* looking between *two subjects* where one is pres-ent only via screened image seems possible here precisely because of the characterizations of the subjects involved" (Manion, 98).

The importance of the gaze in this story is further shown by the detailed descriptions of both Ella's and Trewe's eyes, whose peculiar intensity is also a sign of the two protagonists being mysteriously connected: "She was dark-eyed, and had that marvelously bright and liquid sparkle in each pupil which characterizes persons of Ella's cast of soul, and is too often a cause of heartache to the possessor's male friends, ultimately sometimes to herself" (Hardy, 8). Trewe's gaze has also got something peculiar about it; as Mrs Hooper tells Ella, he is "more striking than handsome; a large-eyed thoughtful fellow, you know, with a very electric flash in his eye when he looks round quickly, such as you'd expect a poet to be who doesn't get his living by it" (17).[4]

Throughout the text, the narrative oscillates between the 'magic', inexplicable event – the figure in the portrait who apparently gets the passionate woman pregnant by an "electric flash in his eye", as if an encounter of the senses had taken place and desire had prevailed over heredity – and its debunking and deglamorization by the ironic description of the protagonist's naiveté. When Ella is given the photograph by the landlady, she decides, "with the subtle luxuriousness of fancy in which this young woman was an adept", to postpone the actual gesture of looking at it, prefiguring her emotions and sensations, and imagining a romantic, and stereotyped, ambiance made of "silence, candles, solemn sea and stars outside" (18). After the 'supernatural' atmospheres of "Schalken the Painter" and "The Portrait", "An Imaginative Woman" takes the reader to a more mundane terrain, in which the portrait becomes the site of a psychological conundrum, and the fantastic metamorphoses into the surreal.

Taking the cue from Doreen Massey's statement that space is "always in process" (2005, 11), I have tried to show how this particular spatial trope of fantastic fiction has changed and developed over a few decades in the Victorian period. As we have seen, these tales introduce an innovative feature into the grammar of the Fantastic by the adoption of the portrait as a chronotope; within its physical space, in fact, time seems to stop, and past and present meet: Rose, Agnes and Trewe come to life through their viewers' gaze, metaphorically breaking the borders of their pictures' frames and stepping into the real world. In the three stories, the cultural "unsayable" (Jackson: 26) enters the perimeter of the fantastic through the image of the portrait, disrupting reassuring certainties about time, space, and identity; but while Oliphant's tale, in the end, provides a comforting closure, Le Fanu's leaves the mystery about Rose's fate unsolved, and Hardy's poses new questions of both a scientific and psychological nature.

Notes

1. We have three versions of the tale: (1) the one that first appeared in *Dublin University Magazine* in 1839 as "Strange Event in the Life of Schalken the Painter", posthumously published in *Purcell Papers* (London, Richard Bentley, 1880); (2) the one included by Le Fanu in *Ghost Stories and Tales of Mystery* as "Schalken the Painter" (1851), and then in *Collected Works* (1977); (3) a reprint of the latter in *Best Ghost Stories of J. S. Le Fanu* (edited by E.F. Bleiber, New York, Dover, 1964), which juxtaposes the two versions. Bleiber's edition – which, although philologically less reliable, is most easily available, is the one used in the present essay.
2. The first story to be published was "A Christmas Tale" (1857), followed by "The Secret Chamber" (1876), but the true corpus of the collection started

with the short novel (or 'novella') *A Beleaguered City* (1879) and continued with 12 more tales, which appeared between 1880 and 1897.
3. In Conrad's "Amy Foster" (first published, by installments, in *Illustrated London News* in December 1901), we find an analogous situation: Amy's child inherits the same expression from his dead father Yanko Goorall: "The little fellow was lying on his back, a little frightened at me, but very still, with his big black eyes, with his fluttered air of a bird in a snare. And looking at him I seemed to see again the other one – the father, cast out mysteriously by the sea to perish in the supreme disaster of loneliness and despair" (Conrad 1986, 240).
4. Norman Page suggests an affinity between this "bizarrely but touchingly spiritualized affair" and the story of another artist, the sculptor Jocelyn Pierston in *The Well-Beloved*, and remarks that, like the latter, Ella Marchmill "projects her intense feelings on an idealized rather than a real object", and behaves like an English Emma Bovary (xv).

Works Cited

Bleiler, Everett Franklin. 1964. "Introduction" to *Best Ghost Stories of J. S. Le Fanu*, edited by E.F. Bleiber, v–ix. New York: Dover Edition.

Calder, Jenni. 2000. "Introduction" to *A Beleaguered City and Other Tales of the Seen and the Unseen*, by Margaret Oliphant, edited by Jenni Calder, vii–xviii. Edinburgh: Canongate.

Carter, Margaret L. 1987. *Specter or Delusion? The Supernatural in Gothic Fiction*. Ann Arbor, MI: UMI Research Press.

Conrad, Joseph. 1986. "Amy Foster". In *Typhoon and Other Stories*, edited with an Introduction by Cedric Watts, 201–40. Oxford: OUP.

Ettorre, Emanuela. 2012. "Liminalità e voyeurismo nei racconti di Thomas Hardy". In T. Hardy, *L'immaginazione di una donna e altri racconti*, Traduzione e introduzione di Emanuela Ettorre, Postfazione di Philip Mallett, 5–19. Massa: Transeuropa.

Hardy, Thomas. [1894/1996] 2008. "An Imaginative Woman". In *Life's Little Ironies*, edited by Alan Manford, 7–32. With an Introduction by Norman Page. Oxford: OUP.

Jackson, Rosemary. 1981. *Fantasy: The Literature of Subversion*. London: Methuen.

Jay, Elizabeth. 1995. *Mrs Oliphant: 'A Fiction to Herself'. A Literary Life*. Oxford: Clarendon Press.

Le Fanu, Joseph Sheridan. [1839] 1964. "Schalken the Painter". In *Best Ghost Stories of J. S. Le Fanu*, edited by Everett Franklin Bleiber, 29–46. New York: Dover Edition.

Le Fanu, Joseph Sheridan. [1872] 1999. *In a Glass Darkly*, edited with an Introduction and Notes by Robert Tracy. Oxford: OUP.

Manford, Alan. [1996] 2008. "Explanatory Notes" of *Life's Little Ironies*, edited by A. Manford, 231–51. With an Introduction by Norman Page. Oxford: OUP.

Manion, Deborah Maria. 2010. "The Ekphrastic *Fantastic*: Gazing at Magic Portraits in Victorian Fiction". PhD diss., University of Iowa. Iowa Research Online. http://ir.uiowa.edu/cgi/viewcontent.cgi?article=5399&context=etd.

Massey, Doreen. 2005. *For Space*. London: Sage.

McCormack, William John. [1980] 1997. *Sheridan Le Fanu*. Stroud, Gloucestershire: Sutton.

Oliphant, Margaret. [1885] 2000. "The Portrait". In *A Beleaguered City and Other Tales of the Seen and the Unseen*, 275–312. Introduction, notes and glossary by Jenni Calder. Edinburgh: Canongate.

Page, Norman. [1996] 2008. "Introduction" to *Life's Little Ironies*, by Thomas Hardy, edited by Alan Manford, xi–xxvii. Oxford: OUP.

Punter, David. 1980. *The Literature of Terror*. London: Longman.

Sage, Victor. 2004. *Le Fanu's Gothic. The Rhetoric of Darkness*. London: Palgrave-Macmillan.

Sullivan, Jack. [1978] 1980. *Elegant Nightmares. The English Ghost Story from Le Fanu to Blackwood*. Athens, OH: Ohio University Press.

Walton, James. 2007. *Vision and Vacancy. The Fictions of J. S. Le Fanu*. Dublin: University College Dublin Press.

Williams, Merryn. 1986. *Margaret Oliphant. A Critical Biography*. New York: St. Martin's Press.

6 Rambles in the Fantastic

Digital Mapping Mary Shelley's *Last Man*

David Sandner

"Futurity, like a dark image in a phantasmagoria, came nearer and more near, till it clasped the whole earth in its shadow".

(201)

Sybilline Leaves: Fantastic Prophecy

Mary Shelley's first and last published works are travelogues: *The History of a Six-Weeks Tour* (1817) and *Rambles in Germany and Italy, 1840, 1842, and 1843* (1844). Her two fantastic novels, *Frankenstein* (1818) and *The Last Man* (1826), are also "rambles", travelbooks in which the main characters trek across real-life landscapes – but only to become, as in the last line of *Frankenstein*, "lost in darkness and distance" (161). Her fantastic creations (the impossible creature; the all-encompassing plague) compel her main characters to rush into radically empty spaces: the white out North where Victor dies and the Creature will build his funeral pyre; the wipe out of total plague death in a desolate Rome at the end of Verney's narrative. Maps fail when no one is left to read them. Shelley employs the technique of the tourist's guidebook to a purpose, mapping, then unmapping the reader in order to intensify our engagement with untranslatable experience, unfolding new perceptions – sublime moments accessed as prophecy, as sf speculation, and as hauntings.

The plague dead weigh on Lionel Verney; *Frankenstein's* undead creature, his dark double, hides in shadow, always near, always secret. Their rambles bring us very pointedly out into the world (to the wild edges of nature, before famous tourist sites, and across multiple geographic boundaries), but the impossible presence of spectral bodies – the oppressive dead, the desolate creature – undermine our relationship to places we thought we knew. For after "the end of the world", to whom does the world present itself? To whom does it belong? In what way, with what meaning? The reader realizes limits, Alpha and Omega, first and last: in *Frankenstein*, we can be replaced by the new Creature, first of a species better, stronger, more durable, possibly smarter; in *Last Man*, humanity slowly, painfully depletes, falling one by one. Who, or what, waits beyond to read of our fall?

Shelley's strange and wondrous introduction to *The Last Man* presents a pre-story about finding the story of the novel. She describes a tourist journey near Naples that ends in the hidden recesses of the Sybil's cave from antiquity. The tourists themselves appear quite ordinary; they seem, in fact, to represent Mary Shelley and her husband, Percy Bysshe Shelley, who truly did travel together in Naples. But the cave tunnels into the heart of the fantastic. There, groping in darkness, their guides too frightened to continue, the curious wanderers find prophetic fragments, unbound leaves from the ancient Sybil's books in languages known and unknown, ancient and modern and *other*, describing events from the past and, remarkably, absurdly, the future (3–4). These leaves cannot possibly mean something, or anything, taken together, yet our narrator insists the novel's linear narrative is an incredible translation and transcription of these leaves – pages randomly chosen in darkness and ordered for us out of no possible order. We are offered a fantastic pastiche told in all languages, and yet *more*, an unbearable excess, until the dream of language fails us like the fall of Babel. What could we possibly be reading? Who could tell it to us?

The dislocation described by *Last Man's* introduction resists the specificity of the geographical movement in the novel itself across a recognizable landscape, largely contemporary to Shelley (but with sfnal elements, most notably balloon travel); her central fantastic trope, the all-killing plague, does not even bear mention in the first volume of her three-Decker. But when it comes, it swiftly empties the landscape of meaning as of people. The narrative's chronology begins 2080. The plague appears in 2092, infecting Europe in earnest in 2093 (172); just seven years later, Verney, alone in Rome, "ascended St. Peter's, and carved on its topmost stone the æra 2100, last year of the world!" (365). But of course it is not the end of the world, just the end of humanity's participation in it. A tension between the known world and a future without humanity (and so unknowable to human readers by definition!) invokes the spectral presence of the fantastic to imagine the world *without* people *in the present* – to realize the totality in which our presence or absence is irrelevant. Her novel's "mapping" – attempts to systematize and so know the world – are revealed and undercut. Alfred Korzybski famously states "the map is *not* the territory" (58) but Baudrillard pushes further: "the map [. . .] precedes the territory" (1). The map does not simply reveal – it creates what can be known in an act of imagination and ideology. Equally, a text can take no necessary precedence over a map in the act of reading. As Anthony Pavlik comments, "literary maps actually reveal their full potential not just in direct association with a text, but through the reader's imagination" (28).

Consider two famous maps from the tradition of fantasy: the detailed map of Middle-Earth from J. R. R. Tolkien's *Lord of the Rings* (1954–55), with its backing appendices; and Lewis Carroll's equally striking map from his quest fantasy narrative poem, *The Hunting of the Snark* ([1876] 2013). Taken together, they present contrasting purposes for fantastic maps.

Following the success of Tolkien's trilogy, epic fantasies, in particular, typically offer a map, usually at the beginning – as an orientation tool for the traveller in new realms (Ekman, 22; Jones, x; Kaveney, 624). Tolkien's fantasy work builds up its peculiar power through a distinctive "thickness" of detail throughout the narrative, testing the patience of some readers, compelling others to invest themselves as fans obsessed with his details, languages, and myths. In "On Fairy-Stories", Tolkien wrote explicitly about how to build and maintain the integrity of a "Secondary World" (140). Maps are useful to his project because they promise the presence of the actual in a dubious but tangible way. The map reinforces the imaginary world's existence, and so has become a common technique for achieving what Coleridge calls "the suspension of disbelief" (264) and Tolkien "secondary belief" (140).

In Lewis Carroll's *The Hunting of the Snark*, the Captain produces "a large map representing the sea,/Without the least vestige of land" to aid his crew on their odd, dangerous quest.

> "What's the good of Mercator's North Poles and Equators,
> Tropics, Zones, and Meridian Lines?"
> So the Bellman would cry: and the crew would reply
> "They are merely conventional signs!
>
> "Other maps are such shapes, with their islands and capes!
> But we've got our brave Captain to thank:
> (So the crew would protest) "that he's bought us the best –
> A perfect and absolute blank!"
>
> (224)

The passage is adorned by an illustration of a map with nothing on it, a map frame of a blank. And, indeed, this "perfect and absolute" map does prove "best", allowing the crew to find the island where the Snark lies; they sail purely into the fantastic because they sail nowhere at all. Maps can be useful when you're lost, if we follow conventions. As Farah Mendelsohn complains, maps might limit fantasy by implying "that the destination and its meaning are known" (4). If you want to be lost in order to find something that can't be found, you're going to have to misread nothing. What is the good of conventions and control if you seek something you can't understand? Tolkien's linear, mapped quest is characteristic of the epic; but Carroll's lunatic quest to nowhere might be more in line with the fantastic's fundamental resistance to hermeneutics, what Rosemary Jackson identifies as its drive to "subvert (overturn, upset, undermine) rules and conventions" (14).

Shelley's sublime introduction, presenting her narrative as fragmentary, unknowable prophecy from both past and future, connects her method to Carroll's; still, her detailed use of place "anchors" her work. She writes, with a purpose, from one way to the other: from the detail and fullness of her contemporary world (enriched with sfnal touches) toward nothingness; she takes and takes away, in an inexorable subtraction, until only one, the last, remains. Then none, as Verney sets sail into a "perfect and absolute blank". In Shelley's novel, the fantastic offers not an antithesis to realist fiction, unmooring us from reality, but a recognition of the actual as incomprehensible, awaiting apprehension. As the story ends, Verney, dedicates the work to us: "THE ILLUSTROUS DEAD. SHADOWS, ARISE AND READ YOUR FALL!" (364). Ghosts, we stand in the dark, holding ancient leaves, babbling mad prophecy.

To chart Shelley's methods, my project offers two components – a digital mapping and this chapter – designed to be complementary, yet to function separately. At **www.viseyes.org/visualeyes?1967**, you can view maps of *Last Man* I produced in VisualEyes5, an authoring tool for dynamic, interactive, web-based visualizations from the University of Virginia's Sciences, Humanities, & Arts Technological Initiatives (SHANTI). My criteria for an authoring tool followed Amy E. Earhart's suggestion to use a "robust mapping tool specifically designed for humanities concerns [. . . . that] allows users to create highly detailed maps, add historical map overlays and images, create robust metadata, and build timelines for temporal modeling" (100, though she uses Neatline). Editor Anne McWhir's notes to the Broadview *Last Man*, and her own end map, "Lionel Verney's World" (368), also proved invaluable. My maps recreate Verney's movements in order to consider spatiality in Shelley more closely. Her better-known *Frankenstein* is equally preoccupied with landscape, but *Last Man* turns more sharply into geography and its relation to the geopolitical. Nations and wars, elections and religious divisions, move her plot . . . until the plague ends plotting. These "worldly" considerations point to a political dimension in her "fantastic" that I will discuss in the final section of the chapter. I argue her work does not seek to estrange us *from* the world, but demonstrates that we have always been so. After the end of the world, when Verney has been confirmed "last", carved the end date on St Peter's, and dedicated his story, why does he sail off on a journey of discovery? The point of the novel lies there, in his – in our – inability to stop reaching, moving.

Datasets: From the Lake District to the Wide World

Mapping *Last Man* produces a series of *competing* maps. Tensions emerge prompting movement over boundaries; but looming in the title, belied for a time by the first's volume's domestic and political concerns, the plague "nullifies all hope of human relationship" (Snyder, 436). In the beginning,

Verney's world centres on the Lake District of north England. He is a young shepherd, and his sister, Perdita, "dwelt in a cottage whose trim grass-plot sloped down to the waters of the lake of Ulswater" (13); their father, ruined, "turned his back on London" and "buried himself in solitude among the hills and lakes of Cumberland" (9). Verney's Wordsworthian occupation and location identify him with nature; he is described as wild, and angry with his banishment from society. He finds himself, typically for her narrative, in one place, yet called to another, larger stage.

Verney's solitude is broken by the appearance of Adrian, and later his sister Idris, the children of his father's late friend, the abdicated King of England (for Britain is now a kingless democracy). Still wealthy, they move into a local estate, and Adrian brings Verney into society. As part of his education, he travels to Vienna (28) for two years, 2081–82, returning to live not in the Lake District but in Windsor, now the once-King's family residence, and also in London, especially Westminster, the seat of government and power. Between 2083 and 2097, aside from two journeys to Scotland and Ireland, and war in Greece, the events of his life consist of constant movement between Windsor, the domestic space of friends and family (Lionel marries Idris) and London, which provides "easy access to the fashionable and political circles of England" (38), especially in the company of the worldly Lord Raymond, a Byronic figure whose "reckless courage and comprehensive genius brought him notice" (31). The tension between these spaces is between love and contentment in the family circle and ambition and power in the social sphere. The retiring Adrian, a Percy Shelley stand in, refuses the power others would give him; but Lord Raymond embodies restless desires for achievement, and off into the wider stage he leaps.

The "supremely handsome" (31) Lord Raymond is elected Lord Protectorate of England; yet his ambitions will not remain in bounds. He ultimately determines to leave his work and go to Greece to fight against the Turks in order to (as he says to entice Adrian to join him): "behold new scenes; see a new people; witness the mighty struggle there going forward between civilization and barbarism" (117). The map again enlarges to bring us to a perceived edge of civilization as defined, with racial and religious prejudice, as the space where Asia and Europe, "Mahometans" (123) and "Christians" (124), meet and war. Raymond, Adrian in tow for a time, leaves and becomes commander of the Athens division, but is captured (at first thought dead, but he rises again), leading his wife, Perdita, with her brother Verney, to travel to Greece themselves in the year 2092.

Ransomed, Raymond begins a campaign for Constantinople, the key city on the border between competing ideologies and world-views. The beginning of the war marks the first mention of the plague, first described as a dangerous, but natural, occurrence, which grips Constantinople. As Verney remarks, "as each year that city experienced a like visitation small attention was paid to these accounts which declared more people to have died there already, than usually made up the accustomed prey of the whole of the hotter months" (137). The war and the plague progress in countervailing directions. The Turks resolved on war when the Greeks marched "from their stronghold in the Morea, acquired Thrace and Macedonia, and had led their armies even to the gates of Constantinople" (123); later, in a mirror-image movement, the "disease has spread in Thrace and Macedonia; and now, fearing the virulence of infection during the coming heats, a cordon has been drawn on the frontiers of Thessely" (173). The cordon fails; soon enough, "The plague had come to Athens" and "Raymond's beloved Athenians, the free, the noble people of the divinest town in Greece, fell like ripe corn before the merciless sickle of the adversary" (175). The enlargement of maps by human agency has reached its outer limit, and now the human world contracts as nature, in the form of the plague, constricts it.

A first mapping of England records Verney's advancement from Ullswater to Windsor and London; a mapping of Verney in Greece tracking Raymond's campaign to liberate Constantinople from the Turks records a mocking counterprogress of the plague back along the track of war. The spread of disease destroys the dominion of the map; disease suddenly fills all space: Verney notes the contagion's preexistence before it enters Europe in the "East" where "the scene of havoc and death continued to be acted [. . .], on a scale of fearful magnitude" (175), but quickly "America also had received the taint" (175) Soon, "the vast cities of America, the fertile plains of Hindostan, the crowded abodes of the Chinese, are menaced with utter ruin" (184). As Verney hopelessly observes:

> I spread the whole earth out as a map before me. On no one spot of its surface could I put my finger and say, here is safety. In the south, the disease, virulent and immedicable, had nearly annihilated the race of man [. . .]. In the north it was worse – the lesser population gradually declined, and famine and plague kept watch on the survivors.
>
> (204)

The "whole earth" convulses against humanity like a body, in a fever, fighting off infection. All humanity is undone, unmapped.

The horrifying but natural explanation, that is, the sfnal speculation of a disease *like* what has come before but more virulent, is confounded with the notion of the plague as fate, a curse. The character Evadne, who loves Lord Raymond but is rejected, dies proclaiming: "I have sold myself to death, with the sole condition that thou shoudst follow me – Fire, and war, and plague, unite for thy destruction – O, my Raymond, there is no safety for thee!" (142). Evadne's curse looms over the narrative, but Raymond dies when he rides into infected Constantinople and sets off an explosion, a trap left by the retreating Turks. Still, a captured Turks spits: "The curse of Allah is on Stamboul, share ye her fate" (150). At one point in the narrative, Verney hears the strange story of a "black sun" (176);

at another, he sees "three other suns, alike burning and brilliant, rushed from various corners" of the sky to whirl around our sun and then into the ocean (290). The sea mounts up, obscuring the sun itself and Verney fears that, somehow, the planet is "turned adrift in an unknown region of space" (290), engendering a "sublime sense of awe" (291). These events present as both natural and supernatural. Verney experiences vertigo as "under our very feet the earth yawned – deep and precipitous the gulph below opened to receive us, while the hours charioted us toward the chasm" (214). The world is void, replaced by the image of the abyss, meaninglessness.

Finally, the novel's world settles into a rhythm as the seasons mark the rise and fall of the disease's ravages. Summer ramps up the destruction of the plague; winter finds it dormant. Despite curses or voids, mapping records the movement of the disease into Europe and toward England. In 2093, "the plague was in France and Italy" (186) – appearing in Leghorn, Genoa, and Marseilles, towns along the Mediterranean. In June of 2094, "symptoms of the plague had occurred in hospitals of [London]" (188). Surprisingly, mapping records another countervailing movement, the march of the remnant of humanity "south" to "the native place for the human race" (255), the origin. Adrian, who would not lead before, becomes Lord Protector (192) and takes the last band of about two thousand, on "the procession of the last triumph of death" (312–13), "to sacred and eternal Rome" (258). The third map records the ironic "pilgrimage" from London to Paris, where the group squabbles and splits, but carries on; Verney alone arrives in Rome. A final, spectral map imagines Verney's plans to circumnavigate the empty world (McWhir, 368). What does it mean, standing on the shore by the Tiber, to watch him go? As Verney sails out of the narrative, we must consider not where Verney went, but what his journey means to us, the reader left behind; the answers lie in Shelley's politics at the intersection of mapping and the fantastic.

The Politics of Fantastic Prophecy

Lee Sterrenburg, taking a once-common view, declares *Last Man* "pessimistic" and "antipolitical" (328). However, Andrea Haslanger notes that Shelley transforms apocalyptic literature by "representing the natural world as flourishing, rather than disappearing" (661), opening what Ranita Chatterjee calls Shelley's "biopolitics" – her critique of the inability of the modern state to see "what lies outside of its law" (35). Shelley's politics lie in what remains *after*; using the fantastic, she represents what refuses anthropocentric determination.

To approach her politics of the fantastic, let me return to the relationship of the fantastic and the sublime, a matter I have developed at length elsewhere (Sandner, *Critical*, 7–46). In literature, both are devices; neither has a necessarily radical politics, certainly. The staunch conservative political theorist Edmund Burke, after all, writes the most famous eighteenth-century treatise *Of The Sublime and the Beautiful* (1757). Terror, Burke writes, is the primary "source of the sublime, [. . .] productive of the strongest emotion which the mind is capable of feeling" (58). Terror arises in fear, for "No passion so effectually robs the mind of all its powers of acting and reasoning as *fear*" (100). The greatest fear is produced, for Burke, by the unknown: Burke's discussion of the centrality of sublime "obscurity" and its production of "astonishment" (99) was used, perhaps to his chagrin, as a blueprint for how to write Gothic literature by Horace Walpole, the writer who invented and named the genre in *The Castle of Otranto* (1764); later Gothic writers modeled their works on Walpole's and consciously deployed Burke's ideas; the Gothic is the first popular literature of the fantastic, and its direct descendants include science fiction, fantasy, and horror. Shelley's *Frankenstein* is, of course, a key crossroads text in this tradition, both a late Gothic but also the first science fiction novel (Aldiss, 153–4).

The modern genres of the fantastic, in brief, arise out of Burke's discussion of the sublime aesthetics of the imagination: the moment when the imagination is confronted and overwhelmed by something not only unknown but unknowable, too great for comprehension. We should note, however, though the sublime itself may be but a tool, apolitical, Burke himself is far from politically neutral. Indeed, he studies "aesthetics" and "feeling" precisely to understand what moves us, as voters, and, importantly for him, as mobs during events like the French Revolution. His claim that our deepest emotion is a fear of otherness can be interrogated as a political claim.

In *Reflections on the Revolution in France (1790)*, a prime document in the history of political theory, Burke argues for the value of tradition, even if repressive, over the chaos of revolution, even if that brings social justice. For Burke, the ideals of the French Revolution, "liberty, equality, brotherhood," are dangerous because, in them:

> All the pleasing illusions, which made power gentle, and obedience liberal, which harmonized the different shades of life, and which, by a bland assimilation, incorporated into politics the sentiments which beautify and soften private society, are to be dissolved by this new conquering empire of light and reason. All the decent drapery of life is to be rudely torn off.
>
> (74)

Importantly, he doesn't claim that tradition is true. The "new" era of "light and reason" might be more true: but he asserts the value of imagination – tradition as a "pleasing", and necessary, "illusion". To remove "the decent drapery" in which we clothe our minds would leave us what we *are* underneath: naked, violent, rude – like so many cockroaches caught out on the kitchen floor when the light's flipped on. It is a dark and discouraging view of humanity, but a politically compelling and influential one (much argued against by, for one, Mary Shelley's mother, Mary Wollstonecraft).

How might a different politics of the fantastic, of being sublimely overwhelmed, be articulated? In Percy Shelley's poem "Mont Blanc", the sublime encounter with the mountain compels a "dizzy rapture", in which his apostrophe to the mountain moves toward personification when, in a key passage, he writes: "Thou hast a voice, great Mountain, to repeal/ large codes of fraud and woe" (99, ll. 80–1). But no mountain speaks; the "voice" is rhetorical, a conjuring meant to engage the mountain's emergent otherness, its untameable weirdness that repeals "large codes of fraud and woe" by giving the lie to our self-importance which frames such codes. "Mont Blanc" takes place on the mountain where Frankenstein's Creature secludes himself; it was written at the same time as Shelley's first novel; it is frequently anthologized with her work. They share, in short, a set of concerns, and methods. The Creature comes down from the mountains and speaks – as if he were its voice. Equally, *Last Man's* sublime plague makes us dizzy, "mocking all assumptions of order, meaning, purpose, and causality" (Snyder, 435), delivering us to an empty world that might "repeal large codes of fraud and woe" if we can hear the impossible voice of the "last man".

Percy Shelley's *Defense of Poetry* performs a dense and lyrical argument for the value of imagination. Poets, he claims, connecting the imagination directly to the political, "are the unacknowledged legislators of the world" (535). They "legislate" by setting the terms for our understanding, and opening the world to the new that reshapes it. But they are unacknowledged because their power is unsanctioned and, finally, sublime – unknowable. "The great instrument of moral good", he writes, "is the imagination". How? First, he writes, in a common enough claim, that the imagination establishes sympathy: we imagine ourselves in the place of another, and so act for others, promoting common good (517). But Percy Shelley offers a more radical idea of the imagination's power. He writes:

> All things exist as they are perceived. [. . .] But poetry defeats the curse which binds us to be subjected to the accident of surrounding impressions. And whether it spreads its own figured curtain, or withdraws life's dark veil from before the scene of things, it equally [. . .] makes us the inhabitants of a world to which the familiar world is a chaos. It [. . .] purges from our inward sight the film of familiarity which obscures from us the wonder of our being. [. . .] It creates anew the universe, after it has been annihilated in our minds by the recurrence of impressions blunted by reiteration.
>
> (533)

He aims his remarks at all literature, but they have special relevance for fantastic literature and its strangeness; if strangely compelling enough, fantastic stories shake us loose to consider other ways of being. We leave "the accident of surrounding impressions", the chance of the moment and space in which we live, and encounter "the wonder of our being". The "fantastic sublime" (Sandner, *Fantastic Sublime*, 49–65) withdraws "life's dark veil", revealing the world anew, but it is also only a figuration, a "figured curtain" drawn over the world. The fantastic conceals and reveals, revealing by concealing, a paradox, confounding, offering nothing certain but newness, in which the imagination "creates anew the universe".

Similarly, Shelley's novel destabilizes reality in order to bring us a closer experience of it – deploying the fantastic as a way to make visible the meaning of the world as present but unknowable, spectral, shot through with the imagination as a necessary tool for apprehending the incomprehensible. Shelley's dramatic "big idea" sf novel destroys "the world" *as humanity images it to itself* in order to get what lies behind figuration (Snyder, 444). After the all-consuming plague, Verney declares: "There was but one good and one evil in the world – life and death. The pomp of rank, the assumption of power, the possessions of wealth vanished like morning mist" (230); and, "farewell to the desire to rule, and the hope of victory; to high vaulting ambition, to the appetite for praise, and the craving for the suffrage of their fellows! The nations are no longer!" (253). Erasing the lines imposed by the map, she interrogates why we marked what we marked in the first place.

When I began, I noted both *Frankenstein* and *The Last Man* move across "map-able" spaces; at the close of both texts, a main character voyages off alone: the Creature, on an "ice raft", was "borne away", "lost" (161); Verney, in a "tiny bark", sails away, "the LAST MAN" (367). Both endings are radically open-ended. But here, at last, we find a contrast: the Creature, hopeless, seeks only to accomplish his death; Verney brings his dog, books, supplies. Verney is on a journey of discovery, to find others and to see the world, however impossible the task. We might reconcile this difference by noting that someone *besides the reader* is left in *Frankenstein* to consider what the final sailing off into "lost-ness" means: Walton. He evidently survives his journey of discovery and returns to his sister, bringing his incredible story with him . . . for we have the story at hand. So, finally, both novels use the fantastic to interrogate our "will to power", seeking, behind the map, what matters. Both end without ready answers to the questions raised. Yet Verney's journey suggests we carry on, strangely hopeful in a strange, strange world.

Works Cited

Aldiss, Brian, with David Wingrove. "Introduction to *Trillion Year Spree*." *Speculations on Speculation: Theories of Science Fiction*, edited by James Gunn and Matthew Candlearia, Scarecrow, 2005, pp. 147–62.

Baudrillard, Jean. *Simulacra and Simulation*, trans. Sheila Fraser Glaser, University of Michigan Press, 1994.

Burke, Edmund. *A Philosophical Enquiry into the Origin of Our Ideas of the Sublime and the Beautiful*, 1757, Dent, 1955.

———. *Reflections on the Revolution in France*, 1790, Arlington House, 1965.

Carroll, Lewis. "The Hunting of the Snark", *Alice in Wonderland*, edited by Donald J. Gray, 3rd ed., Norton, [1876] 2013.

Coleridge, Samuel Taylor. *Biographia Literaria. Selected Poetry and Prose of Coleridge*, edited by Donald A. Stauffer, Modern Library, 1951, pp. 109–428.

Earhart, A.E. "'After a Hundred Years/Nobody Knows the Place': Notes Toward Spatial Visualizations of Emily Dickinson." *Emily Dickinson Journal*, vol. 23, no. 1, 2014, pp. 98–105.

Ekman, Stephen. *Here be Dragons: Exploring Fantasy Maps and Settings*, Wesleyan University Press, 2013.

Jackson, Rosemary. *The Literature of Subversion*, Metheun, 1981.

Jones, Diana Wynne. *The Tough Guide to Fantasyland*, Firebird, 2006.

Kaveney, Roz. "Maps." *Encyclopedia of Fantasy*, St. Martin's, 1997, 624pp.

Korzybski, Alfred. *Science and Sanity*, 1933, 5th ed., Institute of General Semantics, 2000.

Mendelsohn, Farah. *Rhetorics of Fantasy*, Wesleyan University Press, 2008.

Pavlik, Anthony. "'A Special Kind of Reading Game': Maps in Children's Literature." *International Research in Children's Literature*, vol. 3, no. 1, 2010, pp. 28–43.

Sandner, David. *Critical Discourses of the Fantastic, 1712–1831*, Ashgate, 2011.

———. *The Fantastic Sublime: Romanticism and Transcendence in Nineteenth-Century Children's Fantasy Literature*, Greenwood, 1996.

Shelley, Mary. *Frankenstein*, 1818, edited by J. Paul Hunter, 2nd ed., Norton, 2012.

———. *The History of a Six-Weeks Tour*, Hookham, 1817.

———. *The Last Man*, 1826, edited by Anne McWhir, Broadview, 1996.

———. *Rambles in Germany and Italy, 1840, 1842, and 1843*, Moxon, 1844.

Shelley, Percy Bysshe. *Shelley's Poetry and Prose*, edited by Donald H. Reiman and Neil Fraistat, 2nd ed., Norton, 2002.

Snyder, Robert Lance. "Apocalypse and Indeterminacy in Mary Shelley's *The Last Man*." *Studies in Romanticism*, vol. 17, no. 4, Fall, 1978, pp. 435–52.

Sterrenburg, Lee. "*Last Man*: Anatomy of a Failed Revolution." *Nineteenth-Century Fiction*, vol. 33, no. 3, 1978, pp. 324–47.

Tolkien, J.R.R. "On Fairy-Stories." *The Monsters and the Critics and Other Essays*, Houghton, 1984, pp. 109–61.

Walpole, Horace. *The Castle of Otranto, 1764*, 3rd ed., Murray, 1789.

7   Home Is Where the Dark Is

A Literary Geography of Daphne du Maurier's Disturbing Genres

David Ian Paddy

> *It's not for nothing that fantasy exists. It's what makes homes of our houses.*
>
> Milan Kundera *The Joke*

According to crime writer Minette Walters, "One of the reasons I'm such a fan of Daphne du Maurier is that her stories are never comfortable" (2005: vii). Pigeonholed as a mere writer of romances (fellow Cornish writer Arthur Quiller-Couch predicted correctly that critics would never forgive her for *Rebecca*), du Maurier deployed genres only to disturb them.[1] Her tales told in a fantastic vein can be unsettling to read, but they also unsettle expectations by not sitting easily within any readymade critical mode: "she's a complex, powerful, unique writer, so unorthodox that no critical tradition, from formalism to feminism, can digest her" (Auerbach 2002: 10). When her writing turned to the fantastic it was as a disturbing genre that also disturbed genre itself.

Furthermore, far from creating cozy domestic dramas, she produced fictions that challenge the idealized comforts of home. A writer deeply concerned with landscapes and the built environments of houses, du Maurier provides a unique template for theorizing the intersection of spatiality and the fantastic. While du Maurier's work has been considered in such terms as the Gothic, suspense and macabre, and she has been recognized as a writer attuned to the power of landscape (especially given her constant attention to her beloved Cornwall) how these two elements intersect – the fantastic and the spatial – will be the focus of this chapter.

In his classic work of experiential geography, *Space and Place* (1977), Yi-Fu Tuan illuminates the keywords of his title in a way that can provide a starting point for understanding the disturbances of genre and location in du Maurier's work. For Tuan, "Place is security, space is freedom: we are attached to the one and long for the other" (3). In the fantastic scenarios of du Maurier, Tuan's terms come undone. Where a home should be regarded as a place (familiar and comforting), and heading out from home could open up an experience of space (the positive potential of the unknown, with promises of change and renewal), disturbing events *within* place and space undermine the positive traits *of* place and space. Home – as place – no longer feels familiar or comforting, and venturing out – as space – is no longer freedom, but challenge and threat. If Tuan argues that the general tendency of human experience is to turn the unknown of space into the known of place (6), the abstract into the concrete (199), the fantastic in du Maurier's tales reverses this to turn the known of place into the unknown of space, and the promise of space into disappointment. The comforting idea of home is shattered and the opportunity of movement provides no escape.

Du Maurier and the Fantastic

Du Maurier's oeuvre is populated by many of the traditional tropes (and beyond) that we associate with fantastic literature in its most general sense: doubles (*The Scapegoat*), animated objects ("The Doll"), ghost ships ("The Escort"), the blurring of human and animal ("The Blue Lenses"), the breakdown between the real and the imagined ("The Alibi"), ESP ("Don't Look Now"), communication with the dead ("The Breakthrough") and even psychedelic time travel (*The House on the Strand*). Themes of atavism, immortality, the self lost in the other, and psychic powers abound. Her fiction is filled with characters that resemble her grandfather George du Maurier's creation, Svengali. At the same time, her work does not slide easily into given generic categories, and as an author she was loath to identify with any category cast upon her, especially romance. (Notably, she elided easy labels about her gender and sexuality as well.) According to Alison Light: "certainly her work must be a nightmare for the eager compiler of 'genre studies' compendia" (1991: 159).

Take for instance, "The Breakthrough" ([1971] 2006a), a story commissioned by Kingsley Amis for a science-fiction collection. It is along with *The House on the Strand* ([1969] 2003) the closest she came to that genre, but *The House on the Strand* is also an historical novel that features hallucinatory drugs that enable time travel, while "The Breakthrough" concerns pseudo-scientific material rather than cutting-edge hard science. James MacLean, in the story, fits the mad scientist type, who experiments in "telepathy, precognition, and all the so-called psychic mysteries" (2006a: 240), with his ultimate experiment harnessing the energy of a dying boy to break down the boundary between life and death, and open up the potential of immortality. If this paranormal fantasy feels a touch Lovecraftian, it is perhaps more jarring given its grim concrete wasteland location of an abandoned radar experimental station – "The place looked like a deserted Dachau more than ever" (232) – that better befits the landscapes of J. G. Ballard.

Or how about "The Blue Lenses" (1959)? After undergoing an eye operation, Marda West begins to see everyone around her with animal heads, the nurse a cow, the surgeon a terrier, her husband a vulture. After a second operation, their human heads return, but her own is now that of a timid deer. Is this horror? Fantasy, comedy, allegory? Where to place such things? If genre is a kind of house that contains and distinguishes different types of stories, where can narratives like these and others reside?

Patricia García, providing an overview of the criticism of fantastic literature, notes a distinction between two strands – one that sees the fantastic as any form of literature that departs from a mimetic or realistic mode of writing (Kathryn Hume's *Fantasy and Mimesis* (1984) is a good example of this more expansive approach), and the other that claims the fantastic as one specific mode within the broad spectrum of non-realistic literature (Tzvetan Todorov's *The Fantastic* (1975) is the iconic work in this vein). In the analysis of du Maurier that follows, while examples of the fantastic in the general (non-realistic) sense will be noted, the emphasis will be on Todorov's version of the fantastic. One of the remarkable things about that study is that Todorov proposes, in some sense, a genre that does not really exist. It is a hypothesis about a kind of space between genres. So, although it may sound paradoxical, his non-genre of hesitation is the more fitting ground for the ill-fitting nature of du Maurier's disturbance of genres and her genres of disturbance, and for the more radical picture it can help raise about the fantastic use of space.

Todorov describes the fantastic as a work in which an unexpected event emerges within and violates the sensibility of an otherwise consistent textual reality, and this unexpected event leaves the implied reader and often the narrator in a position of hesitation as to what is real and what is not. In a story in which a ghost appears, the reader may hesitate between interpreting the appearance as a product of the narrator's unstable psychology (the uncanny) or decide instead that this is a world in which ghosts are a reality (the marvelous). The fantastic occupies the space of hesitation between the uncanny and the marvelous, when a stabilizing interpretation cannot yet be offered. In this way, Todorov's fantastic is less of a genre or mode than a potential space between non-realistic genres. If, as stated earlier, a genre is a kind of house, the fantastic, in Todorov's model, is nomadic, homeless. It may even bring the house down.

As a test case, three stories – the opening triad of du Maurier's 1952 collection, *The Birds and Other Stories* ("The Birds", "Monte Verità", and "The Apple Tree") – can help us map ways of approaching du Maurier's literature of the fantastic. In "The Apple Tree", a widower is pleased to be on his own, free of his depressed wife, only to be haunted by constant reminders of her in an apple tree just outside his home, which bears her "martyred resignation" (2004a: 114). The more he tries to forget her, the more the apple tree insists on his consciousness, from the firewood made of its branches brought in by the gardener or the tart made of its fruit by the cook:

And whichever way he turned his chair, this way or that upon the ter-
race, it seemed to him that he could not escape the tree, that it stood
there above him, reproachful, anxious, desirous of the admiration he
could not give.

(139–40)

However, only the widower experiences the tree as animated and nightmarish. We tip toward the uncanny: the unreal elements in the story do
not make the reality of the story different from ours; instead, the narrator
seems to project his psychological conditions – guilt, anxiety, inability to
face his own flaws – onto the tree.

Like "The Apple Tree", "The Birds" is a story of nature behaving strangely (and in both a sense of home is under threat), but "The
Birds" seems a better embodiment of the marvelous (or, more precisely,
the fantastic-marvelous) rather than the uncanny. A solitary farmer, Nat
Hocken, who is deeply familiar with the rhythms of the Cornish countryside, notices the sudden aggressive behaviour of the birds and their gang
mentality, before they start killing the human population. Unlike "The
Apple Tree", it is clear that the strange events are actually happening in
the world; something has changed in reality, not in the psychology of the
character. By the story's end, though, the cause for the change in nature
and the land is never explained. This world is like ours, but something
has changed to make it unlike ours.

One of du Maurier's more complexly structured pieces, the novella
"Monte Verità" is narrated by an Englishman and passionate mountain-
eer looking back on the relationship he had with his friend Victor and
Victor's wife Anna. Anna was reluctant to go mountain climbing with
them, but when she does, upon the fabled (and fictional) European Monte
Verità, she disappears, joining an ancient cult that lives within a valley at
the mountain's top. The truth of Anna's fate – has she become one of a
group of perfectly beautiful immortals, or actually a member of a leper
colony – is further complicated by the group's mysterious disappearance
at the end. At the novella's start, the narrator offers three incompatible
theories, as if using Todorov as a guide, leaving the reader with no real
answer from beginning to end.

What these three stories help illustrate is that literature that breaks
away from the expectations of realism can obviously do so in a variety of ways. Todorov's categories help us distinguish those works that
tend toward a subjective breaking point (the uncanny), those with an
objective change (the marvelous), and those that leave us somewhere in
between (the fantastic). Despite these differences, each of these stories
in fact leaves the reader in some interpretive doubt, and this commonal-
ity may point to the strengths of Todorov's model: rather than focusing
entirely on what feels unreal in imagery and event, the defining impact
of the fantastic is in the uncertainty it produces. This sentiment arises in

du Maurier's prefatory note to her short-story collection, *The Breaking Point* ([1959] 2009a):

> There comes a moment in the life of every individual when reality must be faced. When this happens, it is as though a link between emotion and reason is stretched to the limit of endurance, and sometimes snaps. In this collection of stories, men, women, children and a nation are brought to the breaking-point. Whether the link survives or snaps, the reader must judge for himself.
>
> (2009d: v)

What Todorov's model does not offer, though, is a sustained exploration of how spatiality may factor in the considerations of genre and interpretation. As we do start to consider spatiality, a reflection on the three stories just considered shows that, for all their differences, the fantastic produces a fundamental change in the relationship between the characters and the settings they occupy. Place and space become unfamiliar, threatening, destabilizing.

Spatiality and the Fantastic

Whether in a realist or supernatural mode, location is always prominent in du Maurier's work. Often compared with the Brontës, her writing also resonates with Thomas Hardy in its near geographical determinism. Personified landscapes draw in and shape the humans moving through them. Location features largely in her autobiographical accounts as well. Her memoir, *Myself When Young* (1977), is close to being a history of the houses in her life, with an emphasis on the contrast between the London homes of her childhood and the Cornwall she discovered on family holidays, which eventually became her lifelong residence. Numerous also are her accounts of how, near Gribbin Head, she chanced upon and became obsessed with the abandoned sixteenth-century manor, Menabilly, later the inspiration for the Manderley of *Rebecca*. In her essay, "The House of Secrets" ([1946] 2014), she says, "the house possessed me" ([1946] 2014: 139), and "in a strange and eerie fashion we are one, the house and I" (144). Place and identity are inseparable.

Her earliest short stories are often London-based depictions of her late adolescent world of socialite Bright Young Things, an urban realm that forges cruel and manipulative relationships, whether romantic or familial. Cornwall offered instead Tuan's sense of space, of freedom and independence: "The effect was dramatic, her emphasis on the word Cornwall intense. It sounded like a journey to the moon" (*Vanishing Cornwall*, 1972: 3). Later convincing her parents to let her stay on her own at Ferryside, their home in Bodinnick, she wrote her first novel, *The Loving Spirit* (1931), drawn from the world and history she found in the local Cornish fishing villages. Equally inspiring were her finishing school near Paris, with its side trips to Brittany, and later life travels to Italy and Greece. Landscape was a constant inspiration for her imagination.

At the same time, the locations she treasured contained their uncertainties. Although she loved Menabilly, and lived there for decades, she was never its owner, and was turned out in the 1960s. A lover of houses, she usually made them dark and unwelcoming in her fiction. While critics Horner and Zlosnik observe that her focus on Cornwall risked turning her into that belittled category of the regional writer (1998: 64–5), it is just as notable that even though she joined Mebyon Kernow, the Cornish independent party, she always recognized that she was not native to the place, and many contemporary writers in Cornwall would be wary to count her as one of their own. If London is depicted in her fiction as a den of inequity, that doesn't mean her fiction portrays the countryside of Cornwall as a realm of innocence. There is no easy city/country moral binary here. All houses, homes and landscapes rest on shaky ground.

The author Kazuo Ishiguro once said "a novel has to be set somewhere" (2009: 119). This seemingly simple notion proves to be considerably more complex upon reflection, especially considering a work like Ishiguro's own space-shifting dream novel, *The Unconsoled* (1995). Before delving more deeply into du Maurier's particular conjoining of spatiality and the fantastic, it is worth taking a moment to establish some of the basic theoretical premises of literary geography. At the start of *Atlas of the European Novel 1800–1900*, Franco Moretti states "geography is not an inert container, is not a box where cultural history 'happens', but an active force, that pervades the literary field and shapes it in depth" ([1997] 2009: 3). This is to say, in part, that fiction does not simply emerge from a stable spatial context nor do the events within the fiction take place against a neutral background. In Moretti's words, "Space is not the 'outside' of narrative, then, but an internal force, that shapes it from within. Or in other words: in modern European novels, *what* happens depends a lot on *where* it happens" (70).

Moretti distinguishes further between *space in literature* and *literature in space*, between how authors make use of real sites within a text – such as Dickens's version of London – and how literature is disseminated within the extra-textual world. In terms of the latter, we could speak of the role du Maurier and her works have played in Cornish tourism, which may in turn shape ideas and experiences of Cornwall itself (the television series *Poldark* has recently done the same). For our purposes here, the focus will be on the use of *space in literature*, but it is worth keeping in mind how in a popular imagination du Maurier's version of Cornwall has produced a lived experience of Cornwall, most notably in the tourist designation Jamaica Inn.

Humans shape their environments and environments shape humans in turn. We physically reshape places, invest and project upon them meanings, histories and fictions that are frequently in contention. Prior to Moretti, Edward Said spoke of an "imagined geography", of the ways that authors inflect the landscapes they use in their fiction with political perspectives, conscious or unconscious (Said [1978] 2003: 49). If in life a landscape is never neutral, this is only compounded once a landscape enters the realm of literature. Think of the layers of literary meaning laid upon the Lake District and Congo. Real spaces, when employed in fiction, are presented selectively and then represented with new significations. Novels, including realist ones, show not the world, but interpretations of the world.

A psychological perspective is also relevant because in literature, perhaps especially in the fantastic, we are usually faced with the interactive relationship between a landscape and characters, whose perceptions and misperceptions shape the reader's engagement with the location. Inner spaces and outer spaces conflate. If we put literary geography in the terms of psychoanalyst Jacques Lacan, a landscape is at once real, imaginary and symbolic. There is a there there, but it does not speak for itself, and it is hard to encounter any space free of the projections of our imaginations and culturally inherited systems of symbols that give real spaces meaning; yet the world is not just signification, and the real always intrudes back on those interpretations and creations.

A Lacanian perspective would also insist that our spatiality is not just "constructed", but also mediated by desire and fantasy. Paraphrasing Spinoza, Lacan claims, "Desire is the very essence of man" ([1958–1959] 2019: 8). But desire is not our own, it works through us, and, "The function of fantasy is to provide the subject's desire with its proper level of correction or situation" (19); that is, desire runs through us, but it can neither be satisfied nor pinned down, while fantasy is our best effort at trying to organize and situate desire. So a desire for a place or space might motivate a character, who builds fantasies around it, wanting it to fulfill something, do something, stand for something, mean something. We can hear this in du Maurier's own memoir, picturing herself as a child:

> One house, painted red, attracts me. Why is it red? Who lives there? It's on its own, not friends with the other houses. I shall pretend it's mine, and that I live there alone.
>
> (*Myself When Young* 2004d: 6)

She animates the house, projects herself upon it, and builds an imaginary life within it. As we read literature, we may wonder what does a character want from place and space? And, thinking perhaps more fantastically, what does a landscape want from a character?

Since the Paris we encounter in Georges Perec, the Kamakura in Yasunari Kawabata, and the Prague in Bohumil Hrabal are in no way the unfiltered reality of those locations, think how much more complex the notion of a literary geography becomes when we consider the literature of the fantastic. To redeploy Ishiguro, the fantastic also has to be set somewhere. But this opens up new questions. At the end of his general critical overview of the spatial turn in literary studies, Robert Tally Jr. notes that critics tend to focus on the literary use of realistic spaces, but he agrees that attention needs to be given to the use of spatiality in science fiction, utopia and fantasy (2013: 146). In the simplest sense, we can think of a spectrum that goes from imaginative uses of real-world spaces to entirely imaginative worlds presented with their own internal sense of verisimilitude: At one end, Balzac's Paris; at the other, Tolkien's Middle Earth. What interests us here is that much more complex terrain that lies in the middle. For instance, du Maurier's stories "The Archduchess" and "Monte Verità" are set in Europe, with references to countries the reader recognizes as part of our world, but then also includes imagined countries that we would not.

All of this, though, can still presume a fairly stable sense of setting. If the fantastic is not just something imaginary, but a realm of destabilization, then these maps need greater complexity. Patricia García, in her pioneering work, distinguishes between the *Fantastic of Place* and the *Fantastic of Space*, which we may think of as the difference between a story in which a supernatural event occurs within a place (but the place itself does not violate our sense of reality) and a space that is in itself fantastic (it does seem to violate our understanding of how space should work) (2018: 21).

Returning to Todorov can help us further. If, by his terms, the fantastic is the hesitation between the uncanny (that which is psychological, imagined) and the marvelous (that which is supernatural, but real), we might think of spatiality in fantastic literature occupying a similar location of hesitation between the psychological-imagined and the supernatural-real. Something in the fictional world is at odds with readers' notions of their own world. Does that world operate by different rules than our own (a different real), or has the character undergone a kind of trauma that makes them imagine the real world to be stranger than it is (a change in the registers of the imaginary and symbolic)?

Whether this question is resolved or not in the work, the momentary breakdown in the character and their sense of their landscape exposes flaws in a network of signification and desire. Conventional ideas of place and space are called into question, as are our relationships to them. If "genre is itself a sort of map" (Tally Jr. 2013: 55), then the fantastic, in Todorov's sense, is a boundary crossing between genres that can disturb the genres just as it can disturb fiction's act of mapping. The literary fantastic exposes flaws in systems of meaning, identity, desire, and home.

du Maurier, the Fantastic and Spatiality

In the literary geography of Daphne du Maurier, tensions between home and displacement predominate. Characters try to find a home, move or flee from one home to another, or find that something has changed about their home. In each case the known of place ventures into the unknown of space. In each, a sense of the *unheimlich* (the homely become un-homely) takes over by the story's end, leaving the character and reader to wonder if home is really what they thought it was. Because geography is, as argued earlier, invested with the meanings and desires humans give it, places that have become *unheimlich* undergo breakdowns in signification.

Deeply important to du Maurier's sensibility is the fine and vanishing line between a person and the place they occupy, especially houses. In her memoir, she presents the ways that a house, and its history, can imprint upon its denizens:

> Who can ever affirm, or deny, that the houses which have sheltered us as children, or as adults, and our predecessors too, do not have embedded in their walls, on with the dust and cobwebs, one with the overlay of fresh wallpaper and paint, the imprint of what-has-been, the suffering, the joy? We are all ghosts of yesterday, and the phantom of tomorrow awaits us alike in sunshine or in shadow, dimly perceived at times, never entirely lost.
>
> (2004d: 46)

The residents of the past remain within a house, and they, in turn, shape the latest occupants. The autonomous self is mythic once we see the self in its spatial context.

In *The Poetics of Space* ([1958] 1994), Gaston Bachelard speaks to the worlds of difference between the abstract geometry of an architect's design of a house and the lived-in experience of a home: "Space that has been seized upon by the imagination cannot remain indifferent space subject to the measures and estimates of the surveyor" (1994: xxxvi); "A house that has been experienced is not an inert box" (47). For Bachelard, the home is a realm of imagination, and our long-term interactions with its intimate spaces foster and shelter "thoughts, memories and daydreams" (6). The intimate experiences of a house makes it a home, its nooks and turns shape our imagination as much as we shape the house into our own concoctions. When the fantastic comes home, though, this intimate experience is undermined, and it further undermines the conventional semiology of place and space.

The relationship between identity and space is a defining concern of *Rebecca* (1938). While it is not an entirely fantastic narrative, the novel does help illuminate the unsettling nature of spatiality in du Maurier's works. The narrator is a passive, nameless figure, who is initially the paid companion of Mrs Van Hopper, until, in Monte Carlo, she meets and becomes engaged to the wealthy Maxim de Winter; a fairy tale of the poor girl marrying the prince seemingly realized. The narrator is a cipher, whose identity is entirely subsumed into others and the places she is in. She longs to be a character: she "thought of all those heroines of fiction who looked pretty when they cried" (2006d: 41). *Rebecca* is not a romance; it is, however, a novel in which characters know the romance plot and strive for it and recognize their failure within that narrative. Once she is housed in de Winter's estate, Manderley, and expected to assume the role of an aristocratic lady in charge, the narrator is further reminded of the theater of gender and class expectations, and of her own failure in the drama. At the desk of the previous Mrs de Winter, Rebecca, she examines the elegant stationary:

> I put it back in the box again, and shut the drawer, feeling guilty suddenly, and deceitful, as though I were staying in somebody else's house and my hostess had said to me, "Yes, of course, write letters at my desk", and I had unforgivably, in a stealthy manner, peeped at her correspondence.
>
> (86)

Neither the space nor the role it demands belongs to her.

It is of course the dead Rebecca who dominates the narrator's world. Rebecca's devotee, Mrs Danvers, tells her,

> You would not think she had been gone now for so long, would you, not by the way the rooms are kept? You would think she had just gone out for a little while and would be back in the evening. [. . .] I feel her everywhere. You do too, don't you?
>
> (175)

The narrator, who remains without an identity, can only try to occupy the symbolic function of Rebecca. The narrator is other to herself, and she is always made in relation to Rebecca. She is only ever the other Mrs de Winter, and she does not know what Rebecca wants from her. This absence that is not literally present (and not quite a ghost) manifests in the narratives of Maxim and his friends, but especially in Manderley itself.

The novel begins, famously, "Last night I dreamt I went to Manderley again" (1). For reasons we learn later, the narrator literally cannot return to Manderley, but even in the dream she finds "the way was barred to me" (1), because nature has reclaimed the house. If dreams and desires express deeper unconscious truths, this one announces from the novel's beginning that the house is inaccessible in many ways. The narrator recalls that she first encountered Manderley in a postcard as a child (54). It has been romantically idealized, as has a whole picture of the aristo-cratic classes. But the way to that ideal is barred to her. Instead, this is a house that haunts and disturbs, populated by a class that will do anything to preserve its illusions, even defend a murderer. The novel begins and ends on the continent, away from Manderley, because Maxim prefers to repress all memories of Rebecca, and Manderley is Rebecca. All must define their identity in relationship to it and her. Instead of the ideal of an aristocratic house, the dream, with its menacing woods and sense of foreboding, reveals the darkness and deception in the desire for such places.

Written prior to *Rebecca*, "Happy Valley" (1932) presages aspects of the novel, but in a more fantastic manner. Its opening line resembles the novel to come, with its placement of a landscape within a dream: "When she first used to see the valley it was in dreams, little odd snatches remembered on waking, and then becoming easily dimmed and lost in the turmoil of the day" (2011c: 147). In contrast to *Rebecca*, this dream is an actual premonition, a vision of a house that the narrator knows will belong to her in the future. When she meets her husband-to-be and visits the imaginary county of Ryeshire, everything is experienced as déjà vu, as fated. Yet the valley and home of her vision are joyful places, as opposed to the alienation she experiences everywhere else: "It was above all things a place of safety, nothing could harm her here" (147). She often goes there in her mind for comfort, "I'm here, I'm happy, I'm home again" (148).

After they are married, and go to Ryeshire, she heads out for a walk and finds "her valley": "She was not frightened at the realisation of her dream, it was the embodiment of peace, like the answer to a prayer" (153). Moving further in, she finds the house, and peers in to find a boy's room with a photograph on the mantelpiece, only to discover the photo is of herself (with the bobbed hair she will have in the future). She realizes that everything in the house belongs to her: she sees her self outside herself, her self as other. Outside there is a boy, who leads her to a grave. Afterward, the house is found to be derelict. What is first experienced as real within the vision as a pleasure, in reality feels like a dream that has become uncanny. Her desire for an ideal home and place becomes instead an alienating reminder of death. When she comes upon her husband again, she says, "I keep feeling I've lost something and I don't know what it is" (157).

In *The Scapegoat* ([1957] 2004e), John, an Englishman who teaches French history and admires its pre-Revolutionary days, dreams of being accepted as French by the French, but instead experiences anxiety as someone who will only ever be regarded as a tourist: "I was an alien, I was not one of them. Years of study, years of training, the fluency with which I spoke their language, taught their history, described their culture, had never brought me closer to the people themselves" (2004e: 4). All of this changes when he encounters his French doppelganger, Jean, who tricks and swaps lives with him. John soon finds himself taking Jean's place in his dysfunctional family estate and financially troubled glass foundry. While the novel may simply involve the rather extreme coincidence of two unrelated men who are identical in appearance, it is also possible that Jean/John are the same person undergoing a nervous breakdown, overwhelmed by the pressures of home.

The fantastic uncertainty of the situation has an impact on John's relation to Jean's manor. If John and Jean are the same person, then Jean has become alienated from his self, home, and family. If John is a distinct person, he longed to be accepted as French, and now finds his desire to have come true, but the ease with which he can play the role of patriarch and fool Jean's family exposes the empty theater of aristocracy and national identity. It is as if simply being in the house, standing in the function of Jean, makes John Jean. This is reinforced by later revelations that the house had been complicit during the Occupation, which foreshadows Jean and John's occupation of each other's selves and John's occupation of Jean's home. His initial worry over whether an alien's home can become one's own leads to the realization that homes and selves are duplicitous and the ownership of them illusory.

Such illusory ownership is also the subject of "Split Second" ([1952] 1980), in which middle class Mrs Ellis finds her normally orderly day turned upside down. Out on routine errands, she is killed by a laundry van, but she is unaware that she is dead. When she returns to her home, she finds it occupied by multiple tenants and businesses, none of which she recognizes, and no one in the neighbourhood recognizes her, as decades have now gone by. "But my house?" she asks the police, "Those thieves, and my maid Grace, Grace may be lying in the basement. Surely you are going to do something about the house? You won't permit them to get away with this monstrous crime?" (2005b: 248). Comfortable in her routines and her stature, Mrs Ellis is thrust into a strange world – that is and is not her own – to discover the mysterious ephemerality of what we think we possess.

In all of these examples so far, characters assume they can find peace – a break from their crises in identity – in an idealized home. They desire a complete self, and yet dream that an autonomous self can only be found in the right place. Place is crucial to their desires. Think also of the widower in "The Apple Tree", hoping the house free of his wife will become a proper home. But in each of these works the illusions of a house and home are exposed; ideals are brought to earth.

In these works, the ideal of a house is shaken from within, but in others, that same ideal can be undermined by a supernatural force from without, as already seen in the transformations to the familiar nature of the Cornish farmland in "The Birds". In "East Wind" (probably 1926), the titular wind brings a ship from a foreign land to an island far removed from the rest of civilization, "Nearly a hundred miles west of the Scillies" (2011b: 1). Life here is static and ambiguously prelapsarian, "without communication with the mainland, and the people had degenerated into quiet, listless folk, the inevitable result of intermarriage" (1–2). What was unchanging is disturbed by a strange wind from the east – "like a demon let loose upon the island" (6) – that brings with it a ship and strangers, leading the people of the island to behave in new ways: "Something of a madness seemed to fall upon the people of St Hilda's" (7). Change especially comes to the focus couple, Jane and Guthrie, and when Jane expresses greater sexual freedom, Guthrie kills her. The next morning the wind and the brig are gone.

The story leaves the reader with a number of uncertainties, not just whether or not the ship itself was real. Did the ship and the wind create new behavior, or did it unleash already existing repressed desires? Is this unleashing healthy (Jane's sexual liberation), or purely destructive (Guthrie's murderous rage)? The wind comes and it goes, and that is all. As in "Split Second" and "The Birds", a strange force, beyond the subject's control, comes and takes away. And with it, the certainties of home.

+++

In all of the works discussed so far, the comforts of a house (one owns, desires, or visits) become uncanny. In the last of the works to be analyzed, characters have left their homes and homelands for new opportunities, by choice or not. If the stories addressed so far show a familiar place becoming an unfamiliar space, here we venture into an unknown space for the adventure and possibilities of it. An unfamiliar space might present the desire and chance to start again, but it is also possible that this venturing out stems from a need to run away from trauma, and the new hope might prove just as illusory as home, so that space offers no escape.

In "The Pool" ([1959] 2009g), a young girl, Deborah, is visiting the country home of her grandparents with her younger brother, Roger. The father is in London, the mother died during childbirth. Deborah is extremely imaginative, but also prone to moods. Early on, the story establishes a strong distinction in her sense of geography. First, there is the house, which is represented as the realm of the adults. Here, at night, the adults close the windows and the curtains, "They are shutting out the best [. . .] all the meaning, and all the point" (2009g: 137). It is the place of routine, a "pattern of life unchanged", and even their old dog, who "being an animal, should know better" had "forgotten the secrets" (137). In contrast, it is out in the garden, with the pool, near the forest, especially at night, where "the Secret life" can be found (138). Deborah goes to the pool and gives offerings, treating it like a pagan altar. She also personifies everything outdoors: "The garden knew about the promised heat-wave, and rejoiced" (136). What might first be interpreted as part of children's play grows stranger as Deborah heads into the garden at night to meet a mysterious spirit woman, to whom she makes her offerings. If the woman accepts her "tickets", she can venture into the secret world: "The woods had accepted her, and the pool was the final resting place, the doorway, the key" (139). This is a joyous world beyond the order and rules of the house.

At the story's end, Deborah recognizes that she will no longer be granted access to the secret world, and she will no longer be able to see it. It is the house now that pulls her in: "which was real? The safety of the house, or the secret world?" (142). In this postlapsarian echo of Lewis's Narnia, it turns out that Deborah has had her first period, and this step into adulthood blocks her from a more magical place. The reason for her barring remains mysterious to her. Civilization wins over pagan dreamland, but Deborah is only left with bitterness and a sense of loss: "The key was hers, and she lost it" (147). The ability to give birth is announced as a kind of death. In a curious dismantling of some traditional binary oppositions, the loss of Eden means the loss of a kind of knowledge, or at least of imagination. Growing up and joining civilization means more stupidity, less curiosity.

A similar dynamic can be found in "The Lordly Ones" ([1959] 2009f). Ben is a developmentally "backward" child whose family in Exeter treats his non-human howls with anger and impatience ([1959] 2009f: 273). To get away from people and their embarrassment, they head to a holiday home on the moors. It is here that Ben feels welcome, at home, with a non-human family. At one point he hears a caretaker personify the moors, which Ben takes literally, going on to leave food for "the moors". At night he sees "them", and goes to join the spirits that walk about: "He was going to follow the moors, the lordly ones" (284). Just as he is hoping to follow them, and join what he feels to be his real family, he is "rescued" by his human family. Rather than howl, he speaks his first human word – no – in protest. The painful irony is that this demand made in speech, a demand against humanity, makes him more human, and more separate from the primal, pagan realm. In another instance of the postlapsarian order, being human, joining civilization, means dissatisfaction. Gaining a self and a home of one sort requires the loss of another. Both "The Pool" and "The Lordly Ones" feature a child who loses their connection to childhood innocence or, at least something that distinguishes them from the tedium of human normality. Place (family and houses) are horrors and constraints, and having to come into place requires the denial of the freedom and magic of space.

These themes play out in a different manner in du Maurier's earlier work, *Jamaica Inn* ([1936] 2015). At the start of the novel, Mary Yellan must leave her home in Helford because of her mother's death, and live with her Aunt Patience and brutal husband Joss Merlyn at Jamaica Inn on Bodmin moor. Even though she moves within Cornwall, it is as if she has journeyed to another nation:

> The country was alien to her, which was a defeat in itself. [. . .] How remote now and hidden perhaps for ever were the shining waters of Helford, the green hills and the sloping valleys, the white cluster of cottages at the water's edge.
>
> ([1936] 2015: 3–4)

When she arrives on Bodmin moor, she observes: "No human being could live in this wasted country, thought Mary, and remain like other people; the very children would be born twisted" (16). While an unflattering contrast between a new and old home, with such contrasting landscapes, makes sense, it is notable that Mary also recognizes that after her mother's death even her old home could not remain familiar and homely. When a man buys her family's house, she notes: "This stranger from Coverack made her an interloper in her own home" (9–10). Home is no longer a welcoming place, and all she has left are unknown spaces.

Once embedded in the cruel and corrupt realm of Jamaica Inn, Mary has to struggle not to become a passive victim like Patience, overwhelmed by the power of Joss and the monstrous Inn itself. This new space only threatens her identity more. As escape, she frequently roams the wild moors on her own. In this way, the moors offer up space in Tuan's positive sense: even though they are repellant, they are also compelling; they offer a chance of freedom and opportunity. In the second half of the novel, when the darker side of the albino vicar Francis Davey is revealed, this landscape is seen in another light yet again. Mary has an inkling of this perspective early on:

> There was a silence on the tors that belonged to another age that is past and vanished as though it had never been, an age when man did not exist, but pagan footsteps trod upon the hills. And there was a stillness in the air, and a stranger, older peace, that was not the peace of God.
>
> (45)

Resembling a character from Arthur Machen, Davey worships the moor as an ancient pagan force, where "the old gods slept undisturbed" (274). He sees a future coming among the dark tors, where the sham civilization of Christianity will fade and give way to the ways of the Druids and "old pagan barbarism [which] was naked and clean" (318).

Through this atavistic lens, the landscape becomes other, and while we could dismiss this as the mad perspective of the vicar, throughout the novel Mary herself also personifies the spaces around her – the house, the tors, the moors – as if they are living forces. Horrified by Joss Merlyn, she is compelled by his likeness in the brother Jem. These are Merlins, ancient magicians; allied with the nearly unhuman albino. What horrifies her also compels her. Despite her hope that the moors might offer a freedom away from Jamaica Inn (and they do relatively speaking), all of the characters in *Jamaica Inn* are uncanny bodies under the control of a feral, ancient landscape. Its desires are greater than their own, and, in the end, the pagan space denies Mary her freedom.

Though perhaps best known for her works set in England and Cornwall, du Maurier also set a number of works, such as *The Scapegoat* ([1957] 2004e), *The Glass-Blowers* (1963), and *The Flight of the Falcon* (1965), on the continent. "Don't Look Now" ([1971] 2006a) is possibly her best example of a fantastic tale set abroad. An English couple, John and Laura, are on holiday in Venice, trying to heal their relationship after the death of their daughter, Christine, from meningitis. On Torcello, they encounter two strange sisters, one of whom they discover claims to be psychic, and can see their dead daughter with them. While Laura believes them, John thinks it is all a sham. When one of the sisters warns them that their son in England is in danger, Laura flies back to check on him. Soon after, John sees her on a vaporetto with the sisters. We learn later that this was in fact evidence of his own psychic ability as he has had a premonition of Laura's return to Venice for his own funeral: "You saw us [. . .] and your wife too. But not today. You saw us in the future" (2006b: 49). The story ends with John's murder at the hands of a dwarf he thought was a little girl, perhaps even, somehow, his own dead little girl. Although they have left England to try to escape death, they have run directly into it.

The setting of Venice is an integral part of the story. John and Laura get lost in its mazelike streets, reinforcing or creating a sense of confusion – of literally and metaphorically being lost. They find it hard to know what is real and what is merely "a bright façade put on for show" (25). Also, playing on a literary tradition of associating Venice with death (as in Thomas Mann and Antal Szerb), they see "cellar entrances [that] looked like coffins" (19) and think the "whole city is slowly dying" (26). The city is presented as strange, unreal, morose. Perhaps the psychological state of the couple has been projected onto Venice, or perhaps Venice has some kind of supernatural power that draws in John and Laura. The moors, the garden and Venice are anthropomorphized, and given agency, as if they want something from the characters, are stronger than the characters, but also remain at an unbridgeable distance.

Other stories, like "Ganymede", "Monte Verità", and "Not After Midnight," offer variations on this theme of English and Welsh people leaving Britain behind, hoping they might be able to escape a trauma associated with home and reinvent themselves in Crete, Greece, or Italy. But this venturing into space only produces scandal, danger, and death. Where the children of "The Pool" and "The Lordly Ones" sought the magic and freedom of space, only to be thrust back into the horror of familiar place, these adult Britons abroad hope for escape and a new identity in unfamiliar space, only to find those desires denied them as well.

Conclusion: "So You're Back Home Again?"[2]

This chapter begins with an epigraph from Milan Kundera's novel *The Joke* (1967): "It's not for nothing that fantasy exists. It's what makes homes of our houses" (2001: 144). Kundera, like Bachelard, expresses how houses become homes through an act of the imagination and desire. But Kundera implies a darker note; that houses are not really homes.

We wish and will them into a state of coziness, of familiarity. A space becomes a place through an act of desire and imagination, but the narrative of desire that tries to sustain this belief is made of the thinnest cloth. Daphne du Maurier's literature of the fantastic exposes that act of fantasy to the light. The fantastic undermines fantasy. A notable detail about her writing is the frequency with which her narrators speak in the conditional tense – they reside in woulds and coulds. All imagination. The worlds they find themselves in, though – the past-obsessed houses, the unreal moors, the death-driven Venetian canals – are fantastic, yet they manage to bring reality to those floating imaginations.[3] For someone typically pegged as a romance writer, du Maurier wrote a great deal of work about the ways dreams come crashing down. Her use of the fantastic grounds dreams, and exposes the unrealistic nature of desire. Fantastic places become strange spaces, and fantastic spaces bring death to dreams, throwing us back to the houses that are no longer our homes.

Notes

1. "During the 1938 family Christmas in Fowey, Daphne sees her old friend Arthur Quiller-Couch. He congratulates her on her success and seems sincere. But he utters a little phrase that will haunt her for a long time afterward: *The critics will never forgive you for writing* Rebecca" (de Rosnay 2017: 146).
2. Quotation from Brenda Wootton's song, "Cornwall the Land I Love" (1979):

   When I return to home
   People all stop and they say to me,
   "Hello my dear, so you're back again,"
   And I be
   So proud to see the town
   Clock tower of granite and market and quay
   All belong to me.

3. Jacques Lacan, from Seminar I (1953–1954): "the real, or what is perceived as such, is what resists symbolisation absolutely. In the end, doesn't the feeling of the real reach its high point in the pressing manifestation of an unreal, hallucinatory reality?" (1991: 66–7).

Bibliography

Auerbach, N. 2002. *Daphne du Maurier: Haunted Heiress*. Philadelphia: University of Pennsylvania Press.

Bachelard, G. [1958] 1994. *The Poetics of Space*. Boston: Beacon Press.

De Rosnay, T. 2017. *Manderley Forever: A Biography of Daphne du Maurier*. New York: St. Martin's Press.

du Maurier, D. 1972. *Vanishing Cornwall: The Spirit and History of an Ancient Land*. London: Penguin Books.

———. [1969] 2003. *The House on the Strand*. London: Virago Press.

———. 2004a. "The Apple Tree", in *The Birds and Other Stories*. London: Virago Press.

————. 2004b. "The Birds", in *The Birds and Other Stories*. London: Virago Press.

————. 2004c. "Monte Verità", in *The Birds and Other Stories*. London: Virago Press.

————. 2004d. *Myself When Young*. London: Virago Press.

————. [1957] 2004e. *The Scapegoat*. London: Virago Press.

————. 2005a. "Escort", in *The Rendezvous*. London: Virago Press.

————. 2005b. "Split Second", in *The Rendezvous*. London: Virago Press.

————. [1971] 2006a. "The Breakthrough", in *Don't Look Now and Other Stories*. London: Penguin Books.

————. 2006b. "Don't Look Now", in *Don't Look Now and Other Stories*. London: Penguin Books.

————. 2006c. "Not After Midnight", in *Don't Look Now and Other Stories*. London: Penguin Books.

————. 2006d. *Rebecca*. New York: Harper.

————. [1959] 2009a. "The Alibi", in *The Breaking Point: Short Stories*. London: Virago Press.

————. 2009b. "The Archduchess", in *The Breaking Point: Short Stories*. London: Virago Press.

————. 2009c. "The Blue Lenses", in *The Breaking Point: Short Stories*. London: Virago Press.

————. 2009d. *The Breaking Point: Short Stories*. London: Virago Press.

————. 2009e. "Ganymede", in *The Breaking Point: Short Stories*. London: Virago Press.

————. [1959] 2009f. "The Lordly Ones", in *The Breaking Point: Short Stories*. London: Virago Press.

————. [1959] 2009g. "The Pool", in *The Breaking Point: Short Stories*. London: Virago Press.

————. 2011a. "The Doll", in *The Doll: The Lost Short Stories*. New York: Harper.

————. 2011b. "East Wind", in *The Doll: The Lost Short Stories*. New York: Harper.

————. 2011c. "The Happy Valley", in *The Doll: The Lost Short Stories*. New York: Harper.

————. [1946] 2014. "The House of Secrets", in *The Rebecca Notebooks and Other Memories*. London: Virago Press.

————. [1936] 2015. *Jamaica Inn*. New York: William Morrow.

García, P. 2018. *Space and the Postmodern Fantastic in Contemporary Literature: The Architectural Void*. London and New York: Routledge.

Horner, A.; Zlosnik, S. 1998. *Daphne du Maurier: Writing, Identity and the Gothic Imagination*. London: Macmillan Press.

Hume, K. 1984. *Fantasy and Mimesis: Responses to Reality in Western Literature*. New York; London: Methuen.

Ishiguro, K.; S. Matthews. 2009. Interview. "'I'm Sorry I Can't Say More': An Interview with Kazuo Ishiguro." Kazuo Ishiguro. Ed. S. Matthews; S. Groes. London: Continuum.

Kundera, M. 2001. *The Joke*. New York: HarperCollins.

Lacan, J. 1991. *Freud's Papers on Technique: 1953–1954: The Seminar of Jacques Lacan, Book I*. New York; London: W. W. Norton & Company.

————. [1958–1959] 2019. *Desire and Its Interpretation: The Seminar of Jacques Lacan, Book VI*. Cambridge; Medford: Polity.

Light, A. 1991. *Forever England: Femininity, Literature and Conservatism Between the Wars*. London; New York: Routledge.

Moretti, F. 2009. *Atlas of the European Novel: 1800–1900*. London; New York: Verso.

Said, E. W. 2003. *Orientalism*. New York: Vintage.

Tally, Jr, R. 2013. *Spatiality*. London; New York: Routledge.

Todorov, T. 1975. *The Fantastic: A Structural Approach to a Literary Genre*. Ithaca: Cornell University Press.

Tuan, Y. 1977. *Space and Place: The Perspective of Experience*. Minneapolis: University of Minnesota Press.

Walters, M. 2005. "Introduction", in Daphne du Maurier. *The Rendezvous*. London: Virago Press.

8 Place and Space in the Literary Utopia

Patrick Parrinder

According to one recent observer, "Utopian studies remains strongly resistant to the 'spatial turn' in the social sciences" (Bell 2017, 12.11). Although Thomas More's Greek neologism signifies both 'no place' and 'good place', it is the idea of the good society that takes the lead in virtually all discussions of the utopian concept. To outline a utopia is to set out a plan for human happiness, justice, and – in the eyes of some, though not all, utopian scholars – social perfection. But in his correspondence with Erasmus prior to publication More had called the book *Nusquama*, the Latin for 'Nowhere' (Hexter 1952, 99–102), a title that would be echoed in at least two subsequent utopias, Samuel Butler's *Erewhon* (1872) and William Morris's *News from Nowhere* (1890). To emphasize the non-existence of the place described in *Utopia* (1516) is to put More's work alongside such works of fantastic travel literature as Lucian of Samosata's *The True History* (of a voyage to the moon) and Bishop Joseph Hall's *Mundus Alter et Idem* (1607), works whose paradoxical nature is announced in their very titles. It is no surprise, then, that the eye-witness on whom we depend for More's account of the island of Utopia is a returning sailor, Raphael Hythlodaye, whose surname means 'nonsense peddler' (Fortunati and Trousson 2000, 156). *Utopia* is both a major contribution to political thought and, in some respects, a species of nonsense fiction.

A world that is both 'different and yet the same', and that exists only in the mind of the observer, inevitably suggests the analogy of the mirror. Michel Foucault once briefly suggested that a mirror is both a utopia, 'since it is a placeless place', and an actually existing 'counter-site' or 'heterotopia' (Foucault 1986, 24). It is not Foucault, however, but Lewis Carroll who takes us inside a looking-glass world. In *Through the Looking-Glass* (1871) the mirror's two-dimensional surface and its tightly controlled reflection of an external reality are instantly forgotten once we enter the looking-glass's virtual space. As in Carroll's earlier Wonderland, what Alice sees and experiences is 'as different as possible' from the ordinary reality of which it is a fantastic distortion (Carroll 1948, 11). The principles of spatial (dis)organization that Carroll's heroine discovers include the tangled ball of wool, the labyrinth, and the chessboard – the latter being not a static grid, but a scene of forward movement which allows her to progress from her childlike status as a pawn to that of a queen. Carroll's action-and-incident-packed narrative conveys both spatial confusion and a sharply realized sense of unfamiliar places – a sense of bewildering spatial differentiation that is also characteristic of many earlier accounts of fantastic journeys, including Hall's *Mundus Alter et Idem* which (among much else) offers a riot of new and ludicrous place-names. Hall's traveller sets out on 'the ship named The Fantasia' to visit the lands of Crapulia, Yvronia, Viraginia, Moronia, and Lavernia, all of which are part of *Terra Australis Incognita* (Hall 1981, 17). But – since *Mundus Alter et Idem* has been described as 'the first dystopia or satirical utopia in the British utopian tradition' (Fortunati and Trousson 2000, 409) – this suggests a fundamental difference between the literary dystopia and the literary utopia, generic categories which in most respects show a considerable overlap. For *Utopia* and the works most resembling it do not share the emphasis on extreme spatial differentiation that we find in Carroll, in Hall, and, indeed, in most other kinds of fantastic adventure fiction. On the contrary, the geographers Philip W. Porter and Fred E. Lukermann have gone so far as to claim that utopia is both 'aspatial' and 'atemporal' within its boundaries: "The dream of utopists is to annihilate space" (Porter and Lukermann 1976, 216, 210). Why is this?

A utopia must aim to reduce (if not actually to eliminate) spatial difference insofar as it strives to be a society of equals. We can see this, for example, in the land of the Houyhnhnms or rational horses in Jonathan Swift's *Gulliver's Travels* (1726). Not only do the Houyhnhnms (like More's Utopians) hold regular assemblies at which any deficiency in one of the separate districts of their country is "supplied by unanimous Consent and Contribution" (Swift 1949, 265), but they also refuse to make any practical distinction between neighbours and strangers. As Lemuel Gulliver reports,

> Friendship and *Benevolence* are the two principal Virtues among the *Houyhnhnms*; and these not confined to particular Objects, but universal to the whole Race. For, a Stranger from the remotest Part is equally treated with the nearest Neighbour, and wher-ever he goes, looks upon himself as at home.
>
> (263)

The implication of Swift's satire is that, once everyone is content with their level and quality of life, all places will be seen to resemble one another. The utopian fulfilment of desire takes no account of the desire to cherish a particular locality which might make us actually want to regard other citizens as strangers. Space is homogenized to the extent that (as Porter and Lukermann observe) the authors of utopias are oblivious to, or impatient with, concerns that animate geographers: the concept of resource, the look of the land, the organisation of space, the meaning of place, the idea of man in nature and man in landscape, the friction of distance, the economy of location.

(1976, 216)

Time, too, is likely to lose its salience for the utopian citizen who is no longer tormented by unfulfilled (and, within the given social structure, unfulfillable) desires. Many utopias have claimed to represent an end to history, a settled state of human affairs not subject to generational change or the outcome of unresolved conflicts. But the atemporality of utopia was challenged in the nineteenth century by the development of the literary uchronia – a vision of the good society set in an imaginary future rather than in a non-existent but present-day place. Moreover, the unfinished or evolutionary utopia, following the post-Darwinian mindset of H. G. Wells in *A Modern Utopia* (1905), abandons temporal stasis for a streamlined version of history as forward 'progress'. We shall see later how the homogenization of space in utopia gives way to rather different effects in uchronia.

There are, however, counter-tendencies to the annihilation of space and time at work in any literary utopia. To begin with, any narrative utopia must offer an experience of times and spaces in order to hold its readers' attention. There must be some kind of plot or sequence of events, even if this involves no more than a few lines of travelogue in which European sailors stumble upon a hitherto unknown land. In the two paradigmatic Renaissance utopian fictions that will be analyzed here – More's *Utopia* and Tommaso Campanella's *The City of the Sun* (1623) – little is added to this, although both texts take the form of dialogues and, in the case of More, the dialogue is between named participants at a specified place and time. Neither More nor Campanella shows the visitor-narrator from our world interacting with individual utopians, as happens in Francis Bacon's fragmentary *New Atlantis* (1627) and again in *Gulliver's Travels*. Gulliver, for example, is housed (or perhaps we should say stabled) in the residence of a particular Houyhnhnm whom he calls his Master. But beyond his Master's house and farmyard we learn very little about the spatial characteristics of Houyhnhnm-land, and it is only when Gulliver arrives at and leaves the country that we even recall that it is an island. In general, despite the proverbial connection between insularity and the literary utopia, the geographical and ecological peculiarities of island status play little or no role in utopian narratives. The contrast with the richly varied island topography of dystopian fiction is particularly marked. In H. G. Wells's *The Island of Doctor Moreau* (1896), for example, the island's oceanic location, its volcanic origins and topography, its beaches, and its fauna and flora (both native and introduced) all take on crucial narrative significance.

The spatial uniformity of utopian fiction is, if anything, underlined and reinforced by the (often rather sparse) introduction of place-names and the utopian fondness for arbitrarily imposed administrative divisions. There are no named places in the land of the Houyhnhnms, and none apart from the eponym in *The City of the Sun*. Bacon does not name the capital city of Bensalem, his 'new Atlantis', although he mentions another city, Renfusa, as well as the scientific institution of Salomon's House (a large, self-contained research campus at some distance from the capital). More's Utopia has only two distinct place-names, but they are as teasing and whimsical as the name of the country itself. The main river of 'Nowhere' is the Anyder ('waterless'), while its capital is Amaurote (a 'city of darkness', not of light). Amaurote shares the island of Utopia with 53 other unnamed cities, all of which, including the capital, are 'exactly alike' to the extent that the nature of the ground permits (More 1923, 45). Each of the 54 cities forms an administrative unit subdivided into smaller units, all of which the text painstakingly describes. The effect of the municipal divisions, here and in many other utopias, is to replace geographic differentiation with the geometric regularity of a superimposed plan. But this is not merely an idiosyncrasy of the literary utopia, since it follows the logic of historical plantation and colonization, and indeed of human civilization itself.

Utopia, Dohra Ahmad has written, 'was from its very inception a colonial genre' (Ahmad 2009, 19). More's Utopia, originally called Abraxa by its 'rude and rustic' inhabitants (More 1923, 42), was subdued by a conqueror, King Utopus, who brought it to its present state. The builders of the City of the Sun were political refugees who left the mainland of India for the island of Taprobane (Sri Lanka). Both states are, therefore, colonial powers with potentially hostile neighbours. The same is apparently true of the city-state of Plato's *Republic* – otherwise, why would it need military Guardians? – while Plato's later utopian dialogue, the *Laws*, is explicitly a plan for a new colony. Colonization involves both the building of cities and the staking out, division, and plantation of the surrounding rural terrain, replacing its indigenous occupants with an agricultural workforce reorganized and disciplined in order to meet the needs (and greed) of the city. This enforced redevelopment of the countryside is, as archaeologists would now argue, essential to the civilizing process throughout human history (Scott 2017). But there are also graphic and largely celebratory accounts of agricultural industrialization in literary utopias from More to Charlotte Perkins Gilman's *Herland* (1914) and beyond.

Walls, Islands, and Moats

If utopia is ideally a homogenized, unified space, its first necessity is to be set apart from other spaces. Utopias, David Harvey has written, are 'isolated and have sharply defined, impermeable boundaries'; the issue of utopian closure is 'both fundamental and unavoidable' (Harvey 2000, 216). The early literary utopias were either walled city-states, like Plato's *Republic*, or remote and hitherto undiscovered islands. More's Utopia is, famously, an artificial island, thanks to King Utopus' decision to the dig a channel or moat to cut it off from the mainland. The water surrounding any island utopia may be regarded as a wall or line of defence. Other forms of utopian isolation include the underground world such as that of Edward Bulwer-Lytton's *The Coming Race* (1871), the territory ringed by near-impassable mountains as in Butler's *Erewhon* or Wells's 'The Country of the Blind' (1904), and the separate planet such as Anarres in Ursula K. Le Guin's *The Dispossessed* (1974). Yet even in its cosmic isolation Le Guin's anarchist utopia feels the need to assert its boundedness by building a low wall around the spaceport that serves as its one point of contact with the twin planet of Urras which is its social and political antithesis. Anarres is a colony set up by refugees from Urras, and the opening paragraph of Le Guin's novel focuses not on the society they have constructed, but on the spaceport wall (Le Guin 1975, 1).

The relationship between the utopian city and the utopian island (or planet) deserves further clarification. It can be argued that any utopia is either a city or a land centring on one or more cities. That is, utopia is a complex social construct differing in kind from the paradise, arcadia or Land of Cockaigne. It involves both work and the division of labour. (If Swift's Houyhnhnm-land is the exception, this is undoubtedly because his utopians, however rational, are not human.) The division of labour is the founding assumption of Plato's *Republic*, since Plato's definition of justice rests on the idea that everyone should follow their true avocation, chosen from among the wide variety that only a developed civilization can provide. Plato's vision of the civic utopia remains influential even though most of his successors would either qualify or reject the Platonic 'Principle of Specialization' (Annas 1981, 73–4). What such a principle necessarily excludes is any thoroughgoing embrace of the ideal of the 'simple life', though many utopias which might be superficially taken to embody this ideal (such as William Morris's *News from Nowhere*) stop short of actually doing so.

A city is distinguished from a village or agricultural commune by the fact that it houses large numbers of people who either do not work directly on the land, or only do so at intervals (cf. Reader 2004, 16). But if cities give spatial expression to the division of labour, why do they need walls? It may be a truism that a colony or settlement imposed on its hinterland must be prepared for war with its neighbours, but in fact we know rather little about the historical origins of city walls and their armed defence. For although the walls of Jericho (the oldest continuously inhabited city on Earth) are celebrated as military fortifications in the Old Testament, it is now believed that they may have originated around 9000 BCE for the purpose of flood protection (Mithen 2003, 59). Early city walls are associated with grain stores, which needed protection both from floods and from marauders. But were the walls built as much to keep the city's population and its food supplies inside (and thus under the control of a centralized political authority) as to keep intruders out? The earliest nation-states, it is now argued by prehistorians, were cities defined by the walls that made a government and administrative structure possible (Scott 2017, 119). It may be significant that, while Plato's main concern in the *Republic* is with the education of the class of Guardians or defenders of the city, the one form of urban defence that he describes explicitly is the expulsion of unwanted immigrants (the poets); an administrative, not a military procedure.

The first small city-states, except in the rugged terrain of ancient Greece, were soon superseded by empires in which the ruling power asserted its grip over a much larger territory. Empires are potentially continental and global rather than local and insular; they bring together different communities and nationalities and tend to expand in every direction until checked by some impassable boundary. While at best they offer an impersonal and externally imposed system of universal justice, this cannot remove the spatial difference between centre and periphery. A utopia is, therefore, a city, not an empire – an island, not a continent – since empires lack both the closure and the homogenization of space characteristic of the utopian state.

It is true that the utopian city-state may seem to be necessarily divided into central and peripheral spaces by the city's dependence on an external food supply. Perhaps this is why so many utopias set out to reduce and, indeed, to minimize the spatial difference between the city and its surrounding countryside. Not only does modern technology offer the prospect of universal consumption of synthetic foods, but long before that utopian thinkers had been advocating agricultural intensification and industrialization. (The nineteenth-century 'garden city' utopias also involve the quasi-ruralization of the city.) Beginning with More, virtually every utopia aims to destroy and uproot the peasantry, a process that in the modern historical record has led to unspeakable tragedies. The same Thomas More who, in Book I of *Utopia*, deplores the effects of agricultural enclosure on the English countryside, proceeds in Book II to depopulate the Utopian countryside by denying any right of permanent residence outside Utopia's 54 cities. More's agricultural labour force is made up of cohorts of urban conscripts serving for two years, the first year learning from their predecessors, and the second year passing on their knowledge to the next band of recruits. The farmhouses in which they live are little more than barracks. Farming, it seems, is not regarded as a dedicated craft or profession on a level with those pursued by the city-dwellers in their normal lives. More's implied analogy between agricultural and military conscription is made explicit in *The City of the Sun*, where Campanella describes troops of farm labourers marching out each day from behind the city gates. In these and numerous later utopias, the abolition of a peasantry makes it possible to raise everyone to the level associated with city life, whether they live in cities or (as, for example, in *News from Nowhere*) in a largely suburbanized countryside.

Urban Geometries

The geometric regularity of the ideal walled city has been emphasized in literature from the earliest times. There are two persistent models of urban symmetry, based on the square and the circle respectively. Perhaps the most famous example of the grid pattern is the description of the New Jerusalem in the Book of Revelation, influenced no doubt by Roman colonial architecture: "And the city lieth foursquare, and the length is as large as the breadth" (Rev. 21: 16). The four walls of the New Jerusalem are aligned with the points of the compass, and in each wall there are three gates, leading to the streets paved with gold which (it is implied) form a network with intersections at right angles. The cities of More's Utopia also stand foursquare. A second urban model, seen in the ring roads surrounding many modern cities, is an orbital design based on concentric circles. In Assyrian and Babylonian mythology, the City of the Underworld can only be penetrated by passing through seven successive gates, from the outermost to the innermost (Dalley 1991, 156–7). Campanella's City of the Sun is likewise encircled by seven walls, each of which is more heavily fortified than the ones already passed. The grid and orbital patterns may be superimposed to some extent, producing a city with straight streets converging on a single monumental centre. Nevertheless, *Utopia* and *The City of the Sun* provide striking examples of the contrast between the square and the circle as the basis of urban geometry.

More's island itself has a curious geometric shape, since "in the centre, where it is broadest, [it] extends for two hundred miles, and this breadth continues for the greater part of the island, but towards both ends it begins gradually to taper" (More 1923, 41). If this might suggest an ellipse with flattened ends rather like the outline of a round, bulbous potato, Hythlodaye then says that the ends are bent round "to make the island resemble the new moon, the horns of which are divided by a strait about eleven miles across". Inside the two 'horns' or promontories is the 'wide expanse' of an enormous lagoon (41). The result is that the 200-mile breadth of hinterland suggested at first – and more or less taken for granted in More's later descriptions of Utopian topography and agriculture – is one of the work's many contradictions, since the crescent-shaped island could never be more than a thin strip of land between two coasts. Although we are told that the lagoon forms a large harbour and that the opposite coast also contains "numerous harbours" (41), Hythlodaye never acknowledges that Utopia, artificially cut off from its mainland, must be a predominantly maritime nation.

The utopians' capital city, Amaurote, has a central location that makes it "the most conveniently situated" place for the annual assembly of representatives from all 54 cities (42). Architecturally it is identical with Utopia's 53 other cities, another puzzling statement which has been subjected to close analysis by the French philosopher and semiotician Louis Marin. As we have seen, Amaurote is the seat of the national 'Senate' (63), and it also houses a Prince; but just where the ruler and senate reside in a city that lacks a principal palace, a town hall, or any kind of monumental centre, remains a mystery. The city walls form a fortified square on a hillside sloping down to the tidal river Anyder. This square is bisected by another river (the city's main source of fresh water) flowing down through culverts to join the Anyder at a right angle. Like all Utopia's cities, Amaurote is divided into four equal districts, centring on a market-place and composed of streets of uniform terraced houses. (The inhabitants move house every ten years, exchanging their houses by lot.) Each district has a number of communal dining-halls presided over by a community head, the Syphogrant or Phylarch. As Marin notes, these dining-halls are the only buildings potentially capable of housing Utopia's political institutions (Marin 1993, 159–73). It is, therefore, the displacement or suppression of Utopian political space that allows More to state that (despite its necessarily unique situation on a hillside bordering one bank of a tidal river) Amaurote is identical in plan to its fellow-cities. These cities are all built on a grid pattern without any architectural provision to mark the city centre. It follows that within them the contrast of centre and periphery, metropolis and suburb, has no apparent meaning.

As both the capital and the unique city of an inland state, Campanella's City of the Sun offers at first sight a more straightforward example of urban geometry. Not only is it divided into "seven rings or huge circles named from the seven planets" (Campanella n.d., 218), but the city has a "humped shape", centring on a "high hill, which rises from an extensive plain" (217). Each of its concentric rings is bounded by a circular wall containing four gates aligned with the points of the compass, and through the gates run four streets at right angles to one another, converging at the top of the hill, which (reflecting the city's hemispherical topography) is capped by a circular, domed temple. In the vault of the dome are representations of the stars, while above the single central altar there hang two large globes, one with a painted representation of the Earth, and the other of the solar system. It will be seen that the whole city is an affirmation of the Copernican universe and of the roundness of the Earth itself. The citizens live in large palaces joined to the inner side of each of the concentric walls, with arcades or galleries for promenading around the walls and looking down, presumably, on the city's outer rings. Water is pumped up from the bottom of the hill through a network of canals, and every street contains fountains.

The City of the Sun is a theocracy presided over by a high priest – hence the temple at its centre. (The state religion is monotheistic and, though heliocentric, stops short of actual sun-worship.) Not only is the city's architecture a direct expression of its religious creed, but it has a strongly didactic function. The walls function as both schools and libraries, being painted with systematic representations of all the sciences known to this highly learned nation. "[B]oys learn the language and the alphabet on the walls by walking round them" (227). Hence the very nature of Campanella's strictly ordered but communist utopia is inscribed in its urban geometry. The homogenization of space in the City of the Sun may be less than permanent, however, since the walls also serve as an elaborate defence system for a society involved in continual warfare.

Campanella's city is located on the island of Taprobane, but its citizens do not have the island to themselves. They came from India, "flying from the sword of the Magi, a race of plunderers and tyrants who laid waste their country", and they "determined to lead a philosophic life in fellowship with one another" in their new home (225). But they need to defend themselves against both the "other nations of India" to whom they were formerly subject, and the native Taprobanese "whom they wanted to join them at first" (241). The utopians enjoy a highly advanced civilization, whose scientific discoveries include the prolonging of human life up to the age of 200, but they also face repeated uprisings on the part of the dispossessed and displaced local population. Just how these oppressed neighbours view the utopians in their midst may be gathered from the fact that (so far, at least) in the colonial wars on Taprobane "The warriors of the City of the Sun [. . .] are always the victors" (241).

These urban geometries based on the square and the circle do not exhaust the possibilities for the shape and pattern of a utopian city; but for more complex and exotic examples than those found in More and Campanella we need to turn to dystopian fiction. The metropolizes of Hall's *Mundus Alter et Idem* include "the queen of all cities", Pazzivilla, which is "not round or oval, like other cities", but "a cross between a cylinder and an inverted pyramid, plainly composed as a copy of the human body" (88–9). Another of Hall's cities is Zouffenberga, "shaped like a two-handled tankard when viewed from any direction" (89). A later city in the same tradition is the "new Bloomusalem" of James Joyce's *Ulysses* (1922), "built in the shape of a huge pork kidney" (Joyce 1986, 395).

The Return of Place in Uchronia

Not only is space substantially homogenized in the geometric cities of More and Campanella; they are also, in effect, empty of people. Admittedly, we are given the names of various public offices, those of the priests, syphogrants, and the like. In the City of the Sun, there are three princes serving under the high priest – "POWER, WISDOM and LOVE"

(Campanella n.d., 221) – and, under them, magistrates, doctors, warriors, and so on. But these and the rest of the citizens remain an abstraction. We may or may not envy their 'philosophic life in fellowship', but we do not, and cannot, warm to them. Even where, as in *New Atlantis*, specific individuals are introduced, they play the part of representative function-aries rather than personalities in their own right. Modern utopian writers have gone considerably further to reinsert human variety and character-difference into their societies, but the natural home for such qualities is dystopian fiction where the citizens' individual differences are used to reveal and reflect wider social inequalities and political tensions.

There are, however, significant changes to the representation of place and space when we move from utopia to uchronia – to utopias, that is, set in the future rather than in a present-day nowhere. The template for the new genre was set by Louis-Sébastien Mercier's *L'An 2440* (1771), portraying a future Paris. It is true that, in the remote parts of the world visited by Hythlodaye and his successors, there was a degree of sup-pressed analogy with places already known; More's *Utopia*, for example, contains two marginal annotations (possibly written by More's friend Erasmus) comparing the location of Amaurote to London's position on a tidal river (cf. Wegner 2002, 54 and n.). But once it is seen through the eyes of a time traveller rather than a global explorer, utopia, however transformed, is an affective space to the extent that it arouses conscious memories and associations connected to the traveller's previous life and to our own knowledge of the places concerned. This is, admittedly, a side-effect of the widespread shift to uchronia in the nineteenth century and after. The depiction of an idealized future life reflected the advent of mod-ern technologies and ideologies offering the prospect of radical human improvement, while the future dystopia became a vehicle for vehement and usually reactionary polemic. As Oscar Wilde wrote – having said that "A map of the world that does not include Utopia is not worth even glancing at" – "Progress is the realisation of Utopias" (Wilde n.d., 404). Moreover, the future utopia, whether or not it is visited by a time travel-ler from the present, is likely to be a place that itself retains a degree of historical memory. Space in uchronia undergoes a new kind of mirror effect, with superimposed images of the old and the new.

As Dohra Ahmad has noted, in Edward Bellamy's *Looking Backward 2000–1887* (1888) and in Morris's *News from Nowhere* which was a direct reaction to it, there is a "continual sense of doubleness" with cru-cial landmarks appearing as both familiar and unfamiliar. The narrative layering of the new and the old Boston or London means that "the trav-eler as well as the reader must live both times at once" (Ahmad 2009, 37). Morris exploits this effect much more fully and deliberately than Bellamy, whose time traveller Julian West stays mostly indoors discours-ing with his twenty-first-century hosts, the Leetes. Morris's narrator Wil-liam Guest wants to be up and about, and he has already left his house at Hammersmith and taken an early morning swim in the Thames before he realizes that what he thought was an overnight sleep has carried him forward 200 years.

Soon after his swim, Guest is taken by his new acquaintance Dick to eat breakfast in the Guest House, a new building standing on the site of his old home. There is a "frieze of figure subjects in baked clay" on the external walls, and, Guest tells us, "The subjects I recognised at once; and indeed was very particularly familiar with them" (Morris 1970, 10). He does not explain what it was that he recognized, but a strong hint is given two pages later when he notes an inscription inside the dining-hall:

> Guests and neighbours, on the site of this Guest-hall
> once stood the lecture-room of the Hammersmith Socialists.
> Drink a glass to the memory! May 1962
>
> (12)

The inscription itself, regardless of its content, is an artefact of historical memory for the inhabitants of Nowhere, since the date 1962 indicates that it was put up in the immediate aftermath of the socialist revolution which had begun ten years earlier. This is now several generations in the past, and the Hammersmith Socialists belong to an earlier generation still. Yet Guest was one of those ancient socialists, a fact that he does his best to hide from his twenty-first-century companions even though he cannot help constantly revealing it. The future Guest House is one of a series of locations in *News from Nowhere* invested with deep and conflicting emotions, emotions that would have been inconceivable in the earlier utopias. One of these locations, the subject of a whole chapter in Morris's utopia, is the notional centre of the old London, Trafalgar Square.

The square as we know it today, and as Morris himself knew it – with Nelson's Column as its dominant feature – dates from the 1840s, with the four lions being added in 1867. (Only the Lutyens fountains are later additions.) In Morris's twenty-first century, the name Trafalgar has been retained (seemingly due to a lapse in historical memory), but the central monument has been demolished and the square is now an orchard:

> We came presently into a large open space, sloping somewhat toward the south, the sunny site of which had been taken advantage of for planting an orchard, mainly, as I could see, of apricot trees, in the midst of which was a pretty gay little structure of wood, painted and gilded, that looked like a refreshment stall. From the southern side of the said orchard ran a long road, chequered over with the shadow of tall old pear trees, at the end of which showed the high tower of the Parliament House, or Dung Market.

> A strange sensation came over me; I shut my eyes to keep out the sight of the sun glittering on this fair abode of gardens, and for a moment there passed before them a phantasmagoria of another day.
>
> (35)

No sooner has Guest set eyes on the modern open space exemplifying the greening of future London than he is transported to the Trafalgar Square he once knew, above all as the hub of London's democratic and insurrectionary politics. Dick recalls that it had been the scene of a great battle in 1952, which in a later chapter will be described in the words of an eye-witness (presumed to be no longer alive). The maturity of the pear trees overshadowing the road that we know as Whitehall emphasizes once again that the period of violence and civil war is now a half-forgotten past. Not only has a small wooden hut or kiosk taken the place of the overbearing central column, but no new monuments or historical inscriptions have been added. For Guest, however, it is still the scene of the traumatic events of 'Bloody Sunday' (13 November 1887), the large socialist demonstration in which Morris himself took part. The clearing of Trafalgar Square and the plantation of an orchard also has a possible historical precedent not mentioned in *News from Nowhere*. It has been argued that Morris was responding to the demolition by the Paris Communards in 1871 of the ceremonial column in the Place de Vendôme celebrating Napoleon's military triumphs (Holland 2016, 100–1). Morris's vision of a future Trafalgar Square has, in turn, influenced other utopian authors.

The Breaking of the Mirror

There is a second apparent historical precedent for the clearing of Trafalgar Square, which again *News from Nowhere* does not mention. This is reflected in the name of the famous neoclassical church in the corner of the square, St Martin's-in-the-Fields. George Orwell has his character Mr Charrington reflect on St Martin's in *Nineteen Eighty-Four* (1949): "'St Martin's-in-the-Fields it used to be called', he says, 'though I don't recollect any fields anywhere in those parts'" (Orwell 1954, 83). Although he is represented as an antiquarian, Charrington must be unaware that in the Middle Ages St Martin's lay between the separate cities of London and Westminster, in what was effectively an open burial ground. To Winston Smith and his contemporaries, it is now Victory Square and an effigy of Big Brother has replaced Nelson on top of the column. The square is still a political arena of sorts, since Winston and Julia take advantage of the anonymity of the crowd watching a victory parade of Eurasian prisoners. Orwell's dystopian future Trafalgar Square may, however, be indebted to Wells's *A Modern Utopia* rather than to William Morris.

In *News from Nowhere*, the fact that socialist London no longer needs political institutions allows Morris to make his well-known joke about the Dung Market. If this is what the future holds for the Houses of Parliament, what about the city's cathedrals and churches? Morris is silent about London's places of worship, although Guest's final experience in Nowhere is the harvest supper held in an Oxfordshire village church. Earlier, on his visit to Trafalgar Square he noticed the National Gallery but not St Martin's-in-the-Fields. The effective centre of the new London is a different kind of building enshrining historical memory, the British Museum where Guest's informant old Hammond is a retired custodian. Morris, however, makes no attempt to describe the museum or its contents. Despite the travelogue style of narration, Morris's accounts of Guest's journeys from Hammersmith to Bloomsbury and then up the river to Kelmscott are remarkable both for what they include and for what they necessarily omit and gloss over. However laden with historical memory, his future London remains to some extent a non-place.

This effect of utopian vagueness is openly acknowledged in *A Modern Utopia*, where Wells's visitors travel to a transformed London and once again find themselves in a "central space, rich with palms and flowering bushes and statuary", which – as is belatedly confirmed – stands where Trafalgar Square once stood (Wells 2005, 165). *A Modern Utopia* is not technically a uchronia, even though it depicts a world that readers are meant to find futuristic. The narrator and his companion are transported from a walking holiday in Switzerland to an apparently perfect replica of the Earth situated in a different part of the galaxy. The geography and ecology of this parallel world are identical to ours, and the population is so closely matched that the narrator's journey within Utopia leads to a meeting with a senior official, a member of the Samurai or voluntary ruling class, who is his exact genetic double. Only the world's political history has been changed. Utopia, then, has a fragile, transparently virtual existence leading to what Wells admits is an "incurable effect of unreality" (14). The journey to the new London, which remains one of the world state's imperial capitals, might be expected to counteract this unreality, but the city's atmosphere is one of "fairy-like unsubstantiality" (165) and its topography is deliberately sketchy. At no point do we experience the close emotional engagement that Morris's narrator felt in *News from Nowhere*'s future London.

In *A Modern Utopia*, the city's "central space" (it is not described as a square) is passed through daily by a "great swarm of people", students and workers, residents and tourists, on their way to London's "mighty university", its "stupendous libraries" and museums, and no doubt also to the world's ruling council which still meets occasionally at Westminster (164–5). The architecture, typified by the city's "great arches and domes of glass" (165), has an unfocused sublimity in stark contrast to Morris's sometimes pedantically detailed medievalism. From the "central space" there stretches a vista "along an avenue of trees" (contrast the specificity of Morris's mature pear trees) "down a wide gorge between the cliffs of crowded hotels, [. . .] to where the shining morning river streams dawn-lit out to sea" (165). The narrator and his companion stay in one of the hotels and spend some of their time walking through the colonnades and riverside gardens. Early in the final chapter, "The Bubble Bursts", we see them sitting in their hotel courtyard, within view of a colonnade with a "great archway". (Curiously, this might suggest Aston Webb's Admiralty Arch on the west side of Trafalgar Square, now a well-known landmark but designed three or four years after the publication of *A Modern Utopia*.) In the "middle of the place" – again, the nature of the 'place' is unspecified – there is a marble fountain in the form of a "flower-set Triton" (237). A moment later, with "no jerk, no sound, no hint of material shock", the vision of utopia dissolves and the two men find themselves not just back in England (they have apparently returned from their Swiss walking tour) but beside an iron bench in "that grey and gawky waste of asphalt – Trafalgar Square" (237). Soon they are moving "towards the dirt-littered basin of the fountain" (239), and then a cab-horse is hurt in a road accident outside St Martin's-in-the-Fields. The sudden return to the all-too-familiar clamour of shabby, dangerous, and bad-tempered London is startling. The utopian mirror-world has been shattered.

The abrupt disillusionment caused by a return to our own time and place is another effect found in several influential uchronias. It may be said, indeed, that the emotional disjunction here is strictly temporal: that the (almost invariably male) traveller has returned from the virtual world of his remote descendants, reversing what should have been an irreversible journey through the gateway of his own death, to a life in which the future happiness he has glimpsed must remain permanently out of reach. In a curious episode in *Looking Backward*, for example, Julian West is horrified to think that he has returned to nineteenth-century Boston, only to be greatly relieved when he wakes up – still in the twenty-first century – to discover that it was only a bad dream. His virtual utopia is real after all. And yet West, as we have seen, is nearly always in or on the site of what had been his own house in Boston, a sleeper who barely leaves his own bed. Although Wells would adopt the same basic narrative device in *When the Sleeper Wakes* (1898), the nearest analogy in his writings to *Looking Backward* is *The Time Machine* (1895), where the Traveller both enters the future and returns to the present on a machine standing in a laboratory in his own London house. In both *A Modern Utopia* and Morris's *News from Nowhere*, however, the shock of the narrator's temporal return is increased by a spatial displacement, with the Wellsian move from Switzerland to London echoing William Guest's journey from Hammersmith to Kelmscott. Not only is the utopian mirror-world shattered, but we have entered that world at one location only to leave it at another.

The places of entry and exit are, of course related, though in different ways in each text. *A Modern Utopia* takes us, in effect, from the periphery to what are represented as the political centres both of Wells's own world and its utopian parallel. Morris offers us something more like a personal pilgrimage between two sites with a special significance that – though shared with the reader – can have little or no meaning for his utopians. But in each book the journey is also finally something of a descent into hell, with the familiar place (Kelmscott for Morris, Trafalgar Square for Wells) seen as if for the first time in its full ugliness and meanness. What follows this moment of emotional displacement (or, to use the appropriate term from literary theory, cognitive estrangement) is the narrator's appeal to us to begin the work of utopian construction, to realize the beauty and perfection of a world that is now known more clearly than ever before to be non-existent. Thomas More, by contrast, had ended his *Utopia* with the tight-lipped observation "that there are many things in the Utopian commonwealth, which it is easier to wish for in our own states than to have any hope of seeing realized" (More 1923, 122). More's imperturbability here is simply the last (or, given that his work has several appendices, not quite the last) of *Utopia*'s many paradoxes; we shall never know quite how he hoped or expected that his readers would react to his vision of nowhere. What can be said is that, whether or not it offers a basis for political action, the desire to enter the mirror-world first named by Thomas More remains a permanent feature of human imagining.

Works Cited

Ahmad, D. (2009). *Landscapes of Hope: Anti-Colonial Utopianism in America*. Oxford: Oxford University Press.

Annas, J. (1981). *An Introduction to Plato's* Republic. Oxford: Clarendon Press.

Bell, D. M. (2017). *Rethinking Utopia: Place, Power, Affect*. New York and London: Routledge (E-book).

Campanella, T. (n.d.). 'The City of the Sun'. In Henry Morley (ed.), *Ideal Commonwealths*. 10th edn., London: Routledge, and New York: Dutton, pp. 215–63.

Carroll, L. (1948). *Through the Looking-Glass and What Alice Found There*. London: Macmillan.

Dalley, S. (trans.) (1991). *Myths from Mesopotamia: Creation, The Flood, Gilgamesh, and Others*. Oxford: Oxford University Press.

Fortunati, V., and Trousson, R. (eds.) (2000). *Dictionary of Literary Utopias*. Paris: Champion.

Foucault, M. (1986). 'Of Other Spaces'. *Diacritics* 16: 1, 22–7.

Hall, J. (1981). *Another World and Yet the Same: Bishop Joseph Hall's Mundus Alter et Idem*, trans. and ed. J. M. Wands. New Haven and London: Yale University Press.

Harvey, D. (2000). *Spaces of Hope*. Edinburgh: Edinburgh University Press.

Hexter, J. H. (1952). *More's 'Utopia': The Biography of an Idea*. Princeton: Princeton University Press.

Holland, O. (2016). 'From the Place Vendôme to Trafalgar Square: Imperialism and Counter-Hegemony in the 1880s Romance Revival'. *Key Words* 14, 98–115.

Joyce, J. (1986). *Ulysses*, ed. H. W. Gabler with W. Steppe and C. Melchior. New York: Vintage.

Le Guin, U. K. (1975). *The Dispossessed*. New York: Avon.

Marin, L. (1993). *Utopiques: Jeux d'espaces*. Paris: Éditions de Minuit.

Mithen, S. (2003). *After the Ice: A Global Human History, 20,000–5000 BC*. London: Weidenfeld & Nicolson.

More, T. (1923). *More's Utopia*, trans. G. C. Richards. Oxford: Blackwell.

Morris, W. (1970). *News from Nowhere, or an Epoch of Rest*, ed. J. Redmond. London: Routledge and Kegan Paul.

Orwell, G. (1954). *Nineteen Eighty-Four: A Novel*. Harmondsworth: Penguin.

Porter, P. W. and Lukermann, F. E. (1976). 'The Geography of Utopia'. In D. Lowenthal and M. J. Bowden (eds.), *Geographies of the Mind: Essays in Historical Geography*. New York: Oxford University Press, pp. 197–223.

Reader, J. (2004). *Cities*. London: Heinemann.

Scott, J. C. (2017). *Against the Grain: A Deep History of the Earliest States*. New Haven and London: Yale University Press.

Swift, J. (1949). *Gulliver's Travels and Selected Writings in Prose and Verse*, ed. J. Hayward. London: Nonesuch, and New York: Random House.

Wegner, P. E. (2002). *Imaginary Communities: Utopia, the Nation, and the Spatial Histories of Modernity*. Berkeley, Los Angeles and London: University of California Press.

Wells, H. G. (2005). *A Modern Utopia*, ed. G. Claeys and P. Parrinder. London: Penguin.

Wilde, O. (n.d.). *Poems and Essays*. London: Collins.

9 Seeing Things

Competing Worlds in Octavia Butler's *Kindred* and China Miéville's *The City and the City*

Lucie Armitt

Fantasy geography is a way of simultaneously anchoring fiction in a specified location and overcoming what is, for realism, a key impasse: the impenetrability of the narrative membrane dividing differing epochs and spatial zones. According to Rob Kitchin and James Kneale, the traditional concept of "geography as a jigsaw puzzle made up of discrete, bounded spaces" is "dead" (Kitchin and Kneale 2002: 1). In this chapter, I compare the different fantasy worlds inherent in Octavia Butler's 1979 novel *Kindred* and China Miéville's 2009 novel *The City and the City* and explore their respective relationships to the geography of *the* dead. In the process, I explore two related issues: surveillance and its politics and nearness and its relationship to the 'thing', as defined by Martin Heidegger.

Kindred and *The City and the City* are written 40 years apart, but what is striking are their structural similarities in terms of their shared interest in the divisive politics of racial and ethnic difference and their shared structural usage of worlds which are split. In *Kindred*, the central protagonist space-time travels between twentieth-century urban California and nineteenth-century agricultural Maryland. In *The City and the City*, the central protagonist travels between two separate cities, Besźel and Ul Qoma, both having autonomous existence from each other but sharing the same geographical co-ordinates. Although Miéville makes a vague attempt to position Besźel and Ul Qoma somewhere within Eastern Europe, through references such as "There are direct flights . . . from Budapest, from Skopje [in Macedonia], and, probably an American's best bet, from Athens" (Miéville 2018: 88), no more precise regional location is offered. Similarly, although occasional parallels are made with East and West Berlin, the reader is never permitted to fall into the easy mistake of reading *The City and the City* as a fantasy re-visiting of post–World War II Germany.

Both *Kindred* and *The City and the City* are portal fantasy quest narratives, meaning that two competing worlds are established within the setting, movement between them being accessed via an identifiable entry point. In many fantasy narratives portals have a material presence and take up space themselves; this is how the portal works in *The City and the*

City. An architectural enclosure, Copula Hall forms the portal meeting point of the two cities and has a "huge entrance like a made secular cave. The building is much larger than a cathedral, larger than a Roman circus. It's open at its eastern and western sides" (Miéville 2018: 85). Where most portals operate as a membrane facilitating access into a new space, however, Copula Hall facilitates access into the *same* space the traveller has just left, but this time the voyager is permitted to see the 'other' city, previously actively *un*-seen despite that person walking the same streets. Now the traveller becomes "a tourist, a marvelling visitor, to a street that shared the latitude-longitude of their own address" (Miéville 2018: 86). Both novels have first-person narrators and, in *The City and the City*, that narrator is Inspector Tyador Borlú, a detective tasked with solving a murder enquiry that will require him to move from his home city of Besźel into Ul Qoma. In *Kindred*, our narrator is Dana, a black woman who has just celebrated her 26th birthday and is a struggling writer living in California in 1976. To earn money, she works for a casual labour agency, which she joking describes as a "slave market" (Butler 1988: 52) before experiencing the real thing in nineteenth-century Maryland, as she falls through an invisible portal in response to a kind of unspoken call from her ancestor, the white boy (later man) Rufus.

The City and the City is unusual in that the portal is both visible and potentially usable to all, albeit that strict controls are imposed on movement between the two cities. Nevertheless, at the end of the novel Borlú remains trapped on the other side, unable to return home. In *Kindred*, only Dana and anybody else who happens to be in physical contact with her at the time can move between worlds. The fear of becoming trapped is therefore especially acute for Kevin, her white husband, who is stranded in nineteenth-century Maryland during the course of the text, though is able to return to his own time at the end. According to Farah Mendlesohn, in portal fantasies "we ride with the point of view character who describes fantasyland and the adventure to the reader, as if we are both with her and yet external to the fantasy world" (Mendlesohn 2008: 8). Rather than adventure, however, both Butler and Miéville provide us with portal fantasies of violent *mis*-adventure involving gendered violence and the death and near-death of women.

It is that death and near-death that operate as the catalyst for entry (or 'escapism') through the portal. Early on in *Kindred*, Dana explains to Kevin that "Rufus's fear of death calls me to him, and my own fear of death sends me home" (Butler 1988: 50). Later, when Kevin becomes stranded in nineteenth-century Maryland and Dana returns home without him, she reflects: "Kevin might as well be dead. Abandoned in 1819, Kevin *was* dead. Decades dead, perhaps a century dead" (Butler 1988: 113). In *The City and the City*, Borlú's transition through Copula Hall is set in train by the murder of a young PhD student, Mahalia Geary, whose body is dumped under a mattress in open waste ground. Despite the apparent openness of the location, it is described as if cut off: "I could not see the street or much of the estate. We were enclosed by dirt-coloured blocks" (Miéville 2018: 3). Just as Butler's Rufus sees through the portal into Dana's twentieth-century home in California, but has no means of accessing or interpreting that space, so Mahalia's body is surrounded by an architectural impasse and establishes a search for a motive that will end with a folkloric dead end. According to Mark S. Madoff, the locked room mystery is the key "wrinkle of fiction", inhabiting "involuted architectural space" and revolving around "a crime, especially a murder" which presents itself "in a devilishly mystifying way" (Madoff 1989: 49). Although Mahalia's body is discovered outside, Miéville provides us with the external embodiment of such a locked room.

Death is, of course, itself a portal, a state of passing. What is left behind is the corpse, which is surely nothing more than a 'thing'. Borlú tells us that "*Nothing* is still like the dead are still. The wind moves their hair . . . and they don't respond at all" (Miéville 2018: 3–4 – my emphasis). When, in Chapter 2, Borlú's female assistant, Constable Lizbyet Cowri, opines of Mahalia, "She's still a question mark" (Miéville 2018: 23), on one level we interpret this observation as an evaluation of the lack of progress of the case. On another, we recall that Mahalia's actual body-shape, in death, is set "in an ugly pose, with legs crooked as if about to get up", itself evoking a type of material mimicry of the punctuation mark (Miéville 2018: 4). Death is always near to and yet distant from us, a closure and a kind of aperture onto otherness and, in that sense, forms the perfect embodiment of Heidegger's theory of the 'thing'. The thing, he argues, requires a reflection on space-time travel: "All distances in time and space are shrinking", he observes, before establishing that "Near to us are what we usually call things" (Heidegger 1971: 165–6).

Via the portal, we have seen that perceptible nearness is utterly distinct from actual proximity, and vice versa. What sits between these two states is a form of physical or conceptual emptiness. Rufus tells Dana: "You come out of nowhere and go back into nowhere" (Butler 1988: 206), while Miéville's Copula Hall is described as "an emptiness walled by antiquity" (Miéville 2018: 158). While the aperture through which Butler's Dana passes, unlike Miéville's Copula Hall, seems to take up no material space at all, it 'holds' nearness. Thus Dana fears leaving home in 1970s California, "worr[ying] about what might happen if Rufus called me from the car while it was moving" (Butler 1988: 58) and keeps her canvas bag close by her side, packed with small things: underwear, a map, writing implements and "the biggest switchblade knife I had ever seen" (Butler 1988: 45). When she starts to feel the dizziness which heralds the onset of her movement between worlds, Kevin rushes "beside me holding me" and hence is transported to Maryland too (Butler 1988: 58). In that sense, also, Dana becomes both the object passed through the portal and a vessel through which Kevin and their possessions can pass, traveller and conduit, adventurer and 'thing'.

For Heidegger: "The vessel's thingness does not lie at all in the material of which it consists, but in the void that holds" (Heidegger 1971: 169). Beyond the details already given, Dana's life-history is comparatively empty. Her parents are dead, cutting her off from a sense of where she came from, but through her travels to the Weylin plantation she comes to realize Rufus and Alice, a black woman whom Rufus desires but who accedes to his advances only under duress, are her ancestors. She needs to keep Rufus alive long enough to ensure the birth of Hagar Weylin, "born in 1831", from whom Dana has inherited the family Bible (Butler 1988: 28). That connection with Alice almost embodies the physical superimposition of nineteenth-century Maryland upon twentieth-century California. Rufus tells Dana that she and Alice are so physically similar as to be "only one woman", a judgement with which Alice concurs: "I know what he means. He likes me in bed and you out of bed . . . we're two halves of the same woman" (Butler 1988: 228–9). In narrative terms, then, Dana's importance is purely functional. In the act of spilling between worlds, she becomes what Heidegger calls the "offer in sacrifice" (Heidegger 1971: 173) which he identifies as the thing's main function, most obviously when she loses half her arm in her final return home. As Kevin puts it to Dana, trying to rationalize how he explains her injury to the police authorities:

> I said I was in the bedroom when I heard you scream. I ran to the living room . . . and I found you struggling to free your arm from what seemed to be a hole in the wall. . . . That was when I realized your arm wasn't just stuck, . . . it had been crushed right into the wall.
> (Butler 1988: 11)

A very similar form of sacrifice applies to Miéville's dead Mahalia. At first, her identity is wholly unknown, leading to her being described, emptily, as "Fulana Detail . . . the generic name for woman unknown" (Miéville 2018: 10). Even when identified, however, a different kind of void becomes encapsulated by Mahalia: something called Orciny.

Orciny is a place of folklore in Miéville's novel, a fabled state believed by a minority to exist in an interstice between Besźel and Ul Qoma and described to Mahalia's grieving parents as "The third city . . . A secret. Fairy tale" (Miéville 2018: 98). This fabulous 'space between', however, is not simply a place of wish-fulfilment, for what surprises the reader is the level of condemnation attached to belief in it. Initially, the subject is associated with the professional embarrassment of a disgraced academic, Dr David Bowden, in admiration of whose work Mahalia had given a conference paper on the subject, some years before the fictive present of the text. We are told, however, that Mahalia "needed to get her hands on the actual objects" believed to belong to it, a desire that takes her to the study of archaeology (Miéville 2018: 110). In that sense Orciny becomes another of Heidegger's objects of emptiness, into which is poured a seemingly disproportionate amount of anger and violence; after all, both Mahalia and her friend Yolanda lose their lives because of their shared faith in something generally believed not to exist.

There is a kind of double bluff at work in Miéville's novel that leads the reader into another *cul-de-sac*. Precisely because we are told repeatedly that Orciny does not exist, the reader nurtures an expectation that the final revelation will be that it *does* exist, in a fissure or crack in the ground (another kind of portal, perhaps) between Besźel and Ul Qoma. It is this fissure that underlines the importance of the archaeological dig upon which Mahalia is basing her PhD thesis. We learn that "digs are constant in Ul Qoma, research projects incessant, its soil so much richer than [Besźel's] in the extraordinary artefacts of pre-Cleavage age" (Miéville 2018: 75). Mahalia's supervisor jests that there are false rumours about the 'magic powers' of such artefacts (Miéville 2018: 110) and, later in the novel, refers to the shadow (but probably fake) existence of

> seductively vague references to the pre-Cleavage locals, these peculiar men and women, witch-citizens by fairy tale with spells that tainted their discards, who used astrolabes that would not have shamed Arzachel or the Middle Ages, dried-mud pots, stone axes that my flat-browed many-greats grandfather might have made, gears, intricately cast insect toys, and whose ruins underlay and dotted Ul Qoma and, occasionally, Besźel.
>
> (Miéville 2018: 181–2)

Miéville's terminology is worthy of especial attention, because of its relationship to these fissures. Cleavage is another synonym for a split or rupture, out of which may emerge something or nothing and into which something or nothing may be inserted. Note Borlú's demonstration, later on in the novel, of the means via which Mahalia 'returned' things dug up from the archaeological site to what she then believed to be Orciny. Standing at the edge of the archaeological dig, with a simple fragment of wood in his hand, he drops it into his trouser pocket, explaining that his pocket contains a hole:

> I walked a few steps in the crosshatch, dropping the thankfully unsplintered wood down my leg. . . . I stood as if contemplating the skyline and moved my feet gently, letting it onto the earth, where I trod it in and scuffed plant muck and dirt onto it. When I walked away, without looking back, the wood was a nothing shape, invisible if you did not know it was there.
>
> (Miéville 2018: 315)

So Borlú describes how Mahalia, having removed items of treasure from the drawer of the artefact warehouse, would replace them with 'twists of paper, stones, the leg of a doll' (Miéville 2018: 317), in other words more objects devoid of significance. Like Heidegger's jug, the drawer and the wrappings take on significance only in terms of what they are presumed to contain, such that, paradoxically, only once they have been checked and found to be empty do they become worthless. As Heidegger also observes, the role of the jug is to anticipate and take meaning from that emptiness: "The twofold holding of the void rests on the outpouring. . . . Even the empty jug retains its nature by virtue of the poured gift" (Heidegger 1971: 172). In that sense, Mahalia's PhD thesis has been another empty vessel, a decoy providing her with a reason to exist in this space. As her supervisor, Professor Nancy observes, "Honestly I was a little, a little bit disappointed. . . . She was a 'grind', we'd say" (Miéville 2018: 107–8).

That functional, frictional noun 'grind' reinforces the sexual reading of violence that sites the woman, again like Heidegger's jug, as a vessel which not only contains and gives shape to oppression but seems to provide a narrative rationale for it. That image of the woman's body as a site of splitting is implied partly by Miéville's choice of the word 'cleavage', a word in itself often synonymously used as a synecdoche for a woman's chest, which takes definition, not from her breasts, but the (empty) space between them. Unlike the breasts, which are functional vessels filled with milk and emptied by the infant (as the pejorative slang term 'jugs' itself implies), Mahalia embodies the 'wasted' woman and that definition is carved across her chest and face, in a clear attack on her individual identity. One of Borlú's colleagues addresses the first cavity in her chest as a conversational presence: "Well, hello cause of death" (Miéville 2018: 8), before Borlú himself continues by describing her facial lacerations. These extend across her cheek and under her jaw line so deeply as to run "half the length of her face" and "under the overhang of her mouth, it jagged ugly and ended or began with a deep torn hole in the soft tissue behind her bone" (Miéville 2018: 8). Later, more grinding attaches itself to Mahalia in "a bunch more scrapes and whatnot on the body" which the same colleague considers to be "consistent with dragging her along. The wear and tear of murder" (Miéville 2018: 28).

Similarly violent lacerations are carved through Dana's body in *Kindred*, when she is beaten by the white patroller who tries to rape her early on in the novel; when she is whipped by Tom Weylin for trying to run away; when she is whipped in the fields by Evan Fowler, the white overseer for lacking skill in cutting crops. In an archaeological article based on the recovery of domestic items from slave plantations, John Solomon Otto and Augustus Marion Burns III note that the overseers were usually "the sons of yeoman farmers" who, despite living in similarly impoverished circumstances to the slaves, "collaborated with the planter family in preserving the slave system" (Otto and Burns 1983: 188 and 197). Branded "mean low white trash" by Sarah in the cookhouse, the overseers in Butler's novel "drew simple, unconflicting emotions of hatred and fear" from their black neighbours (Butler 1988: 138 and 230). It is the overseer who beats Dana across her breasts as she turns to look him in the eye, again as if in direct assault against her womanliness. Eventually, Dana turns to self-laceration, slitting her own wrists to force her return to 1970s California, as if in direct acknowledgement of the fact that her split role must be matched by a severance of the flesh.

In *The City and the City*, we have seen this interstice to have a geographical as well as a fleshly application. In addition to Orciny, another emergent body erupts in the form of Breach. Simultaneously an organization and a transgression, 'Breach' occurs when an inhabitant of either Beszel or Ul Qoma refuses to 'unsee' the other city, thus crossing (even in sight) the lines dividing one from another. The manner in which the two cities interface is complex and irregular in form and the term Miéville attributes to that intersection is 'crosshatch'. Thus, walking through the streets of Beszel, Borlú tells us that

> The length of BudapestStrász, patches of winter buddleia frothed out from old buildings. It's a traditional urban weed in Beszel, but not in Ul Qoma, where they trim it as it intrudes, so BudapestStrász being the Beszel part of a crosshatched area, each bush, unflowered at that time, emerged unkempt for one or two or three local buildings, then would end in a sharp vertical plane at the edge of Beszel.
>
> (Miéville 2018: 53–4)

The members of Breach, whom Miéville calls avatars, are attributed with uncanny characteristics. At the suggestion that Mahalia's murder might have been a crime subject to Breach (at that stage it is thought she may have been murdered in Ul Qoma, but her body dumped illicitly in Beszel), Cowri responds: "Breach, boss. I don't want that shit in the picture. Where the fuck you getting this spooky shit from?" (Miéville 2018: 56). Even the bodily movements of these avatars seem ethereal, seemingly emerging from nowhere in a manner that recalls Butler's character Rufus's aforementioned assertion that Dana "come[s] out of nowhere and go[es] back into nowhere". Following a road traffic accident in Miéville's novel, in which a van in Ul Qoma skids across a crosshatched area into buildings and pedestrians in Beszel, instantly "Shapes, figures, some of whom perhaps had been there but who nonetheless seemed to coalesce from spaces between smoke from the [traffic] accident . . . controlled, contained, the area of the intrusion" (Miéville 2018: 81). Later, when Borlú commits his murder of Yolanda's assassin, chasing him through crosshatched streets, the assassin in Beszel, Borlú in Ul Qoma, our narrator knows he must stop him before he reaches an area of Beszel which is 'total' or inaccessible from Ul Qoma. Just as Dana looks around at the overseer on being whipped on the back, facing him in an act of indignation, only then to be whipped across her breasts, so, as Yolanda's assassin nears his exit point, he turns to meet Borlú's gaze and gives "a tiny triumphant smile", in response to which Borlú shoots him in the chest. Instantly,

> unclear figures emerged where there had been no purposeful motion instants before, only the milling of no ones . . .
> '*Breach.*' A grim-featured something gripped me so that there was no way I could break out, had I wanted to. I glimpsed dark shapes draped over the body of the killer I had killed. . . . A force shoving me . . . in directions that made sense in neither city.
> (Miéville 2018: 285–6)

As Borlú faces the reality of his transgression, he tells us: "I went under into black, out of waking and all awareness, to the sound of that word", before continuing by noting that the state into which he is propelled is "not a soundless dark", but "a dream arena where I was quarry" (Miéville 2018: 286 and 289). This description of falling unconscious resonates with echoes of Butler's Dana, not simply in the manner in which she describes the dizzying bodily effect of sinking through the time-space portal, but in the realization that her passage through the portal renders her vulnerable to being hunted by white patrollers, white overseers, Rufus and Weylin.

Thus, as the parallels already alluded to suggest, the notion of breaching equally manifests itself in *Kindred*. The *Collins English Dictionary* gives the following definitions of the term breach: "a crack, break, or rupture . . . a breaking, infringement or violation of a promise . . . any severance or separation . . . an obsolete word for wound . . . to break through or make an opening, hole" (*Collins English Dictionary* 1991: 195). When we consider these multiple meanings, we see how perfectly they fit Butler's narrative. The 'crack, break or rupture' reminds us of the role of the portal in Butler's novel. The 'breaking, infringement or violation of a promise' applies when Rufus pledges to post Dana's letters to Kevin, then known to be living in the North, but Rufus conceals them, undelivered, in his trunk. The 'severance or separation' is both what happens to Dana and Kevin when they become stranded apart in time and space and what is inflicted on Dana's arm as it becomes crushed into the wall at the end of the novel. That ruptured return home typifies the disorientated relationship with home characters in both novels face throughout. Hence, irrespective of whether characters in Miéville's novel 'belong' to Besźel or Ul Qoma, walking even their own streets involves a strangely foreign experience, whereby certain buildings, people and vehicles must be actively 'un-seen'. Similarly, Dana and Kevin, travelling home together from nineteenth-century Maryland, find that home does not actually feel like home. Dana considers: "The time, the year, was right, but the house just wasn't familiar enough. I felt as though I were losing my place here in my own time. Rufus's time was a sharper, stronger reality" (Butler 1988: 191).

In the context of the crime novel, Philip Howell reflects on the peculiar relationship between the detective and the city streets:

> The problem of 'knowing' the city is . . . in large part a matter of understanding the qualifications involved in any claim to that knowledge. What the mysteries of the city enjoined, and detective and crime fiction continue to endorse, but what certain strains of radical urban social theory disavow, is . . . the epistemological gap in our knowledge of the city.
>
> (Howell 1998: 364)

In both of these novels, that estranged sense of familiarity widens rather than narrows the sense of defamiliarization, as homesickness brings up precisely such a "discernible gap in one's knowledge". Where one might conventionally fill such a space with map reading, maps prove problematic in both novels. Though, once Dana has discovered Rufus has not posted her letters, she arms herself with historic and modern maps of Maryland to try to aid her escape from the Weylin plantation, such maps simply affirm their futility. Alice, Dana notes, "couldn't read a map" but managed to remain at large for days, whereas Dana only manages a few hours before re-capture, despite knowing "about towns and rivers miles away" (Butler 1988: 177). A similar view of maps is found in *The City and the City* where, on the wall above one of Borlú's colleague's desks, is a "large scale map of Besźel and Ul Qoma", but "To avoid prosecution the lines and shades of division were there – total, alter, and crosshatched – but ostentatiously subtle, distinctions of greyscale" (Miéville 2018: 56). In other words, in these novels maps establish visual geography only to draw attention to its actual limits. Specifically in the context of fantasy, Kitchin and Kneale argue that "empty spaces, places of fog and mirrors, labyrinths" require readers to "make sense of space through a variety of forms of mapping" (Kitchin and Kneale, 9) and, here, mapping eventually takes the figurative form of leaked CCTV footage. As Borlú peers at precisely the kind of "fug of ghost lines and crackles" on the footage that Kitchin and Kneale associate typically with fantasy geography, he repeats the question "What am I looking at?" in the manner of one who, presented with a map, may be unable to read it. Eventually, aided by one of his colleague's patient deciphering, he makes out the identity of the van which he then realizes transported Mahalia's body legally between Besźel to Ul Qoma and back through the Copula Hall, utilizing the correct paperwork (Miéville 2018: 131–3). As such means of transportation is entirely permissible, the ironically named 'Oversight Committee' refuses to invoke Breach at this point, hence setting in train the series of events which will result in Borlú being required to cross over the border into Ul Qoma and continue the search to its conclusion, ultimately committing Breach himself.

Closed circuit television images bring to light one more way in which sight, oversight, occluded sight and unseeing connect up the various aspects of these novels that interest us here. In Butler's *Kindred*, 'seeing' predominantly holds the key to political oppression, from Jake Edwards and Evan Fowler's role as white overseers, to Rufus's ability to see through the portal into 1970s California, to Liza, the Black informant, who tells Rufus and Master Weylin that Dana has escaped. Only Weylin's disempowered wife, Margaret, learns to 'unsee'. As Kevin says to Dana: "I saw three little kids playing in the dirt back there who look more like Weylin than Rufus does. Margaret's had a lot of practice at not noticing" (Butler 1988: 85). In *The City and the City*, as noted before, 'unseeing' is taken to a political level, citizens of one city actively 'unseeing' the buildings, traffic and inhabitants of the other, threatened otherwise with Breach. Not so different from *Kindred*, however, while the citizens of both cities are busy unseeing, afraid of inadvertently committing Breach, Breach is simultaneously closely and continually watching them. As Borlú says to Cowri:

> "We need to be careful". . . . There was another set of long moments when neither of us spoke. We looked slowly around the room. I do not know what we were looking for but I suspect that she felt, in that moment, as suddenly hunted and watched and listened-to as she looked like she did.
>
> (Miéville 2018: 150)

In *Kindred*, when Dana comes across a group of Black children playing 'slave markets', her shocked reaction is articulated in terms of distance and proximity. First she says to Kevin: "Let's get closer. I want to hear what they're saying". Surveying them, but now at closer hand, she hears a young boy reiterating in 'play' the very words used by the white trader when he was bought with his mother. Instantly, Dana "turn[s] and walk[s] away . . . tired and disgusted" (Butler 1988: 99). When Kevin accuses her of "reading too much into a kids' game", he continues with the observation: "We're in the middle of history. We surely can't change it" (Butler 1988: 100). As Lyon observes, "surveillance often involves participation in which the watched play a role" (Lyon 2007: 15–16). While these children play at being transformed from people into things, Dana both refuses to accept this game as "a thing" and reflects, again, "I never realized how easily people could be trained to accept slavery" (Butler 1988: 101). A remarkably similar scene occurs in Miéville's book, when Borlú thinks back to a time when children played 'Breach'. Though he acknowledges that "It was never a game I much enjoyed", he never-theless observes that "I would take my turn creeping over chalked lines and chased by my friends, their faces in ghastly expressions, their hands crooked as claws. I would do the chasing too, if it was my turn to be invoked" (Miéville 2018: 46). According to David Lyon, an expert in surveillance,

> "In traditional societies, people are typically available to each other in person. . . . For most of human history such co-presence has been the context in which social interaction and exchange have taken place". What holds people together in social relationships is the trust emanating from "looking each other in the eye".
>
> (Lyon 2001: 15–16)

In *Kindred*, Dana reminds us that, in nineteenth-century Maryland, Black people never look white people in the eye, for fear of being considered insolent. In the case of Miéville's novel, the same indirect gaze applies to citizens of Besźel and Ul Qoma respectively, as they walk alongside and around each other on the same streets but in different cities. Even when driving,

> Though the traffic cultures are not identical, for the sake of the pedestrians and cars who have, unseeing, to negotiate much foreign traffic . . . we all learn to tactfully avoid our neighbour's emergency vehicles, as well as our own.
>
> (Miéville 2018: 114)

In the reality beyond these texts, surveillance is both a growing source of fear and a growing means via which the establishment regulates its citizens. Lyon argues that "Surveillance always carries with it some plausible justification that makes most of us content to comply" and both texts reflect this view (Lyon 2001: 3). Walking the streets of Ul Qoma as a visitor from Besźel, Borlú is aware that "Ul Qomans unsee me because of my clothes and the way I hold myself, double-take and see my visitor's mark, see me" (Miéville 20–18: 172). In *Kindred*, Dana bemoans, on more than one occasion, the ease with which nineteenth-century Black characters come to accept their subordinate role in society. Sarah, who runs the cook-house "had done the safe thing – had accepted a life of slavery because she was afraid", despite having had three of her four children sold (Butler 1988: 145). This compliance persists today in certain contexts which connect the detective work of Miéville's novel with the racial politics of Butler's. In a twenty-first-century essay on Black police officers in New York, Liyah Kaprice Brown notes that the relationship between the police force and the Black community still remains defined by "the legacy of slavery", especially in relation to questions of surveillance (Brown 2004: 760). She continues: "Despite the nearly forty years of desegregation, the Black community can cite countless stops, frisks, strip-searches, botched raids, and certainly unanswered calls as evidence of 'business as usual'" (Brown 2004: 793). Aware of the duplicity of her own situation, Dana tells Kevin:

> You might be able to go through this whole experience as an observer. . . . I can understand that because most of the time, I'm still an observer. . . . It's nineteen seventy-six shielding and cushioning eighteen nineteen for me. But now and then . . . I can't maintain the distance.
>
> (Butler 1988: 101)

Hence we return to the concept of nearness (here in terms of time and social reality) with which Heidegger introduces our understanding of the 'thing'.

When Lyon more recently reflects on the role popular culture, including literary culture, plays in surveillance, he observes that "It is clearly a mistake to assume that the imaginative world of [popular culture] exists in an entirely separate realm from everyday reality" in relation to that surveillance (Lyon 2007: 157). In other words, literature becomes the 'thing' that, in Heidegger's terms, shows us directly (albeit as observers) that "everything present is equally near and equally far . . . no abridging or abolishing of distance brings nearness" (Heidegger, 177). Thus, to return to the impenetrability of the narrative membrane that divides realist epochs and spatial zones, we have seen how fantasy geography both abridges the distance of time and abolishes the distance of space in these novels. By travelling through the portals with Dana and Borlú, we have been able to explore in detail the politics of gendered violence, placed under a fantasy lens while retaining its critical connection with political realism. That lens simultaneously brings the other world into a closer focus (Heidegger's state of nearness) and opens up an intermediary space of social critique between both realms, in part encapsulated in the presence of the dead woman as question mark. The end result is an interrogative narrative friction in which fantasy geography breaches the conventions of space and time, in order to open up new apertures through which readers are enabled to see things afresh.

Works Cited

Brown, Liyah Kaprice (2004) 'Officer or Overseer?: Why Police Desegregation Fails as an Adequate Solution to Racist, Oppressive, and Violent Policing', *New York University Review of Law and Social Change*, 29; 757–95.

Butler, Octavia (1988) *Kindred* (London: The Women's Press).

Heidegger, Martin (1971) 'The Thing', in Martin Heidegger (ed.), *Poetry, Language, Thought*, trans Albert Hofstadter (New York: Harper and Row), 163–82.

Howell, Philip (1998), 'Crime and the City Solution: Crime Fiction, Urban Knowledge and Radical Geography', *Antipode*, 30, no. 4; 357–78.

Kitchin, Rob and James Kneale (eds) (2002) *Lost in Space: Geographies of Science Fiction* (London: Continuum).

Lyon, David (2001) *Surveillance Society: Monitoring Everyday Life* (Buckingham: Open University Press).

Lyon, David (2007) *Surveillance Studies: An Overview* (London: Polity).

Madoff, Mark S. (1989) 'Inside/Outside, and the Gothic Locked-Room Mystery', in Kenneth W. Graham (ed.), *Gothic Fictions: Prohibition/Transgression* (New York: AMS, 1989), 49–62.

Mendlesohn, Farah (2008) *Rhetorics of Fantasy* (Middletown, CT: Wesleyan University Press).

Miéville, China (2018) *The City and the City* (London: Picador).

Otto, John Solomon and Augustus Marion Burns III (1983) 'Black Folks and Poor Buckras: Archaeological Evidence of Slave and Overseer Living Conditions on an Antebellum Plantation', *Journal of Black Studies*, vol. 14, no. 2; 185–200.

10 Of Borders and (W)holes

Porous Geographies of the Fantastic in China Miéville and Nora K. Jemisin

Nicoletta Vallorani

Realists of a larger reality.

(U.K. Le Guin)

The alternative is to demand the impossible.

(N.K. Jemisin)

Porous Realities

The Fifth Season (2015), by Nora K. Jemisin is set in a post-post-post-apocalyptic context: the world has already ended, several times, and the point is it cannot be mended. The question is rather how to survive in a space unfit for human and animal life. *This Census-Taker* (2016), by China Miéville, develops against an impervious environment, in the aftermath of a terrible war, in a context where life is both very hard and totally hopeless. In both narratives, genre-belonging is an open issue: both hybridize fantasy, science fiction, New Weird, dystopia, and a number of speculative and adventurous subgenres whose coexistence in the same narrative is a critical challenge. Even at a closer look, both stories keep their own ambiguity in terms of which genre they fit into.

Strangely enough, even though they couldn't be farther apart in many respects, the two narratives seem to provide plenty of evidence pointing to that notion of *Fantastic of Space* that García focuses on in her *Space and the Postmodern Fantastic in the Contemporary Literature*: the impossible does not merely happen in space, but it is spatial (2015, 9). More specifically, I believe that both texts develop a specific imagery around the notion of "architectural void", appearing in García's title and shaped in different ways by the two authors. Starting from this assumption, I will consider two liminal dimensions, of which I posit their intense analogic nature: the border and the hole. I will trace the appearance and the exploitation of these spatial dimensions to see how they interlace with each other in the two works by Jemisin and Miéville.

The notion of border is probably the most familiar, used and abused as it is today in different fields; at the same time, and precisely because it is so much used, it appears semantically ambiguous. By definition, the border is drawn to mark the territory of a specific community, distinguishing and separating it from any other space. Symbolically and in practice, it means ownership, familiarity, and protection. What is beyond the border is unknown, unseen, and possibly dangerous (and it is, therefore, an architectural void). However, at the same time, the border may become an oppressive reality, a claustrophobic, impassable limit to one's own freedom. Borders are made to be crossed and, historically speaking, they *have been crossed* in the path of defining the individual and/or collective journey of identity. They are porous, but only when they are located in a free world, otherwise they become watertight. Their nature depends on the characteristics of the community they enclose, and they change with it.

Quite similarly, the hole is an ambiguous metaphor. It is posited as a dangerous feature of space, the lack of something, a frightening, possibly devouring, intrusion of darkness in a totally luminous (symbolically and topographically) world. But the hole may also be fascinating. It hides something that is unknown and therefore needs to be found out. And the hole alludes to the whole: what is complete, logical, explicable, appeasing. It could even be said that without the porous existence of the *holes*, no *whole* could be possible. Holes are the negative space, the space that is not there.

In the effort of engaging the two *topoi* in direct dialogue, I realized that all borders run along holes: they separate the enclosed community from the external blank spaces that are physically and symbolically unknown and unknowable. Unexplored lands and uncivilized cultures are perceived as holes, voids, the land beyond "leones" where the travellers haven't travelled yet. The border is the limit, because "by setting boundaries to the world, the architect constructs a space in which man could dwell" (García 2015, 1). The border therefore becomes the designated place of transition, a threshold to the Unknown. Following this line of thought, it may be posited that each border implies a hole, and you can survive the danger represented by the hole or not. Whether it limits the safe space of a nation or represents the door to safety for people beyond it, the border marks an act of passing that may be successful or not. In the real world (whatever that means), migrants die in the water border that is the Mediterranean Sea. Women trying to cross the Mexican borders are often raped and killed in and around Ciudad Juarez. African American people have sometimes disappeared while trying to reach the democratic north crossing border after border.

In my work here, I assume that the hole is necessarily part of any border, and it may happen that, in the holes that are part of the fabric of borders, things and beings may get lost, swallowed by darkness. I want to develop my assumption by comparing two texts that seem to be quite different in several respects. *The Fifth Season*, mostly considered a fantasy novel, was authored by Nora K. Jemisin: a woman and an African American author living in the US. *This Census-Taker* is the latest published novel by China Miéville: a Englishman born and bred, living in London. National and gender belonging often imply a different gaze upon the real world, and different kinds of imaginations. Moreover *The Fifth Season* is the first episode of a monumental trilogy while *This Census-Taker* can be defined a novelette: a very simple almost Gothic or Weird tale versus a very complex dystopian construction, bordering the fantastic.

However, the two books were published practically at the same time, they both deal with a particular notion of dystopia (technically post-apocalyptic though related to fantasy), and both focus very closely on the social and natural environment and potently resist any final answer or simplistic prophecy. Both call into play the most traditional (and still, in my opinion, most effective) definition of fantastic literature:

> The fantastic occupies the duration of this uncertainty. Once we choose one answer or the other, we leave the fantastic for a neighbouring genre, the uncanny or the marvellous. The fantastic is that hesitation experienced by a person who knows only the laws of nature, confronting an apparently supernatural event.
>
> (Todorov 1975, 25)

But they distance themselves somewhat from Todorov as not very effective – as Rosemary Jackson maintains – in considering the "social and political implications of literary forms" (Jackson 1981, 6): both authors have a "political" profile, in the sense that they tend to consider literature and art as ways to produce an impact on the community or at least to show what's wrong with it. And both – I don't know to what extent in full awareness, but this aspect is ultimately not relevant – deal with the kind of Fantastic of Space Garcia introduces in her *Space and the Postmodern Fantastic in Contemporary Literature* (García 2015, 9).

I will show that borders and holes acquire specific relevance in the two novels, though in different ways. In Miéville, the hole is exploited as "a paradigmatic form of fantastic transgressions of space": it "makes the *body* disappear from its exterior; it swallows it up" (García 2015, 41). It makes the space porous, challenging the defining and protecting function of the boundary. For the protagonist of *This Census-Taker*, leaping over the hole means crossing a border at the risk of falling into the darkness of the Unknown. Surviving implies entering a new realm of existence and possibly accessing adulthood. Miéville's and its connection to a *limen* to be crossed highlight the fact that borders are intrinsically polysemic. They do not have two sides but they show the fictive nature of the act of drawing boundaries (Balibar 2002, 76) that mostly consist in a *"world configuring function"* (Balibar 2002, 79). This function is also clear in *The Fifth Season*, where the main activity of the characters consists in passing fences, facing defensive walls (or building them), crossing thresholds, in search of shelter impossible to find. The Earth of Jemisin's trilogy is in fact built on the operation that Ètienne Balibar defines as the act of territorializing (or re-territorializing, in *The Broken Earth Trilogy*), because to territorialize means to

> assign "identities" to collective subjects within structures of power, therefore to categorialize and individualize human beings (and the figure of the "citizen", with its statutory conditions of birth and place, its different sub-categories, spheres of activity, processes of formation, is exactly a way of categorizing individuals).
>
> (Balibar 2002, 4)

In the case of Jemisin's trilogy, this is done in a land where no belonging appears to be possible.

As a last comment, I will add that I am keeping within the realm of the fantastic, even though it must be clear that the two *topoi* of border and holes do have important implications in terms of biopolitics. Though keeping this awareness in the back of my mind, my objective here is to see how the Fantastic has been echoing the current emphasis on borders, border crossing, holes in the fabric of the civilized world, blank spaces and unseen identity in two different continents in the Western world.

Heart of Blankness

Holes are a central issue in *This Census-Taker*. What is, according to García, the prototype of the fantastic space (García 2015, 37 ff) appears as the hub of this unusual investigation about a crime that may have never been committed, because the corpse that is not to be found anywhere and the possible killer performs in all respects as a loving father. From the structural point of view, Miéville in fact writes a sort of *Bildungsroman*, recalling the perverse process of growing up of the "child" appearing at the beginning of Cormac McCarthy's *Blood Meridian* (1985). And in that case, too, the protagonist does not seem to have a first name, a proper family, a loving context and a "normal" life. The Gothic flavour is the same, though Miéville keeps a shorter measure and sets his story in an undefined post-apocalyptic space rather than on McCarthy's Mexican border.

In the complex geography of this very unusual novelette by China Miéville, the landscape appears at least as mysterious as the characters and even in the full light of the day, it proves slippery and not fully definable, unsettling, and unreadable. Apparently, the author builds a quite traditional city-vs-country topography and soon transforms each place into a sign, exploiting the semiotics of the landscapes to produce a new language (García 2015, 17). There is nothing unusual in this process except that, while normally the topographic sign is decoded sooner or later, in this case each sign – and the hole in particular – keeps its mystery, and this is a new development in the narratives of space. Meaningfully enough, this lack of a final decoding marks the most successful examples of fantastic literature in recent times: explanations, be they natural or supernatural, are made redundant and "there is a foregrounding of the impossibility of certainty and of reading in meaning" (Jackson 1981, 28).

From a more practical perspective, at the beginning of the story, the protagonist lives a secluded life on a hill, together with his family. The isolation increases the mystery surrounding the three-member community that the kid mostly inhabits. The hill is impervious, and from there it takes time to reach the city, an urban conglomeration split in two by a river, defining the north and the south of the area.[1] The protagonist's mother was born in the south, which means a different status in terms of culture, belonging, traditions etc.:

> "I'm a south-towner", she said, "I grew up over there. On the other side. Look at it".
>   We rarely crossed the bridge. When we did, we would go only a very short way into the streets on the other hill. Where the shops and the people seemed different to me.
>
> (Miéville 2017, 36)

The kid's mother is rather mysterious about her upbringing, and only seldom takes the kid to the southern section of the city. The river is in fact a border, and the bridges are dangerous, liminal spaces:

> Houses built on bridges are scandals. A bridge wants to not be. If it could choose its shape, a bridge would be no shape, an unspace to link One-place-town to Another-place-town over a river or a road or a tangle of railway tracks or a quarry, or to attach an island to another island or to the continents from which it strains.
>
> (Miéville 2017, 26)

In the city, when in trouble, the kid finds a new kind of community, a group of peers who want to save him and try to rescue him on several occasions but for some reason ì fail. They live in a sort of ghetto space in the most dilapidated part of the city, near the bridge: one of the marginal "areas belonging to that which society doesn't want to see: the poor, the immigrant, the neglected or abandoned" (García 2015, 38).

From the point of view of architecture, the house where the kid lives appears rather unusual: it "had three storeys that grew less and less finished as they rose, as if the builders had lost spirit the further they were from the soil" (Miéville 2017, 3). The vertical movement towards the sky has apparently been interrupted, and it almost counteracts the mysterious depth of the hole, a space inspired by another vertical movement, oriented towards the centre of the earth. The area around the house and the one around the mouth of the hole are the two hubs of the kid's horizontal and frantic movement. Both the house and the hole prove incomprehensible to the kid, though for different reasons. The house is the place where he should find shelter but particularly after his mother's disappearance, frightens him to death. In the house, something unexpected and mysterious happens and the kid is unable to get a clear vision of his father's responsibility in the possible murder of his wife. In the case of the hole, the kid's inability to explain what happens is more explicit. On several occasions, the kid is on the verge of understanding but the process is never completed: as happens in the true fantastic narrative, he nearly reaches "the point of believing" proving faithful here to Todorov's formula according to which "it is hesitation that sustains it's [the fantastic's] life" (Todorov 1975, 31). In its darkness, the hole proves impervious to the gaze exactly in the same way as the jungle bordering the river seemed mysterious and unreadable to Marlow's gaze in Conrad's *Heart of Darkness* (Conrad and Kimbrough 1988).

There was supposed to be a holy old woman or man living in a cave no more than an hour's walk from our door, just below the zenith, and I remember once glimpsing the beat of a brown cape like a shaken sheet, but whether that cloth was worn on bony vatic shoulders I can't say. I can't even say *if I truly saw it* (Miéville 2017, 9).[2]

Enveloped in this mysterious atmosphere and protected by some curious tricks of the eye, the hole becomes in fact no more than an architectural void, something missing, a blank space. It has upper borders (its mouth) but *it is also* a border (separating light and darkness): Paradoxically, it helps the kid to make out good from evil, and to ultimately distinguish what is real (i.e. the disappearance of his mother) from what can only be imagined (i.e. the murder of his mother).

Quite soon, for the protagonist, facing the hole means being obliged to consider the fact that he is no longer a child. And jumping beyond it leads him to find out that he is able to take care of himself, and to be brave enough to disobey his father.

> The hole watched me, above its discards and the insides of the hill. (. . .) It wasn't my friend or my enemy. It was only a rip full of stones and old things.
>
> (Miéville 2017, 123–4)[3]

Replicating the Conradian blank spaces that can swallow whoever tries to unveil their mystery (Conrad 1928, 10–18), Miéville's hole is a void in a void and it leads nowhere. More simply, and disturbingly, it is a bottomless pit devouring everything in its silence (Miéville 2017, 15), and hiding the kid's mother, or her corpse, among other disposable objects.

"He killed her and he put her in the hole", I whispered. "He puts the things he kills in the hole. Sometimes he kills people and he puts them in there too".

(Miéville 2017, 62)

On receiving the kid's statement, the officers want to be shown the hole, but watching it does not solve the problem: the darkness of the hole cannot be pierced. Any knowledge is impossible. Therefore, as García states, "The hole embodies an ontological and epistemic uncertainty: it is a blank space, a domain that has not been codified yet" (García 2015, 38). It becomes obvious why, at the end of the story, the kid decides to jump over the hole: in the same way as Kurtz decided to "step over the edge", the kid experiences his own rite of passage facing the darkness of the hole and showing he is able to defeat the same darkness that his father nourishes. His final transgression – a more elaborated border crossing that results in a positive ending – makes him into an adult and prepares his decision to leave the house and start out on a journey towards identity.

Again there is some overlapping between Miéville's plot and what García states, theoretically, about the meaning of the hole in fantastic literature: "the transgressive function" of this feature of the landscape results from the fact that

The fantastic hole can be understood as a heterotopic form in that it is the physical form of the non-empirically perceptive or rationalised; that which does not fit within a given sociocultural frame. Furthermore it is a liminal space that transgresses binaries, articulating absence and presence, oscillating between lack and excess of meaning.

(García 2015, 39)

Within this perspective, all the kid's frantic movements are a way of coping with the most important symbolical crossing in human life: the process of passing from childhood into adulthood. To go beyond the hole is to become whole:

I was there, in the dark, beyond the gap.

(Miéville 2017, 125)

The epiphany that follows, again, evokes Conrad's insistence on the ambiguity of the gaze, given here through a specific emphasis on the personification of landscape:

Very slowly the light in the cave mouth waned and I was more able to see the entrance itself, now that glow no longer effaced it. It was like an open eye, I thought – then I thought *No, it's like a closed eye*.

(Miéville 2017, 128)

The image of the cave as a closed eye concludes the story. No knowledge seems to be possible. In a very Conradian fashion, the kid experiences the horror and survives it, starting a new phase in life. The mystery stays unveiled, however, and the oscillation between absence and presence rather than the dichotomy light/darkness makes for the slippery quality of this *topos*. Ultimately, rather than the absence of space, the hole is the potential presence of any space.

The Earth Is Broken

This potentiality is at the core of *The Fifth Season*. There, the basic idea consists in imagining the Earth as a planet devastated by constant earthquakes, endlessly filling up chasms and opening new, mysterious and dangerous holes. The landscape created through this hypothesis is rooted in "the most common understanding of the word 'hole'" that easily "relates to cavities in material structures" (García 2015, 38). Published one year before *This Census-Taker* and equally experimental in terms of style and point of view, Jemisin's novel in fact multiplies the single hole appearing in Miéville, interweaving the exploitation of this trope with an intensified use of the notion of border, both in geographic and in symbolic terms. In her totally unfamiliar post-apocalyptic Earth, Jemisin creates a space that is both tragic and ironic. The prevailing landscape is made up of chasms, precipices, and cliffs. The area where life is more or less possible is called "the Stillness", though far from being still and in fact devastated by uninterrupted seismic and volcanic activity. Any cartography has become useless, since the profile of the territories is changing endlessly, but even so the novel opens with a map of the world, provisional though it is. The fact is, that this world is not on the verge of ending, but already has ended, collectively, and individually, for the protagonist of the story:

> Let's start with the end of the world, why don't we? Get it over with and move on to more interesting things. First, a personal ending. There is a thing she will think over and over in the days to come, as she imagines how her son died and tries to make sense of something so innately senseless.
>
> (Jemisin 2016, 1)

Now, a key aspect of Jemisin's vision in the trilogy is that there is no specific demarcation between the personal and the "natural", a word collectively designating all that belongs to the realm of natural events. The Earth, personified as a "Father" and in all respects behaving as a living creature, has lost his child, just like the protagonist, Essun, and he wants to take revenge against the human or partly human beings that he deems responsible for this loss. His revenge is merciless, because

"Father Earth thinks in ages, but he never, ever sleeps. Nor does he forget – *Tablet Two, 'The Incomplete Truth,' verse two*" (Jemisin 2016, 231). In the same way as Father Earth curses the inhabitants of the planet with an endless cycle of destruction, the so-called normal human beings systematically oppress and discriminate the *orogenes*, who are biologically and by birth endowed with a special connection to the Earth. Ordinary people fear them and their power, which consists in a specific and rare talent that comes at a cost. *Orogenes* have power over the earthquakes, a power that can mean both salvation and destruction. They are different, "other", and, for this very reason, hated. Jemisin's reference to the African American people and their condition in US society is quite obvious.[4] In this respect, she is following in the footsteps of Octavia Butler. An African American woman choosing science fiction as her field, Butler was the first one to challenge a basically male-oriented genre, proving extremely successful.[5] Jemisin starts from there and produces the vision of a whole planet where the issue of discrimination is rooted in biology (one is born an *orogene*), but also consolidated by a defensive need (a "feral" or very young *orogene* is extremely dangerous for the survival of a community). *Orogenes* are also the first to understand the reason for Father Earth's rage. Drawing on their training as well as on their personal research on the subject, they find out that Father Earth – presented as a space endowed with agency, to use Garcia's definition (García 2015, 26) – has lost his child because of the senseless actions of the pristine inhabitants of the planet (Hurley 2018, 468). Syenite as an adult and semi-trained *orogene* is told the whole story by her mentor Alabaster, who is not unveiling a secret but simply explaining and piecing together the tales of the "lorists", the storytellers keeping the memories of the world through symbolic oral narratives:

> Syenite frowns. He's said things like this before, things that hark to the lorists' tales about orogenes – that they are a weapon not of the Fulcrum, but of the hateful, waiting planet beneath their feet. A planet that wants nothing more than to destroy the life infesting its once-pristine surface. There is something in the things Alabaster says that makes her think he *believes* those old tales, at least a little. Maybe he does. Maybe it gives him comfort to think their kind has some purpose, however terrible.
>
> (Jemisin 2016, 146)

At least in part, Jemisin draws on her origins for this vision. The idea that planet Earth is a live and sentient being is an integral part of many traditional African cultures, and in this mythological reservoir, all living creatures on the planet's surface are connected in the web of life (Ikeunobe 2014, 2–7). The order of nature, therefore, is not to be broken; there is no kind of life that is better than others, and human beings are not supposed to be the most relevant of all creatures. Consequently, when the original balance is interfered with, the consequences are bound to be terrible, and they will result in the punishment of whoever the Earth deems responsible. While other living creatures are unable to feel the rage of Father Earth, though suffering its consequences, the orogenes are endowed with a profound, inner relationship with the planet they inhabit, a relationship that is there from birth, perceivable even when they are no more than children.

> There are boring parts, like when the Imperial Road along which they ride passes through endless fields of kirga stalks or samishet, or when the fields give way to stretches of dim forest so quiet and close that Damaya hardly dares speak for fear of angering the trees. (In stories, trees are always angry.)
>
> (Jemisin 2016, 84)

In terms of the dynamics of space, this concept of life on the Earth implies that in Jemisin the notion of the "object" as an inanimate and unchanging entity does not exist. Even normally inorganic entities become living beings: so they become dynamic signs, continuously semantizing and resemantizing the space they inhabit. Literally "Space *is* the Fantastic" (García 2015, 2), and it makes for a radically new conception of humanity. The very definition of the protagonist – Damaya/Syenite/Essun – as a human being is controversial. She seems to relate with space in a way that is very deep and that will, in the following episodes of the trilogy, imply some forms of symbiosis. When she first appears as Essun, she has the look and attitude of a strong woman:

> She is forty-two years old. She's like most women of the midlats: tall when she stands, straight-backed and long-necked, with hips that easily bore two children and breasts that easily fed them, and broad, limber hands (. . .) her skin is unpleasantly ocher-brown by some standards and unpleasantly olive-pale by others. One midlatters, Yumenesces call (called) people like her.
>
> (Jemisin 2016, 10)

She is a non-white woman – a visible difference that marks the most widespread ethnicity in Jemisin's world – and she is an *orogene*, therefore dangerous. The despising word used to define the orogenes – "rogga" – clearly reminds readers of the word "nigga", and it has the same flavour: It is a dehumanizing word for someone who has been made into a thing (Jemisin 2016, 134). In the same way as the natives in *Heart of Darkness* (Conrad and Kimbrough 1988, 39), *orogenes* are useful when and if they have been "instructed", and the Fulcrum is a space projected to educate them and to make clear the kind of hierarchical obedience they have to show towards mentors and Guardians if they want to survive. The Fulcrum is misleadingly comfortable:

> After that Syen takes her leave of Feldspar, then heads out of Main, the administrative building. Main sits amid a cluster of smaller buildings at the edge of the sprawling, half-wide expanse that comprises the Ring Garden. The garden is acres wide, and runs in a broad strip around the Fulcrum for several miles. It's just that huge, the Fulcrum, a city in itself nestled within the greater body of Yumenes like . . . well. Syenite would've continued the thought with *like a child in a woman's belly*.
>
> (Jemisin 2016, 65)

In fact, the place results from the clumsy blending of a prison and a constrictive shelter. There, *orogenes* are kept away from "normal" human beings until they are perfectly able to control their talent. When they've completed their basic education, their talent is to be used to serve the Fulcrum in missions that essentially consist in quelling earthquakes and preventing land movements that might be dangerous for people and/or for economic enterprises. They are always under the authority of the Guardians, and they may suffer a terrible death if they disobey their mandate.

Disobedience is the capital sin – from the Bible onwards and particularly for women. So the first harsh punishment appearing in the novel concerns the violation of a secret (a door that should never have been opened is opened) and the unauthorized visit to a specific part of the Fulcrum. The place beyond the forbidden door hosts a mysterious hole:

> At the core of it, however, there is indeed a depression. That is an understatement: it's a huge, tapering pit with flat-sided walls and neat, precise edges – six of them, cut as finely as one cuts a diamond. "Evil Earth", Damaya whispers as she edges forward along the walkway to where the yellow lights limn the shape of the pit.
>
> (Jemisin 2016, 319)

Again, the hole is given as a forbidden place, possibly dangerous, in any case secret and dark. It is enclosed in walls, and these walls are not supposed to be crossed (in the same way Miéville's kid was not allowed to go to the cave alone). The walls mark a border, replicating a notion that appears very often in *The Fifth Season*. In the first few pages of the novel, for example, the protagonist is portrayed while trying to get out of her own, protected community because people living there are on the verge of discovering that she is a *rogga*. She therefore experiences, in factual terms, the inner duplicity of the border, which becomes very clear in this context. The fantastic space described by Jemisin reveals the basic feature of suffering frequent earthquakes; this condition imposes the continuous drawing and redrawing of the map of inhabitable land. The builders choose a place and define the borders of the new "comm", in the same way as, to protect themselves, the human beings build houses and enclose them in fences designed to last until the next "shake". They territorialize, deterritorialize, and reterritorialize – borrowing this notion from Deleuze and Guattari's logic of deterritorialization – drawing borders that have the double function of protecting the people *inside* from the earthquakes and keeping *orogenes* (and other undesirable mutants) *out* of the community. Therefore the border is not only a protection, but also becomes a strong agent in determining exclusion (Mezzadra and Neilson 2013, 14). After finding out that his son has been killed by his own father because he was suspected of being an *orogene*, thus revealing that Essun herself has orogenic talents, the protagonist has to get out of the community before being lynched. She becomes dis-located (Balibar 2002, 16) and she is torn between the automatic need to protect the community she has been living in for a long time and the awareness that she should be out of this very community to make it safer.

> "Rask isn't letting anyone leave or come in". Rask is Rask Innovator Tirimo, the town's elected headman (. . .)
> "First guard the gates", you whisper. It is a rasp. You screamed a lot after that dream of Jija.
>
> (Jemisin 2016, 20–1)

In this respect, and quite obviously, the borders work as a Janus-faced device of inclusion and filtering, admitting or rejecting people according to the pre-defined requirement of the inhabitants stated by the community (Mezzadra and Neilson 2013, 7). Essun was admitted to the comm of Tirimo on the grounds of what she pretended to be, and because she wanted to hide her previous life as an *orogene* trained in the Fulcrum. When her secret identity is unveiled, she is "filtered out" of the community, and the next comm she will be admitted to "filters her in" precisely because she is an *orogene*, and may be of some help in the project of the comm itself. Between one crossing and the other, Essun experiences the no man's land, a blank space where people are fighting, one against the other, for their own lives.

> Not many people are out and about. Rask must have finally declared an official lockdown. During lockdown the comm's gate are shut – and you guess by the people moving about near one of the wall watchtowers that Rask has taken the preemptive step of putting guards in place. That's not supposed to happen till a Season is declared; privately you curse Rask's caution. Hopefully he hasn't done anything else that will make it harder for you to slip away.
>
> (Jemisin 2016, 46)

The Third Season, as well as the two following books in the series, is scattered with examples of border-crossing into the wasteland or from the wasteland into an ephemeral shelter. The fact that the story is told – by means of a sophisticated stylistic device – through the gaze of a woman and by an African American author makes the narrative choices even more meaningful. From Huxley's *Brave New World* (1932) to *Gattaca* (Niccol, 1997), the unknown has always been presented, in a genre Jemisin flirts with, as more fascinating that one's familiar world. *The Third Season* keeps the idea of describing the exploration of something that is new (and possibly forbidden) but it adds to this commitment to the defence of the environment and a deep, intense, highly political commitment to African American history in the States. In this respect, Jemisin replicates the use that Octavia Butler made of Science Fiction, in particular in *Kindred* (Butler 2003), another novel where border-crossing in space and time is the dominant device in the plot.

Borrowing Walters's definition, both in Jemisin and in Butler borders may be considered as "a sort of meta-issue, capable of condensing a whole complex of political fears and concerns" (Walters 2011, 141). These fears and concerns cannot be thought of in global terms but tend to be specific to each specific community, in the same way as each border produces a specific kind of foreigner or stranger. In his reflection on this topic and going back to Bauman's position on the same issue, Balibar repeats that "All societies produce strangers", then adding that the mechanism of production is unique to each community and cannot be replicated in a different context (Balibar 2002, 32). Within the context of Jemisin's vision, the kind of fantastic space that is imagined produces the *orogenes* as undesirable others because of their biological ability to fruitfully interact with the place they inhabit. At the same time – and differently from Miéville's protagonist – the *orogene* main character of *The Fifth Season* proves unable to get out of the hole where she is endlessly rejected. She "stepped over the edge" facing the same architectural void given as a central metaphor in *This Census-Taker*. Both narratives, therefore, challenge the idea of a space explicitly built to "protect" human beings, and propose a fantastic vision that appears totally new.

Notes

1. Miéville tends to privilege for "Split Cities [. . .] Budapest and Jerusalem and Berlin, and Beszel and UlQoma" (Miéville 2011: 90). Even though he develops this kind of landscape in full in *The City and the City*, the idea appears in many works of his.
2. The "uncertainty of the gaze" shown by the kid is deeply Conradian and it recalls Marlow's inability to identify the arrows when his boat is attacked: they are "sticks", then "little sticks", then "things" and finally "arrows" (Conrad and Kimbrough 1988, 47).
3. Again a Conradian reference, this time to the famous passage of the black shapes, in *Heart of Darkness* (Conrad and Kimbrough 1988, 21–1).
4. This attitude is made clear right from the beginning through the dedication appearing at the beginning of the novel, reading: "For all those who have to fight for the respect that everyone is given without question".

5. Butler was in fact the first African American Woman to win important awards with her stories, most of which are set in a land closely resembling Jemisin's future (in particular the Xenogenesis series and the unfinished Parables). Among others, Butler won the Hugo Award for her short stories in 1983 and the Nebula Award in 1984.

Bibliography

Balibar, Étienne. 2002. *Politics and the Other Scene*. Phronesis. London: Verso.

Butler, Octavia E. 2003. *Kindred*. 25th anniversary edition. Black Women Writers Series. Boston: Beacon Press.

Conrad, Joseph. 1928. "Geography and Some Explorers." In *Last Essays*, 10–18. London: J.M. Dent & Sons.

Conrad, Joseph, and Robert Kimbrough. 1988. *Heart of Darkness: An Authoritative Text, Backgrounds and Sources, Criticism*. 3rd edition. A Norton Critical Edition. New York: Norton.

García, Patricia. 2015. *Space and the Postmodern Fantastic in Contemporary Literature: The Architectural Void*. Routledge Interdisciplinary Perspectives on Literature 31. New York; London: Routledge, Taylor & Francis Group.

Hurley, Jessica. 2018. "An Apocalypse is a Relative Thing: An Interview with N. K. Jemisin." *ASAP Journal*, September 2018, pp. 467–77.

Ikeunobe, Polycarp A. 2014. "Traditional African Environment Ethics and Colonial Legacy." *International Journal of Philosophy and Theology*, December 2014, pp. 31–42.

Jackson, Rosemary. 1981. *Fantasy, the Literature of Subversion*. New Accents. London; New York: Methuen.

Jemisin, N. K. 2016. *The Fifth Season: The Broken Earth*. London: Orbit.

Mezzadra, Sandro, and Brett Neilson. 2013. *Border as Method, or, the Multiplication of Labor*. Durham: Duke University Press.

Miéville, China. 2011. *The City & the City*. London: Pan Books.

Miéville, China. 2017. *This Census-Taker*. London: Picador.

Niccol, Andrew. 1997. *Gattaca*. SF. USA.

Todorov, Tzvetan. 1975. *The Fantastic: A Structural Approach to a Literary Genre*. Cornell Paperbacks. Ithaca, NY: Cornell University Press.

Walters, William. 2011. "Foucault and Frontiers: Notes on the Birth of the Humanitarian Border." In *Governmentality: Current Issues and Future Challenges*, edited by Ulrich Bröckling, Susanne Krasmann, and Thomas Lemke, 138–64. New York: Routledge.

Contributors

Lucie Armitt is Professor of Contemporary English Literature at the University of Lincoln, UK. She has been publishing on fantasy and the literary fantastic since 1991 and has a particular interest in the relationship between women, bodies, and space. Her principal publications include *Fantasy* (Routledge, New Critical Idiom, 2020); *Twentieth-Century Gothic* (University of Wales Press, 2011); *Fantasy Fiction* (Continuum, 2005); *Contemporary Women's Fiction and the Fantastic* (Palgrave Macmillan, 2000); *Theorising the Fantastic* (Arnold, 1996); and *Where No Man Has Gone Before: Women and Science Fiction* (Routledge, 1991).

Maria Teresa Chialant was Professor of English Literature at the University of Salerno. Her main fields of research are the nineteenth- and twentieth-century novel, NeoVictorian Studies, and "the Fantastic". She has written extensively on Dickens and Gissing, and published articles on M. Oliphant, H. G. Wells, J. Conrad, E. M. Forster, and R. West. She has (co)edited several collections of critical essays, which include *Time and the Short Story* (Peter Lang, 2012), and she has contributed to international volumes and journals; the most recent ones are *Dickensian Prospects. E-rea* (13.2, 2016) and *Mapping the Imagination: Literary Geographies* (3.2, 2017). Her publications include the Italian translation of four late-Victorian texts and Rose Macaulay's *Non-Combatants and Others* (Edizioni Scientifiche Italiane, 2018).

Patricia García is a Ramón y Cajal researcher at the Universidad de Alcalá (Spain). She has previously served as an associate professor in Hispanic and comparative literature at the University of Nottingham. Her research focuses on narrative spaces and their intersection with other fields, in particular with urban studies, feminisms, and with representations of the supernatural. She has directed the project *Gender and the Hispanic Fantastic* (funded by the British Academy) and has been a fellow of the Helsinki Collegium for Advanced Studies (2018–2019) with a EURIAS fellowship. She is a member of the Executive Committee of the *European Society of Comparative Literature*, of *ALUS: Association for Literary Urban Studies*, of the Spanish Research Group on the Fantastic (GEF, Grupo de Estudios de lo Fantástico), and of the editorial board of the academic journal *BRUMAL: Research Journal on the Fantastic*. Her most notable publications include the monograph *Space and the Postmodern Fantastic in Contemporary Literature: the Architectural Void* (Routledge, 2015).

Matthew Gibson is Associate Professor of English Literature at the University of Macau. He is the author of *Yeats, Coleridge and the Romantic Sage* (2000), *Dracula and the Eastern Question: British and French Vampire Narratives of the Nineteenth Century Near East* (2006), and *The Fantastic and European Gothic: History, Literature and the French Revolution* (2013). He is also the co-editor with Neil Mann and Claire Nally of *W. B. Yeats's "A Vision": Explications and Contexts* (2012) and more recently, again with Neil Mann, of *Yeats, Philosophy and the Occult* (2016), and, with Sabine Lenore Mueller, of *Bram Stoker and the Late Victorian World* (2018).

C. Bruna Mancini is Associate Professor of English Literature at the University of Calabria. She is interested in translation studies, media studies, gender studies, and cultural studies. She published essays on Shakespeare, on the contemporary rewritings of the Shakespearian texts, on eighteenth-century women writing, on fantastic cinema and literature, on gothic, on monstrosity, on city and narration, on space. In 2005, she published *Sguardi su Londra. Immagini di una città mostruosa*. For Liguori Editore, in the book series 'Angelica' in 2003 she edited and translated *L'Amante Mercenario /The Mercenary Lover* by Eliza Haywood with an Introductory essay, and in 2006 she edited and translated *Angelica, ovvero Don Chisciotte in gonnella/Angelica, or, Quixote in Petticoats* by Charlotte Lennox with the Introductory essay. In 2009, she co-edited with Romolo Runcini, *Universi del fantastico. Per una definizione di genere* (Napoli, ESI) and in 2013 she edited and translated *L'inconscio letterario* by Eric Rabkin for Solfanelli Editore. In 2015 she published the translation of *The Shelter/Il rifugio* by Caryl Phillips (Napoli, Liguori). Since 2014, she is leading a research group at the Department of Humanities of the University of Calabria on "Spaces, Power, Canon. From maps, to literary cartographies, to cyberspace". In 2020, she has published *Spazi del Femminile nelle letterature e culture di lingua inglese tra Settecento e Ottocento* (Mimesis) and has co-edited *Declinazioni del fantastico. La prospettiva critica di Romolo Runcini e l'opera di Edgar Allan Poe* (Liguori), *Millennium Ballard* (Morlacchi), *Migrazioni. Percorsi interdisciplinari* (Mimesis). She is co-director of the series "Margini" for the Publishing House Mimesis.

David Ian Paddy is Professor of English Language and Literature at Whittier College, and teaches courses in modern and contemporary British literature, James Joyce, Celtic literature, critical theory, the European novel and science fiction. He is the author of *The Empires of J. G. Ballard: An Imagined Geography* (Gylphi 2015) and articles on Angela Carter, Niall Griffiths, Jackie Kay, and Jeff Noon. His research interests are in literary geography and the relationship between literature and national identity.

Patrick Parrinder is Emeritus Professor of English at the University of Reading and the author of many books, including *Utopian Literature and Science* (2015) and *Nation and Novel* (2006). His work in the field of science fiction and utopian studies grew out of his lifelong interest in H. G. Wells, on whom his first book was published in 1970. He is President of the H. G. Wells Society and also General Editor of the 12-volume *Oxford History of the Novel in English*. He lives in London.

David Punter is Professor of Poetry Emeritus and Senior Research Fellow in the Institute of Advanced Studies at the University of Bristol, UK. As well as hundreds of articles and essays, he has published many books on the Gothic as well as other areas of literature. His best-known work is probably *The Literature of Terror*; his most recent book on the Gothic is *The Gothic Condition*. His other books include *Writing the Passions*; *Rapture: Literature, Addiction, Secrecy*; *Metaphor*; *Modernity*; and *The Literature of Pity*. He has also published six books of poetry.

David Sandner is a professor of English at California State University, Fullerton, where he teaches Romanticism, popular literatures, and creative writing. He is author or editor of *Philip K. Dick: Essays of the Here and Now* (2020), novelette *Mingus Fingers* (2019, co-written with Jacob Weisman), *The Treasury of the Fantastic: Romanticism to the Early Twentieth Century* (2013, co-edited with Jacob Weisman), *Critical Discourses of the Fantastic, 1712–1831* (2011), *Fantastic Literature: A Critical Reader* (2004), and *The Fantastic Sublime* (1996).

Nicoletta Vallorani is Professor of English Literature and Cultural Studies at the University of Milan. Her specializations include visual studies, gender studies, and queer studies. She recently authored *Anti/corpi. Body politics e resistenza in alcune narrazioni contemporanee di lingua inglese* (2012), *Millennium London. Of Other Spaces and the Metropolis* (2012), and *Nessun Kurtz. Cuore di tenebra e le parole dell'occidente* (2017). She is included in *The Routledge Companion to Crime Fiction* (2020), with an essay entitled "Crime Fiction and the Future". She is the project leader of *Docucity. Documenting the metropolis*, on documentary filmmaking and urban geographies and she co-directs the online journal *Other Modernities* (http://riviste.unimi.it/index.php/AMonline).

Index

Page numbers in italic indicate a figure on the corresponding page. Page numbers followed by 'n' indicate notes.